Spirit in Health

Spirit in Health

Spiritual roots in modern healing

The social and medical sciences
enlist ancient mind-body spiritual techniques

Robert Fripp

Shillingstone Press

SPIRIT IN HEALTH: *Spiritual roots in modern healing*
(*Social and medical sciences enlist ancient mind-body spiritual techniques*)

By Robert Fripp

http://RobertFripp.ca | @RSPFripp

Shillingstone Press
125 Southvale Drive
Toronto ON, M4G 1G6
Canada

Copyright Robert Fripp 2009, 2017
First print edition 2009, 2nd print edition 2017
ISBN 978-0-9780621-8-7

Cover design by Robert Tombs, Ottawa
Text font: Baskerville, 10 and 12 pt.

Notice of Rights
All rights reserved. No part of this publication may be reproduced, stored in a retrieval system, uploaded or transmitted in any form or by any means, electronic, mechanical, recording or otherwise without the prior written consent of the author. Short excerpts may be used in reviews or quotations; but no person, company or organization may offer this book, or any part of this book, for sale or reuse without the author's written permission.

Spirit in Health follows *The Becoming* (John Hunt Publications, U.K. 1998), a book of essays describing our cosmic and organic origins. An allegorical creation myth accompanies those essays. Novelist John Fowles wrote the foreword. In 2001, Paulist Press (HiddenSpring imprint) published an illustrated, revised North American edition of *The Becoming* under the title *Let There Be Life* ISBN 978-1587680045

The text combines U.S. spelling and British punctuation. Each is more rational than the alternative. Canadian compromise moderates both.

Spirit in Health is dedicated to
Carol, Will and Eric Fripp, to Satwant Gill;
to Jeff Crelinsten, Ron Freedman;
and to parents, grandparents, friends and family
who struggled harder and died younger.

BOOKS BY ROBERT FRIPP
(Robert Stephen Parker Fripp)

The Becoming (John Hunt Publications, U.K. 1998)
Sixty scientific essays explain our cosmic and organic origins.
An allegorical creation myth accompanies the essays.
British novelist John Fowles wrote the foreword.

•

Let There Be Life (HiddenSpring imprint, Paulist Press, 2001)
This is a revised edition of *The Becoming* for North America.
61 line cuts. ISBN-13: 978-1587680045

•

Design and Science: the life and work of Will Burtin
(Lund Humphries, London; Ashgate Publishing, New York, 2007)
This richly illustrated book traces the career of Will Burtin,
who pioneered several design fields. Co-author R. Roger
Remington.

•

Dark Sovereign
This full-length tragedy is written in English as it stood in 1626.
Dark Sovereign challenges Shakespeare's polemic, *Richard III*.
With Arden-style footnotes and commentary.
(Shillingstone Press, 2009)

•

Wessex Tales
Eight thousand years in the life of an English village
Forty short stories set in Wessex, Volumes 1 and 2
(Two books)

•

Contents

From ancient times

1. Spirits of old ~ 3
*The fall and rise of spirits and shamans
Definitions*

•

Spirits in the world around us

2. People of the north ~ 19
The drum is our horse: Siberia / Among the Inuit

3. Visions, dreams, masks and drums ~ 35
The vibrant world of North America

4. Revelations, vibrations, a matter of balance ~ 55
Central and South America

5. From the recesses of time ~ 68
Europe: fertility and redemption

6. Heal till it hurts ~ 85
Southern Africa: magical people, the Bushmen

7. 'Bring all things into being!' ~ 92
The Dreaming as an instrument of change: Australia

8. Where the spirits never died ~ 103
Southeast Asia: Hong Kong, South Korea and Nepal

Continues over ...

•

SPIRITS AT WORK IN MODERN HEALING

9. THE HEALING SHAMAN:
SHAMANS, DOCTORS AND DISEASE ~ 119
*Studies show that modern psychotherapy
and shamanic therapies are equally effective*

10. HEALING: THE NEED TO BELIEVE ~ 128
*Modern research discovers what native healers knew all along:
Many physical ills, heart attack and cancer among them,
have deep-seated psychological causes
for which shamanic treatments can be effective.*

11. THE FEMININE TOUCH: WOMEN AS HEALERS
THE TWENTY-FIRST CENTURY MUST BE FEMALE ~ 140
*Myths describe the loss of women's shamanic power in ancient times.
In some cultures female healers still dominate.
In others, female power is on the rise again.
Female shamans speak.*

•

A TIME OF TRANSITIONS

12. EVERYTHING IS ENERGY / ENERGY IS EVERYTHING ~ 155
*A time for vision and forward thinking.
Prometheus is once more struggling to be free.*

13. TO HEAL THE WORLD:
THE WORLD TREE SPROUTS AGAIN.
CONCLUSION ~ 160
*Black Elk's vision. A healing environment.
Positive interviews describe the role of shamans in the modern world*

•

BIBLIOGRAPHY ~ 173
ENDNOTES ~ 181
INDEX ~ 187

Spirit in Health: Background

As a current affairs television producer, I spent time describing the failings of the human condition. Visits to native communities in Canada during those years dealt with social problems. On a positive note, those visits made me aware that native peoples are fighting significant odds to re-assert the worth and vitality of their spirituality and rebuild their cultures. It came as a shock to me to recognize that the worldview of primal peoples ('First Nations' in Canada) is not only different in degree from the 'majority culture'; the worldview of primal peoples is conceptually different.

Leaving television, I started a magazine for an information technology company. It explained high performance computing in scientific research and engineering. Redemption for the human condition may not lie with information technology but, remarkably, solving a problem in advanced scientific research demands computer-generated visualizations conceptually resembling the visions sought by shamans. Approaches to scientific revelation seem to be converging with Animists' vision quests and their shamans' pursuit of visions.

Strands on Animist spirituality began coming together. My wife, Carol Burtin Fripp, produced a live-to-air television discussion series, *Speaking Out*, on TVOntario from 1977 to 1991. She addressed many 'new' approaches to the healing arts, i.e. the 'placebo effect', and tumor visualization by cancer patients in order to destroy them. (Dr Carl Simonton spoke to this). Other guests included Dr E. Fuller Torrey, author of *Witchdoctors and Psychiatrists*, and James Lovelock of *Gaia*. These programs showed that much that was new was in fact very old.

It remained to write *Spirit in Health*. It explores traditional spiritual approaches to healing, first looking at healers' roles in the pre-historic Animist world and the reasons for their downfall. Following chapters describe traditions and practices by region, (Siberia and Inuit, North America, Europe, Australia, etc.). We explore spiritual techniques that may be applied to mental and physical health in modern medicine. *Chapter 11* describes the fall of women from dominant spiritual roles they held through much of pre-history. Interviews with female shamans tell us that feminine spiritual power is rising again. The conclusion links Animism, modern science and the quest for environmental health.

Spirit in Health shows parallels between shamanic thinking and modern approaches to problem solving. For example, the Australian Aboriginal concept that translates poorly as the 'Dreamtime' finds unexpected expression in work by the European Community's Forward Studies Unit.

The book brings the nature of Animist beliefs to life for a Western audience. Many indigenous peoples never lost their ancestors' values; rediscovering them has come as release and a joy. Now, Westerners are exploring the ancient shamanic methods of catharsis and healing.

What were those methods? What was shamanism? It was not a religion, not even a belief system. It is a method by which shamans in pre-religious, Animist communities invoked spiritual force: they asked spirits for aid in the hunt, for wisdom, healing and knowledge of plant and animal powers. Lore preceded law. Shamans used spirit-powers to heal physical and mental complaints in pre-technological times.

Spirit in Health explores the mind of the healer from origins in the ancient hunter's world leading to modern medical therapy. Although modern health professionals employ shamanic techniques, the word 'shaman' has been scrupulously banished from the vocabulary of the healing arts. (For clarity's sake, *Spirit in Health* uses 'shaman' where the word is appropriate in a general sense. Chapters devoted to specific cultures use regional terms.)

A third theme explains, not what we have, but what we lack. The juggernaut called Progress sucks a spiritual vacuum behind it, creating a sense of loss that is hard to express. For many, the rapid advance of progress results in a quest for lasting values. The Sixties' counterculture was an obvious manifestation of this spiritual backlash, when youth found value in Earth, flowers, music, dancing and song. Searching for role models, the counterculture discovered indigenous peoples just when those peoples were struggling to avoid cultural annihilation. Many subsequently succeeded in rebuilding their damaged cultures and their pride. One consequence has been a sustained and growing interest in the ancient healing methods and spiritual values of shamanism. I hope *Spirit in Health* may help.

Robert Fripp,
Toronto, 2017

FROM ANCIENT TIMES

1

Spirits of old
THE FALL AND RISE OF SPIRITS AND SHAMANS

In the 1630s a Jesuit missionary, Father Paul LeJeune, studied the work of aboriginal healers in an area stretching from Lake Huron through Quebec and Labrador. LeJeune reported in his book *Relations* that native healers, men and women, believed a significant cause of disease to be

> 'the mind of the patient himself, which desires something, and will vex the body of the sick man until it possesses the thing required. For they think that there are in every man certain inborn desires, often unknown to themselves, upon which the happiness of individuals depends. Shamans, as they think, have a divinely imparted power to look into the inmost recesses of the mind'.[1]

Three centuries later and half a world away, physicians in New South Wales met in 1935 to discuss why Aboriginal patients failed to recover after apparently successful operations for appendicitis and other ills. The doctors, failing to take their patients' belief system into account, had been treating Aborigines' physical ailments without recognizing a spiritual component in disease. Their patients, on the other hand, knew that the first cause of their illnesses had been projected into their bodies by bad magic or a hostile spirit. They needed reassurance that the 'object' or 'agent' had been drawn out of their bodies, and only a 'clever-man' could do that. Once this was understood, doctors encouraged clever-men to suck offending 'objects' from post-operative patients' bodies and hurl them away in the sand. Then the patients healed.

Clever-men, medicine-men, shamans and mudang (female healers of Korea) have much in common. They practise ancient arts that heal patients by spiritual means. As such, they are members of the first learned profession in the history of human society. What does this ancient and complex profession involve?

The oldest, most widespread spiritual belief of the human species holds that everything—the cosmos, humans, plants, rocks, energies, and air—is alive and possessed of spiritual force. This Nature-rooted worldview is known as Animism. For Animists, Nature is a living web of spirits outside time and space; it is a part and parcel of being, a constant lesson in living. In Animist cultures the healer, male or female, acts as intermediary between humans and the spirit worlds.

Principal among their activities, skilled shamans learn the power of healing from the cosmic forces they encounter in those spirit worlds. Plants, animals and spirits speak to them, teach them and guide them in advice they should give, diagnose their clients' problems and tell them how they should heal. To a shaman, rocks, soil and wind are imbued with the same spirit-energy as living things. Every thing that exists is alive, and as such can be called upon for advice or for help in healing.

Between five and three thousand years ago, Animists and their shamans began to be pushed aside or absorbed by new, major world religions.

The modern spiritual view in much of Europe and the Middle East involves created beings and a Creator: His people and their God, an I and a Thou. This duality extends to the mystery of the natural world where creation is seen as a struggle among divine forces to impose order on chaos. Thus the age-old struggle by Man as the earthly surrogate of 'God', to master Nature and build where nothing stood before. As Genesis puts it: 'Be fruitful, and multiply, and replenish the earth, and subdue it: and have dominion over ... every living thing that moveth upon the earth'. That is the modern Western view.

God as such does not exist for many Asians. Instead, all creation is bound together by two opposing, complementary forces. The totality of things may be represented by the circle of *yin* and *yang*, balancing in harmony with each other. Neither is complete without the other. Taking it further, true spirituality depends upon leaving one's ego behind, abandoning the notion of self and recognizing one's being as part of the One that flows through every thing. Buddhism does not apportion a 'soul' to each human being. Rather, each person is a sharer in a universal consciousness that always was and always will be.

Without exception the principal world religions are less than four thousand years old. Before they usurped the spiritual stage, our ancestors' cosmic outlook was based on some form of Animism, interpreted for people by the spiritual specialists in each community, the shamans.

Spirits of Old

In our own time shamanism remains an active force around the great northern ring of Eurasia from Lapland to Siberia, south across China, Korea, northern Japan, central Asia, and down into Indonesia. Shamanism retains what are perhaps its most ancient forms among the Bushmen (San) people of southern Africa's Kalahari Desert, and in Aboriginal Australia. Practised by most indigenous peoples of the Americas from the Canadian Arctic to Tierra del Fuego until the missionaries arrived, the old traditions are on the rise again. Even where Animist healing has been absorbed into such modern religions as Buddhism and Taoism, its ancient influences are still clear, remaining a potent force in Nepal, for example.

WHAT IS A SHAMAN?

Shamans, women and men, are custodians and practitioners of age-old techniques with which they maintain and restore health and spiritual wellbeing for their clients and communities. Although the lost, dark world of the Old Stone Age conceals shamanism's origins, one focus of its practices is clear: lacking the benefits of technology, shamans applied the full force of the human mind to the task of healing. Their techniques were mental and spiritual, as well as physical. Remarkable similarities in beliefs and practices all over the world suggest that thousands of years of trial and error led practitioners everywhere to reach the same successful conclusions. These similarities also suggest that mental principles governing shamanism are fundamental to the human mind.

| Lacking technology, shamans applied the full force of mind

Shamans are distinguished from members of other healing arts by their ability to drop at will into an altered state of consciousness which Mircea Eliade, one of the twentieth century's leading religious scholars, calls 'ecstasy'. In this ecstasy, or trance-state, a shaman's soul is said to leave his or her body and journey to one of two main spirit-realms, the Lowerworld or the Upperworld, which anthropologist Carlos Castaneda describes as 'non-ordinary reality'. By transcending ordinary reality in this way a shaman helps his patients escape their bondage in the physical dimension of our Middleworld—and that includes the temporal reality of sickness.

| Soul loss

In shamanism, misfortune or ill health may result from losing one's spiritual guardian or parts of one's soul, which is worn away and carried off by the stresses of life. The loss of one's spouse, career, or serious shock such as rape can precipitate illness that, in shamanic terms, indicates soul loss. Then a shaman has to journey to the spirit worlds to wrest back his client's soul.

On a spirit-journey to the Lowerworld, shamans typically visualize themselves slipping down a tunnel through the earth, a tunnel that may begin at a tree-root, an animal burrow, a hollow tree or a spring. (Mandalas fit here, too. They will come later.) A journey to the Upperworld may start with a shaman visualizing himself rising into the air from the top of a tree or in a column of smoke. (The use of male pronouns reflects a shortcoming of the English language. Many shamans are female.)

During a trance-induced spirit-journey a shaman experiences visions in which spirits from the otherworlds advise and aid him in his battle against hostile spiritual powers. A good shaman leads his people by example, showing by efforts on his clients' behalf that they are not spiritually isolated. Through their shaman, sufferers can call upon the powers of the spirit world in their struggles against death and disease.

Given the span of time and geography through which the shaman's calling has evolved, it is no surprise that their skills have been pressed into many services. Apart from the central role as healer, a people's traditions may put their shaman to work as priest, seer, mystic, magician, psychologist, judge, advocate, civic leader and historian of tribal lore. Shamans may be called on to change the weather, name newborns, secure a supply of fish or game, and preside over rites of passage into this life or out of it. Long before Joseph took on the role for an Egyptian Pharaoh in the Book of Genesis, shamans interpreted dreams.

Many roles, parts

As scholars of Nature, shamans study the lives and properties of animals and plants, getting to know them well, for these make powerful medicines, spirit helpers, or hostile powers. With their wide experience of spiritual life, shamans can converse as easily with otherworlds of spirits as with mortals. And they do, seeking answers from spirits about the maze that is a human mind: they delve into it to repair clients' souls that were lost or damaged in times of panic or despair.

THE MAKING OF SHAMANS

Some are born to be shamans, some receive a call in adolescence or mid-life, but in the end good shamans must be made. Long, often arduous training in ecstatic techniques transforms an initiate's mind until he is able to detach from roots anchored in a single time and place. When he disciplines himself to shift at will from an ordinary state of consciousness to an altered state—anthropologist Michael Harner uses the term 'shamanic state of consciousness' (or 'SSC')—he will gain direct and intimate insights (in/sights) from his journeys through the spirit worlds.

Attaining that state may call for a pilgrim's struggle through all sorts of hells. Depending on the customs of his culture, initiation may throw a novice into spiritual dismemberment and dislocation. Deprivation, fasting, isolation, or hallucinatory drugs such as *ayahuasca* (*yagé*) force a novice to reconstruct his mind and soul in a way that permits him to acquire wisdom and experience from the otherworlds. This theme of spiritual dismemberment is a recurring feature of shamanic initiations all over the world; it represents the tearing down of the frail, limited ego that can see no farther than death: the mortal body. This is then reassembled, being reconstituted by spiritual helpers as a temple empowered, transformed (em/powered, trans/formed) by the Divine. (For example, the Egyptian god Osiris was torn apart by Seth, and then reassembled by Isis with greater spiritual powers.)

| Shamanic state of consciousness

Not only will a competent shaman learn to communicate with spirits during his/her rigors of instruction, he will also learn to control them and put them to work for himself or his people, until they become his SPIRIT HELPERS—'familiars' in medieval Europe, *rai* to Australia's Aborigines, *apErshat* to the Inuit; *manitou* to the Ojibway; *tsentsak* to the Jívaro of the Peruvian Amazon.

Ecstatic transformation allows a shaman to recognize the spirit world in all its changing shapes. It lets him put his insights to good use by diagnosing with the spirit-gift of a 'strong eye', or directing the powers of his spirit helpers. The adept shaman may be time-lost in the great primordium; he understands the songs in rocks, vibrations from the earth, the energies of trees—and puts them to good, healing use. But just as his specialist knowledge sets him apart, a shaman has to apply himself and his knowledge to the mundane world and set about the task of serving his community. The cycle must return full circle. The spirit-code demands no less.

VISIONS or DREAMS make some shamans; a CRISIS OF MIND gives birth to others. Asian shamans in general, and Siberians in particular, are 'reborn' to a calling as healers in response to an ill-defined crisis or nervous implosion.

St Paul's conversion to the cause of Christ was induced by a heavenly light accompanied by the celestial voice of Jesus, following which Paul was blind for three days. Prophets of every conviction before and since have had similar moments of terror, followed by lifetimes of insight and certainty. When Moses came down from Mount Sinai with the Ten Commandments he appeared to the Israelites as a man transformed. 'When Moses came down from Mount Sinai ... Moses wist not that the skin of his face shone. ... When Aaron and all the children of Israel saw Moses ... they were afraid to come nigh him'. (Exodus 34:29)

This 'flash' of ENLIGHTENMENT (en/lighten/ment) seems to be essential for the making of some shamans. The invocation 'Lighten our darkness!' was a shamanic precept for thousands of years before it strayed into a Christian prayer. A shaman on soul voyages examines darkened worlds that other mortals never see. He is a seer (see/er), one whose insights reach far beyond the perceptions of others. For most of us, 'seeing' involves looking outwards. For shamans it involves looking inwards—or rather, looking past limitations of the senses to discern a greater consciousness beyond/within. The essential training of a shaman is not intellectual; it is hard-won of experience and often suffering. Thus the re-making of a shaman's mind trains him or her to find spirit-influence in the dark recesses of his cosmos, perception beyond the visible spectrum, beyond conscious thought, beyond intellect, a kind of 'focused intuition'. As the shamanic classic, the *Tao Te Ching*, puts it:

> 'Without going outside, you may know the whole world.
> Without looking through the window,
> You may see the ways of heaven.
> The farther you go, the less you know.
> Thus the sage knows without traveling;
> He sees without looking;
> He works without doing'.[2]

Anthropologist Michael Harner compares the oldest sense of the English word 'enlightenment' to the Inuits' Inuktitut word *qaumanEq*,

> 'the mysterious light which a shaman suddenly feels in his body, inside his head, within the brain ... which enables him to see in the dark, both literally and metaphorically speaking, for he can now, even with closed eyes, see through darkness and perceive things and coming events which are hidden from others; thus they look into the future and into the secrets of others'.[3]

That was also how Arctic explorer Knud Rasmussen described Inuit shamans in 1929,[4] as women and men able to transcend material dimensions to journey through space, time or walls.

Enlightenment is fundamental to the shamanic state among primal peoples. In Australia, initiates are said to have been dismembered and born again, their guts replaced by crystalline quartz; when a Wiradjeri man achieves enlightenment, his people celebrate his passage by sprinkling him with a sacred 'water' of quartz sand, 'solidified light', Eliade calls it. Later in a shaman's career he will be able to pull quartz crystals, his *atnongara*, from his body at will. Among Northern clans these crystals may represent his 'strong eye', his diagnostic power.

Harner, who spent two years with the Jívaro on the eastern slopes of the Ecuadoran Andes, tells how Jívaro shamans radiate an aura visible to other shamans[5] during trance-state journeys of exploration in the otherworlds. Centuries earlier, and more than a thousand mountainous miles away, the similar 'radiating energy' (*cizin*) of a priest's enlightenment was depicted in Mayan art by lines or feathers radiating as an aura from an icon's head.

From before the age of biblical prophets until now, mighty shamans have been born out of dark days of sickness, visions, seizures, grief, depression—and flashes of blinding light. Women, wolves, eagles, bears and trees, amongst other beings, appear to 'newly inspired' souls in crisis, dragging them back to health and staying on in the psyche as their first spirit helpers. Crisis, and the anxiety it brings, may not be sought but, equally, it has often proved to be the essential catalyst for change and insightful rebirth as a shaman.

The INITIAL 'CRISIS' which many shamans experience is not a nervous breakdown, although to people not born in shaman-supportive cultures it must appear to be. Joseph Campbell describes these episodes as 'normal' for a gifted mind smothered in a mundane world.

Early researchers thought that shamanism began as an Arctic phenomenon that spread around the world. They blamed some shamans' often bizarre personality shifts on extreme cold, endless winter nights, solitude, or a lack of vitamins that supposedly gave rise to mental illnesses such as Arctic hysteria or shamanic trance. But scholars point out that shamans-to-be often start off in life as persons who are extra-sensitive to events around them, at once impatient with their fellow humans and receptive to the sacred character of spirit-worlds. The tradition is as old as faith: Jesus fasted in the wilderness, King David and John the Baptist took to the Wilderness of Judea, Mohammed to a cave, many prophets to the 'wilderness', Buddha to a Bodhi tree, Merlin to the woods.

The antennae of such sensitives are tuned and trembling, the vibrations of the universe received on every frequency. For many spiritual novices the period of crisis or self-doubt is the means of coping, by which a spirit is hardened till the noises of the cosmos can be reined in, channeled, harnessed, sequenced, and put to use. Just as a rough gemstone must be polished to evoke its brilliance, so the rebuilt psyche of one who awakens to his shaman-self will be harder, clearer, healthier than it was before.

In myth and in practice, many cultures have accepted 'death-in-life' crises as springboards to a higher state. 'Rebirth' has been basic to spiritual wellbeing since early times, finding modern expression in the challenge of Christian fundamentalists: Have you been reborn in Christ? Myth and history provide other examples: 'At the point of death a man's self is reborn', St Francis said.

Death-in-life |

Shamanic cultures say much about death-in-life and subsequent rebirth. A late nineteenth century Bushman, Xhabbo (Dream), described how Moon sent Hare to earth with a crucial message to all humans: 'As I in dying am renewed again, so shall you dying be renewed again'.[6] Among the Dené of northern Canada, all sorts of individuals pick up shamanic powers in the course of a long life until, as anthropologist Marie-Françoise Guédon expressed it, 'in dying, one becomes a shaman'.[7] The author Karen Armstrong writes,

> 'Psychologists tell us that ... isolation and deprivation not only brings about a regressive disorganisation of the personality, but that, if it is properly controlled, it can promote a constructive reorganisation of deeper forces within a person. At the end of his ordeal, [a] boy has learned that death is a new beginning'.[8]

The shaman dwells at the heart of human experience, the better to heal the sick, pour comfort on suffering, predict and interpret the demands of spirits, bring prosperity to the community—and throw light on the darkest mysteries, whether they lurk at the centre of a patient's inner being, or come as thunder-voiced malignant spirits in a cold, mid-winter night.

Success in THE HUNT was essential to the survival of all early human cultures. More than 35,000 years ago a Neanderthal hunter killed a mammoth in what is now Lower Saxony. The position of a yew-wood spear unearthed among the mammoth's bones suggests that the victorious hunter had to scramble around beneath the maddened beast to kill it with a thrust to the belly. The hunter's success required strength, skill and good luck that must have been all too rare. The man who killed that mammoth, and others in his hunting party, had to marshal their strength, their energy and their courage beforehand, perhaps by ritual dancing and exercise, working themselves into a high state of exaltation. Success called on courage, and courage on success. Both demanded physical and spiritual preparedness.

Spirits of Old

Hunters also had to invoke beasts' consent to kill them, a formidable spiritual task, and a practice unchanged from the time of cave art to the twentieth century. In 1924, the explorer Rasmussen described how Inuit hunters invoked whale spirits in order to let those animals be taken.

Anthropologist Edmund Carpenter, who worked among the Inuit for many years, described how, when a hunter makes an effigy of a hunted animal,

> 'perhaps he does this with the illusion of being able to possess the animal through the medium of its effigy, but he himself explains his effort as a token of thanks for food or services received from the animal's spirit'.[9]

Across the world, in Africa's Kalahari Desert, writer Laurens van der Post wrote about an incident that might have happened in the Stone Age, except that it took place in 1960. A decorated soldier with years of jungle warfare behind him, van der Post shot at a steenbuck about twenty yards away intending to feed a party of starving Bushmen. He fired, and fired, emptying his magazine at a standing target without so much as grazing the buck. Nor did the animal run at the sound of the gun. The two Bushmen in his party, one of whom was starving, were highly amused. Van der Post's translator, Dabé, consulted the other Bushman and reported that magic protected the steenbuck. That night, an 'old father' explained to van der Post what every Bushman knew, that a 'steenbuck person' stood behind a hunter when he aimed and 'pulled at his arm and made him miss'.[10]

The steenbuck story makes clear that a hunt took place on many planes, not just in the breath-tearing, muscle-wrenching, bruising chase, but also in remote reaches of the mind. Omens, dreams and visions had to be sought and interpreted if a hunter were to be prepared spiritually against the hazards and long odds, whether the quarry was a steenbuck or a mammoth. What the hunt demanded in strength and in the skill of Nature's ways must often have been augmented by recourse to altered states of consciousness. Men had to hunt to live, and they had to do it over and over again. The constant demand on emotional resources must at times have made spiritual dimensions more pressing, intense and real than the material one. Thus the otherworlds of spirits. And thus the shaman.

Hunter and hunted

The tale of the steenbuck, repeated over and over across the wastes of time among primal cultures, suggests the deepest relationship between hunters and hunted. Once, myths tell us, humans and animals spoke together and animals took human form; all life was one. In a shamanic state of consciousness, or the Aborigines' Dream Time, all Nature is still one.

'[L]ines between species and classes, even between man and animal, are lines of fusion, not fission, and nothing has a single, invariable shape', is how Edmund Carpenter describes Inuit mythology. Theirs is 'not a concept of becoming, not even metamorphosis, but rather a sense of being, where each form contains multitudes'.[11]

Modern science began making sense of shamanism when quantum mechanics proposed that, by observing something, the observer affects that which is observed. After missing the steenbuck, van der Post sat on the edge of a Kalahari saltpan to watch the evening fall. 'I was convinced that, just as the evening was happening in us, so were we in it, and the music of our participation in a single overwhelming event was flowing through us'. Thus the quantum physicist, the saint and the hunter-soldier-traveler.

THE FALL OF ANCIENT SHAMANISM

Revered and feared as they are in their own societies, shamans are also men and women apart. A lifelong student of mythology, Joseph Campbell points out that, historically, shamans thrived in hunting cultures where personal initiative, daring and enterprise were called for. A hunter-gatherer's life will not sustain large settlements, so hunting peoples live as they always have, in groups of no more than forty to fifty souls. Belief systems in Old Stone Age hunting clans—worlds of spirits made manifest by shamans—were intensely personal.

The fall of shamanism

But when hunting peoples settled down to become farmers, the new social order demanded teamwork, not individualism, and the shaman and his reputation slid into a long decline. As the hunter's old ways surrendered to settled villages and fields in the New Stone Age, a part of the shaman's realm surrendered, too. Agriculture attracted people to fixed settlements, and with them came the need for rule. Fixed settlement demands order, hierarchy, and a specialist priesthood imposing discipline, rituals and justification—namely, its local god.

The opposing spiritual tensions dividing human populations in changing times are described in the Greek myth of the fall of Prometheus. On one hand Prometheus, the intransigent, tough-minded magician, was an outcast in his own society. The 'titan power of the shaman' ignored the dictates of the gods or God, for he was older, wiser and stronger in spirit than the upstart god-myths barring his way. On the other hand, Prometheus (the 'man of forethought' in Greek) was opposed by come-lately priests claiming creation as the product of their gods, and hence themselves.

The Book of Genesis handles this transition in the story of the brothers Cain and Abel. Abel remained a nomad, roaming freely with his flocks; Cain became a farmer, a settled man. 'Abel was a keeper of sheep, but Cain was a tiller of the ground' (Genesis 4:2). When God preferred the nomadic Abel's sacrifice, his jealous brother killed him. As metaphor, the story suggests that the farmer usurped the nomad's 'golden age', blocking the herdsman's paths, laying claim to what had been common land. Fifteen hundred years after Genesis was written, St. Paul commented that Abel, 'being dead, yet speaketh' (Hebrews 11:4). So he does. This biblical story represents the greatest social and cultural shift in human history.

In the fifth book of the Old Testament, written about twenty years after Genesis, we discover the death-knell of shamanism in the land of the Israelites, as given by God to Moses: 'If there arise among you a prophet, or a dreamer of dreams, and giveth thee a sign or a wonder, and the sign or the wonder come to pass ... that prophet, or that dreamer of dreams, shall be put to death' (Deuteronomy 13:1, 5).

> Gods displace spirits & shamans

Here lies the basis of the ancient shaman's challenge to authority, and of his defeat. Shamans held that *humans* created the later gods, whereas shamanic authority is drawn from the spirits of the larger cosmic worlds. The shaman holds that, in the time of his ancient spirit-sense, mankind reached out long ago and, as a partner in creation, helped shape his world.

Since the old primal belief was that words, poems and songs were powerful in creating the reality to which they gave voice (or which gave them voice), New Stone Age priests, by naming their gods, breathed life into them, (literally in/spired them), made them real. Then, having real/ized their gods, rising priesthoods promoted their deities as voices of authority. Religious doctrine became weapons of social control.

There was no room in the settled, conformist world of agriculture for individualists, 'men of forethought'. Daring and prowess demanded of hunters became antisocial qualities in the new scheme of things. New hierarchies, doctrines and deities were promoted above challenge from below. Gods displaced the spirit-world of shamans, becoming the sole divine 'realities': man's gods alone were cast as creators of the earth, the heavenly lights, the sea and all that therein is.

A NEW AGE RISING

The rise of Agricultural Man and his gods was imposed thousands of years ago. Times hang on the cusp of change again. In much of the world shamanism never died. Missionaries and colonial governments buried it a while, but, like hot embers beneath cold ash, the old spiritual disciplines needed only a breeze of change to catch a new grip on life.

A new age of shamanism is rising from the ashes of the old, not only among primal peoples. Perhaps it reflects a reaction to materialism in our age. Perhaps it stems in part from the failure of religious institutions to address the spiritual needs of changing, threatening times. Shamanism's rise also reflects a realization by millions that 'business as usual' has become a threat to our planetary envelope; this same unease has forced environmental concerns onto international political agendas, where they will stay for decades to come.

Traditional shamanism never laid claim to be a religion. Shamanism was, and remains, a *method* by which initiates enter altered states of consciousness in order to communicate with, learn from and direct the actions of Nature through her spirits. The one and only point of focus for all shamans was Nature and the natural world. It is to that same ancient, Nature-centered value system that the rest of the human species is slowly struggling to return.

The essential reign of Nature is returning to take its place in the human value system. Prometheus, the 'man of forethought', is tugging free and a new enquiring restlessness is stirring in the human breast. How does the ancient legend of Prometheus end? The rough, unbridled man of forethought is finally restored to Olympus, there to become an advisor, a seer to the gods and, restored to influence once more, to animate men from Nature's clay.

Definitions

Animism is an ancient, once universal belief that all things, including objects like rocks, water, wind, mountains, and natural phenomena such as lightning and volcanoes, are imbued with vital energies. The cosmic spirit of existence washes through each and every thing. Every thing that has material or ethereal presence is alive.

As New Stone Age cultures developed agriculture they removed themselves from raw, life-long dependence on the whims of the hunter-gatherer's natural world. Animist beliefs were replaced in agricultural cultures by priest-led religions that brushed aside Nature and her spiritual world. Instead, the priests demanded adherence to community gods or God. But a significant proportion of the human population continues to hold Animist beliefs.

Shamanism: All shamanic peoples are Animists, but not all Animists practise shamanism. Shamanism constitutes an ancient, worldwide and remarkably consistent spiritual discipline in which sensitives enter an ecstatic trance-state to communicate directly with spirits. In this state shamans transcend material space/time and journey spiritually to Upper and Lower spirit worlds. Here they learn from spiritual contacts, return with power animals (guardian spirits) for clients, and search out and wrest back clients' missing spirits and souls. In this trance state, or even in dreams, a shaman's spiritual contacts may teach him or her the healing arts, which he uses for the benefit of single clients or a whole community. Shamans may be called upon to carry out other functions, too, everything from bringing rain to ensuring a plentiful supply of game. But whatever a shaman is called upon to do, he does it as an instrument of the cosmic power endowed him by his contacts in the spirit worlds.

Spirits: A natural world in which every object or phenomenon is endowed with cosmic force makes itself manifest to human perception through spirits. Water and rocks have spirits, as do earth, mountains and air. Spirits are not abstract beings to people in Animist or shamanic cultures. Spirits are simply the manifestations by which shamans and sensitive people experience the cosmic world. 'Spirits are anything you see with your eyes closed', says anthropologist Michael Harner, and 'spirits represent the healing power of the cosmos'. Psychiatrist Roger Walsh writes, 'Spirits are the way in which shamans and mediums interpret their experience'. Spirits are the mind-forms (visions) which a seer experiences. Humans, rooted in our senses, have to visualize spiritual things in order to perceive them, making spirits the intermediaries—the interface, in a computer age—between cosmic power and those humans privileged to share and use it.

This thought links spirits with visualization and perception: Rudolf Steiner was a Western man of esoteric and sometimes practical ideas. He claimed that he could visualize spirits during waking hours. Here he writes about training one's sense of perception:

> 'Just as, in the body, eye and ear develop as organs of perception, so a man may develop in himself spiritual organs of perception through which the soul and spiritual worlds are opened to him.'

SPIRITS IN THE WORLD AROUND US

2

People of the North

THE DRUM IS OUR HORSE: SIBERIA

Siberia unfolds across one hundred and ten degrees of longitude, one quarter of the Asian landmass. Many ethnic groups practise shamanism here. Man and the spirits are alive and alert to each other in Siberia.

Siberian shamans often serve as a blueprint against which to compare the rest of the world. Siberia was a nurturing home for shamanic method way back in the Old Stone Age. The word *saman* (shaman) originates in the language of Siberia's Tungus people.

Russians call their Denisova cave in Siberia the 'Cradle of Humanity'. Digging through six metres of sediment, archaeologists have found 22 layers of distinct human cultures going back 282,000 years, including '80,000 items include tools, arms [and] ornaments'.[12] In 2016 the dig found a 50,000 year old bone needle. Here, ancient Denisovans interbred with Neanderthals and more modern humans. Geneticist Svante Paabo states, 'From the molecular anthropological point of view, this is the most important place in the world'.

282,000 years: Animist beliefs and shamanic practices may go back that far, and further.

In the first half of the twentieth century it was sometimes thought that Siberia was the cradle for shamanism everywhere. More likely, similar practices arose from subconscious human needs and abilities over and above distinct tribal and regional cultures. Siberian practices tell much about shamanic methods around the globe.

Fifteen thousand years ago, the Siberian climate was warmer than it is now. Pollen analysis shows willow, spruce, pine and birch trees growing along the coast of the Arctic Ocean, several hundred miles north of their present range. Bones of large mammals tell us that hunting was good, and it is reasonable to expect that wildfowl flourished, migrating north to spend summers in the coastal marshes. Along the River Lena and its tributaries—a region centered on the modern town of Yakutsk—Stone and Bronze Age Yakut hunters scratched hundreds of animal drawings, notably elk, into the walls of cliffs. Many survive. The animals are depicted running wild or being hunted, wounded and killed by deadfall traps, or herded into palisades.

Consider the scale. A tiny human settlement lay like a pinprick in a vastness of forest. The ring of white birch trunks at the edge of the clearing emphasized the brooding darkness among encircling trees. In search of release, the eye would be drawn upward to the ring of sky whence came the changing seasons, storm and weather. One imagines how the sense of isolation might have encouraged a mind to seek assistance in the spiritual world.

Dwarfed in their cosmos, how did hunters in their scattered hamlets view their fellow beings in this shared creation—the beasts they preyed upon, the animals they killed? Not as prey. That is the view of ethnologist Evelyne Lot-Falk, whose classic study of Siberian hunting peoples offers a fluent analysis of the 'spirit of the hunt'.[13]

Early hunters saw the whole natural world as a province of spirits— if not as the physical embodiment of spirits made manifest. In such a world, Nature herself is forever in motion and material forms are fluid: animal, plant and mineral manifestations represent changeable forms within one creation. The modern notion of classifying organisms into related species and groups falls away. All are but shades of the One. Nothing is certain. One moment a moth in flight is what it seems to be; then, landing, it disappears (dis/appears), seemingly becoming rough bark on a tree. One moment a shallow river is clear. But, drop a scrap of food and water spirits fashion a horde of minnows gorging themselves till the food is gone. Then the minnows go too. Everything that is, is alive, or may take life; and a common bond fastens everything that lives. Time, in a world of change and cycling seasons, appears circular: the past infuses the present, and the future overtakes the present in a constant beginning-again.

In the ancient space/time of Animist societies the hunt constituted a struggle by hungry men against the spirit-backed domain of Nature's world. Humans had no divine right to triumph. Survival was triumph enough. To succeed in a world of large quadrupeds required a combination of technical proficiency honed by spiritual discipline, a commitment not unlike that of competitive martial arts today. As Lot-Falk points out, the hunter's world demanded that technical skill and spiritual empowerment be indissolubly linked: the latter fired the former, guided the arm, propelled the weapon, closed the trap on the hunted.

Long ago, the human mind gave rise to systems of belief about origins, cosmologies. The Yakut peoples of central and western Siberia share a threefold cosmology common to many Animist societies: the Upperworld is heaven; the Middleworld is the here and now of solid earth; the Lowerworld is where the earthy spirits dwell. Linking this trinity of worlds is the Tree of Life, its roots anchored and sustained in the Lowerworld, its trunk pushing up through the Middleworld of mortals, its branches thrusting into the heavens of airy spirits and gods. The vision of the Tree of Life is fundamental to Siberian shamanism. Rooted at the centre of the cosmos, at the midpoint of our Middleworld, the Tree of Life symbolizes the spirits' intention to spread happiness to each and every living thing on earth. In *Yakutia*, his 1925 book on the life and beliefs of this ancient people, Russian scholar A.P. Okladnikov includes a description of the tree's role, taken from traditional Yakut epic verse:

'Lonely grew the many-branched
Holy tree of happiness …
Nourished with the juices of this tree,
Bathing in its enlivening flow,
The weak grow strong,
They grow, the small filled out,
The sickly were made whole.
Such was the purpose of that,
For the happiness of the living created,
Blesséd regal tree'.[14]

In the Tungus tradition, shamans' souls were reared in such a tree—the higher in the tree, the more powerful the shaman. So profound was the role of 'Tree' in Siberia that the ancestral shaman-spirit responsible for choosing novices was said to live in the roots of a birch identified by local shamans. In some communities the rim of a novice's drum had to be cut from a tree visited by airy spirits, i.e. struck by lightning. Wood inhabited by such a powerful spirit was the obvious vehicle to transport a shaman in his trances to otherworlds.

'Tree' is also the habitat of birds at rest. The similarity between birds' aerial freedom and a shaman's spiritual flight was already a natural motif when willows still grew on the Arctic shore. Bird-ness illustrates the immortal freedom of each human soul. Joseph Campbell points out that the Buriat word for a shaman's bird or animal protector spirit comes from a verb meaning 'to change oneself, to take another form'. Flying geese carved from mammoth ivory have been found at a Stone Age hunting camp near Lake Baikal. In turn, those figures suggest a shaman drawn at the Lascaux cave in France, whose staff is topped by a bird. Fifteen thousand years later, birds and the sacred tree remain principal motifs on the dress of modern Siberian shamans.

The realities of health and sickness, of the cosmic tree, birds, and elk, which the Yakut hunted—all these creative and sustaining cosmic qualities had to be understood, interpreted and, in so far as it was possible, directed through a shaman's spiritual contacts in other-worlds.

No matter how skilled, a shaman could not function without first having been accepted by his or her community. People had to *believe* in a practitioner's powers. The term 'tribal sanction' remains true of healers in all cultures, be they shamans or medical doctors.

Only those with shaman-ancestors were accepted as novices among his people, said Tungus shaman Semyon Semyonov, in 1925. 'The gift descends from generation to generation'.[15] Among Buryats, ancestor-spirits always hoped to find shaman-potential among their descendants' children. The ancients tutored suitable candidates while they slet.

In Siberia, novices were often found among those who did not fit society's accepted norms. They were men and women smitten with a deeper, more profound sense of the world's spiritual values than the usual, thick-skinned run of mortals. The American psychologist William James coined the term 'tender-minded' for the shamanic personality type. Shamanic peoples believed that psychic energies tended to concentrate in these tender-minded individuals, rather than in ordinary souls. Visions, seizures, periods of bizarre behavior, illness or depression, staring eyes—such characteristics often indicated novice-potential. Dark days of trauma turned the course of many lives, creating mighty shamans. Such people were often left to stray for a time, lonely, on the fringes of their society, tugged in opposing directions by mundane demands and the calling of higher worlds. For a novice this was a time of instruction by spirits, not to be interrupted too soon, but Siberian peoples eventually took charge and apprenticed the candidate to an experienced shaman for months or years, waiting for a moment of enlightenment or until shaman elders were satisfied, at which point some sort of consecration followed.

Healers need tribal or cultural sanction

A novice's initial 'crisis' seems to have been the norm in Siberia, though by no means universal. In the 1880s, the Yakut shaman Tiuspiut confided to anthropologist V.M. Mikhailovskii:

> 'When I was twenty years old, I became very ill and began to see with my eyes, to hear with my ears that which others did not hear or see; nine years I struggled. ... I became so ill that

I was on the verge of death, but when I started to shamanize I grew better'.[16]

Some got the call in mid-life more by accident than design. Around 1920 a Tungus shaman told anthropologist Lev Shternberg that,

> 'Up to the age of twenty I was quite well. Then I fell ill, my whole body ailed me, I had bad headaches. Shamans tried to cure me, but all of no avail. When I began shamaning myself, I got better and better'.[17]

For many, a vision of self-dismemberment brought initiation to an end. In Siberia and central Asia, spiritual reincarnation through a vision of one's own dismemberment was an ancient tradition, the death-in-life experience by which a shaman earned spirit-powers. Yakut shaman Pyotr Ivanov described a typical vision-making of a novice:

> 'The candidate's limbs are removed and disjointed ... the bones are cleaned, the flesh scraped, the body fluids thrown away, and the eyes torn from their sockets. After this operation all the bones are gathered up and fastened together with iron'.[18]

G.V. Ksenofontov recorded a similar Yakut spirit death and birth:

> 'The evil spirits carry the future shaman's soul to the underworld ... cut off his head, which they set aside (for the candidate must watch his dismemberment with his own eyes), and cut him into small pieces, which are then distributed to the spirits of the various diseases. Only by undergoing such an ordeal will the future shaman gain the power to heal. His bones are then covered with new flesh, and in some cases he is also given new blood'.[19]

As late as the 1950s, a Hungarian researcher, Vilmos Dioszegi, recorded the vision of the shaman Kyzlasov:

> 'In my dreams I had been taken to the ancestor and cut into pieces on a black table. They chopped me up and then threw me into the kettle and I was boiled ... When I came to from this state, I woke up. This meant that my soul had returned. Then the [master] shamans declared: "You are the sort of man who may become a shaman" '.[20]

Around the world, novices' death-in-life accounts seem interchangeable. Comments from Greenland, Sarawak, Australia, European folklore, Greek myth and many primal peoples of the Americas would fit here, and only scholars might spot the substitution. Modern research by psychiatrist Charles Tart suggests that, with training, a mind can be repatterned until, with practice, it can indeed shift into an altered—shamanic—state of consciousness (SSC), dropping in and out of the SSC at will. The blinding flash or dismemberment vision represents the moment a mortal becomes a shaman: colors are enhanced, senses overwhelmed and the mind uncovers depths and perspectives it never encountered before. To cross to a shamanic state of consciousness is a willed shift into new worlds.

Christians recall such a blinding flash. Saul, smitten blind on the road to Damascus, changed from persecuting Jesus to becoming a disciple named Paul.

In Siberia, as in other parts of the world, a shaman's preferred vehicle for soul-flight was his drum. This was so crucial to spirit journeys that, when some peoples cut the drum's hoop from the wood of a birch selected by experienced shamans, the tree was left standing, alive. As for the drum-skin, before using his drum the novice was sent off to wander the trails of the animal that had given its life. Be it deer, elk or goat, the beast's spirit had to be thanked. Only then was its hide effective as the shaman's carriage into spirit-words.

Excluding effects of psychedelic drugs, shamans used the potent effects of monotonous rhythm—of verse, song, rattle or drum—to support them on journeys into the SSC. A constant, unstressed drumbeat was the usual vehicle on which shamans journeyed into otherworlds. The drum is still a vital tool, and a shaman's badge of office, a symbol of his spiritual attainment and of ecstatic journeys between worlds. 'The drum is our horse', Siberian shamans say. Across Arctic Eurasia the drum is known as a shaman's horse, roebuck, deer, mount or steed.

> 'The drum is our horse'

Drumming sets up alpha and theta waves in human brains, patterns associated with creative thought or going to sleep. Measurements made at spirit dances of Canada's Coast Salish people found a theta frequency from four to seven cycles a second, the optimal rate for inducing trance states. In one experiment, ten minutes of drumming put a shaman into an altered state of consciousness comparable to that attained by a Zen master after a full six hours of meditation. It has been estimated that a majority of novices can experience a successful spirit-journey on a first attempt if a drumbeat of 200 to 220 a minute supports them. One result of such an altered state of mind is that the brain begins to make beta-endorphins, the body's natural painkillers.

To journey in the shaman-state may be an important step in one's personal development, but it is just a beginning. *Support* is what a shaman's life's endeavor is about. The major thrust of shamanic practice must be to assist the dis-spirited, heal the sick, and uphold the wellbeing of a shaman's people. As a drum supports the shaman's journey into the otherworlds of the SSC, so the shaman in turn supports his own community.

Joseph Campbell describes the Yakut shaman, Aadja, flying to rescue a soul:

> 'Riding—as they say—on the sound of his drum, [the shaman] must sail away, on the wings of trance, to whatever spiritual realm may harbor the soul in question, overwhelm the guardians of that celestial, infernal, or tramontane place, and work swiftly his shamanistic deed of rescue'.[21]

Since, in shamanism, illness may result from soul loss or the loss of a power animal or guardian spirit, a shaman's spirit-journeys are the vehicle by which an individual's—or a community's—health and welfare must be retrieved.

The drum is central to a shaman's role in many parts of the world where its rhythm represents its owner, spirits to which he or she must travel, and the patient on whose disease (dis/ease) these spirits pronounce and prescribe. All healing instructions and techniques pass as dialogues between the shaman's traveling soul and otherworld spirit-beings. The spirits diagnose, recommend, and prescribe. The shaman then effects a cure, but the healing power comes from the spirits via the booming, driving rhythm of the drum. Nor are spirits' instructions limited to healing single patients or providing therapy to a community. A shaman's encounters with spirits may lead to foreknowledge of coming events or instructions for a successful hunt. Spirits can be invoked to change the weather, drive hunted creatures into traps, and provide fish, fruit, game, and the wisdom for living.

Yakut epic poems equivalent to Homeric verse speak of women in important roles. These *olonkho* refer to women as 'white' shamans for the color of their costumes, hung with rings and silver bells.

> 'We stand before you,
> Blesséd she-shamans of the light
> With pure thoughts, with cleansed bones'.[22]

'Cleansed bones' implies the women's rebirth as shamans after dismemberment visions, and the shaman-state made them pure. Purity meant more than chastity: spirits voiced their truths and channeled wisdom through chaste persons in matters of healing or the hunt.

A powerful Yakut spirit was Baay-Bayanay, 'the spirit master of the dark forest and the ruler of the animals dwelling in its depths'. Baay-Bayanay had a female aspect as the giver of children. Female spirits were responsible to see that birds and animals reproduced. Ancient cliff drawings in Yakutia still show the female aspect of the Grandfather spirit attired in a dress with hair braids.

A hunter appealed to the male aspect of the Grandfather for success. He could invoke Baay-Bayanay, through a shaman, to lead herds of elk to traps or palisades. In *Yakutia*, Okladnikov records a hunter's invocation:

> 'Turn a male elk with branching antlers towards me, lords, my grandfathers! Lords my grandfathers, drive [it] as if to the crossbow; drive [it] as if to my snare'.

Baay-Bayanay replied through the shaman's throat:

> 'For a hunter of my party, why should I not bring some of my long-shanked ones to thy deadfall!'[23]

The shaman kept uttering the spirit's voice, then held up several fingers to show how many elk the hunter would take.

Shamanism is alive and well in Siberia. The world-tree may be battered, 'with slightly rubbed bark, with bare branches and top bent askew', like the spiritual state of the world. But, in one Altayan epic, an 'Orpheus' figure comes into the earth, playing a wooden pipe so sweetly that 'green silk leaves sprouted on the dry branches, [and] innumerable flowers bloomed on the barren earth'. If ever was a time when the cosmic world tree must spring back to life, that time is now.

'THE ONLY TRUE WISDOM LIVES FAR FROM MANKIND'
~ AMONG THE INUIT ~

One February night in the early 1920s, a shaman-hunter from Iglulik, at the northwest tip of Hudson Bay, expressed the most moving and comprehensive view of Inuit (Eskimo) attitudes to life, belief, the cosmos and the spirit worlds. For several evenings, explorer Knud Rasmussen had questioned Aua about taboos encompassing everything from work to diet to childbirth. Regarding these taboos, Rasmussen repeatedly asked 'Why?' but no one ever answered. At length Aua invited his guest outside and pointed across the ice. Moonlight revealed hunters returning from seal blowholes empty-handed. So fierce was the wind that, from time to time, it stopped men in their tracks. Now it was Aua's turn to put questions.

'Why these constant blizzards and all this needless hardship for men seeking food for themselves and those they care for? Why?'

Rasmussen could give no answer.

Aua took him to a house where a woman and children sat shivering, the blubber lamp barely alight, giving no heat. 'Why should it be cold and comfortless in here? Kublo has been out hunting all day, and if he had killed a seal ... the place would be warm and bright and cheerful. Why should it not be so? Why?'

Rasmussen could give no answer.

Next, Aua took him to a snow hut where his sister, Natseq, had been placed in isolation. Her 'malignant cough' made it plain that she must soon die. Aua asked, 'She has lived a long life and given birth to healthy children, and now she must suffer before her days end. Why?'

Rasmussen could give no answer.

Back in his snow-house the shaman explained, 'You see, you are also unable to give a reason when we ask why life is as it is. And so it must be. Our customs come from life and turn towards life; we explain nothing, we believe nothing, but in what I have shown you lies the answer to all you seek'.[24]

The shaman's response to the explorer's questions explained a way of being that had guided the Inuit for generations along a path of least resistance through an unforgiving material world.

Prohibitions, behavior patterns which one must avoid—taboos[25]—represent the negative aspect of a four-point code for harmonious co-existence with the spirit world. On the other hand, offerings, prayers and purifications constitute essential observances. Success in the hunt demands no less. To hunt is to disturb the order of Nature, to attack its animal spirit.

The hunt therefore demands spiritual preparation and reparation. For that reason a hunter must approach the hunt in what Lot-Falk describes as a 'state of grace', like a priest to a sacrifice.

The Inuit led a traditional life for thousands of years. Hunters traveled to their traps or seal-holes, standing silent and still for hours at a time to kill—if the spirits so willed—then returned to the icehouse or the summer tent. In winter the horizon was lost in darkness. At any time visibility could be blanketed by storm, leaving no clear line between land and sea-ice, earth and air. Explorers have described days when a man could see no farther than the tip of his dog-whip, but still the Inuit traveled, navigating by winds present and past (assessed by the cuts and lines of wind-drift), the slopes of land, the sounds of gulls or grinding ice. Furthermore, a traveler had to keep looking over his shoulder, committing to memory the mirror image of his outward journey, or he might never return.

Rasmussen, who understood and spoke several Inuktitut dialects, traveled across the Arctic in the 1920s, west from his native Greenland, across Canada to Alaska. At Nome, he asked the renegade Najagneq if he believed in spiritual powers. The Innu told him:

> 'Yes, a power we call *Sila* ... a strong spirit, the upholder of the universe, of the weather, in fact all life on earth—so mighty that his speech to man comes not through ordinary words, but through storms, snowfall, rain showers, the tempests of the sea, through all the forces that man fears, or through sunshine, calm seas or small, innocent, playing children who understand nothing. When times are good, Sila has nothing to say. He has disappeared into his infinite nothingness and remains away as long as people do not abuse life but have respect for their daily food'.[26]

Discovered after his death, Rasmussen's note reads: 'Najagneq's words sound like an echo of the wisdom we admired in the old shamans we encountered everywhere ...'

As a word, *Sila* is 'difficult to define or even to translate', but Rasmussen offered three senses: the universe; weather; and 'a mixture of common sense, intelligence and wisdom. ... In the religious sense, *Sila* denotes a power that can be invoked and applied by mankind'.[27] Anthropologist Edmund Carpenter, who lived among Inuit in the 1960s, rendered *Sila* as 'thought' and 'outside', which hints that thought is not born of a mind but may be the agent of an external force. Humans give voice to Thought— but Nature must speak it first.

When Nature spoke, man had to respond correctly. Spirit-sense pervaded every aspect of Inuit culture. Souls of humans and animals, living and dead, the spirits and the powers of crushing natural forces—all these had to be taken into account, though they could neither be understood nor controlled. Man had to kill to live, but in doing so he laid himself open to reprisal from an animal's spirit if he did not observe proper respect for it. Failure to do so could cause bad weather, sickness or death. The Mother of the Sea Beasts, Takánakapsâluk (Sedna[28]), might take reprisal by withholding her beasts from the hunt. Besieged in a frigid world of peril, Aua explained taboo by telling Rasmussen why things were as they had to be:

> 'We do not believe, we fear! We fear elements with which we must fight in their fury to wrest out food from land and sea. We fear Sila. We fear cold and famine in cold snow huts. We fear Takánakapsâluk, the great woman at the bottom of the sea, who rules over the beasts of the sea. We fear the sickness that is daily amongst us. Not death. But suffering. We fear the souls of the dead, of human and animal alike. We fear the spirits of earth and air ...' [29]

Among the Inuit, shamanism was the bastion against a harsh natural world, but the spirits' help did not come easily. Shamans had to toil to gain enlightenment and win the aid of spirit-helpers, often by suffering. The initiation of Inuit shamans, male and female, is a tale of freezing, fasting and privation that sounds incredible. But a novice's first quest must be to gain help and wisdom from the spirits. Such a quest has driven shamans of every culture into the wilds, to seek visions in solitude, far from their communities.

West of northern Hudson Bay lie the Barren Grounds, sometimes called the most hostile place of human settlement. The brief summer supports low-growing berry bushes. After that the windswept barrens offer what the name implies. Here, a shaman of the Caribou (or Willow-folk) Inuit, Igjugarjuk, told Rasmussen:

> 'The only true wisdom lives far from mankind, out in the great loneliness, and it can be reached only through suffering. Privation and suffering alone can open the mind of a man to all that is hidden to others. Therefore a shaman must seek his wisdom there'.[30]

Years after that conversation, a photo-spread in *Life* magazine brought world attention to the struggle of the Caribou people. In 1958, famine struck, forcing the Royal Canadian Mounted Police to evacuate survivors to permanent sites west of Hudson Bay. For Igjugarjuk, in the first decades of the twentieth century, even the Barren Grounds did not impose privation and suffering sufficient to bring helper spirits to a novice. Haunted from youth by voices of unknown beings, it was clear to his community that the young Inuk must one day become an *angakoq*, a shaman. In winter he was put in a tiny snow hut, where he fasted for thirty days and 'sometimes died a little'. Near the end he was visited by a being 'in the shape of a woman' who became his helping spirit.

The rigors of initiation were not restricted to men. Igjugarjuk's sister-in-law, Kinalik, was hung out on tent poles for five days in mid-winter, then taken down and shot—before being revived. Allowing for exaggeration, it is clear that novices' sufferings were powerful tools in turning the minds of mere mortals into those of great shamans, capable of visiting and talking to the denizens of spirit-worlds.

In a land of near night for half of each year, the Inuktitut term for shamanic enlightenment, *quamanEq*, takes on special meaning. Aua had had little choice in the manner of his calling. An accomplished female shaman, Ardjuaq, foretold before his birth that he would be an *angakoq*. She had also prophesied his profound knowledge of the physical and spirit worlds. But after Aua's first attempts to seek enlightenment failed,

> 'I sought solitude, and here I soon became very melancholy. I would sometimes fall to weeping, and feel unhappy without knowing why. Then for no reason, all would suddenly be changed, and I felt a great, inexplicable joy, a joy so powerful that I could not restrain it, but had to break into song. ... In the midst of such a fit of mysterious and overwhelming delight I became a shaman, not knowing myself how it came about. But I was a shaman. I could see and hear in a totally different way. I had gained my *quamanEq*, my enlightenment, the shaman-light of brain and body, and this in such a manner that it was not only I who could see through the darkness of life, but the same light also shone out from me, imperceptible to human beings, but visible to all the spirits of earth and sky and sea, and these now came to me and became my helping spirits'.[31]

From that point on, the light of Aua's transformation drew new spirit-helpers to him as a candle-flame draws moths.

Enlightenment takes strange, perhaps literal, forms. A Point Barrow woman, Uvavnuk, was out in the dark one evening when she was struck and entered by a fireball. In that moment she perceived a great light, lost consciousness and became a mighty shaman. She described the spirit that

People of the North

entered her in the fireball as a bear on one side, a human on the other. From then on, when in trance, Uvavnuk glowed with enlightenment. 'Nothing was hidden from her'. At other times, when the trance left her, she no longer glowed and had no special pwers.

This 'shaman-light of brain and body' results from an ability to tune to frequencies of spirit worlds. As in Siberia, attaining that point may drag novices through visions involving dismemberment of their mortal bodies and subsequent rebirth, an experience Rasmussen was startled to discover in his talks with Inuit shamans:

| Mental repatterning. New ways to perceive.

> 'Before a shaman attains the stage at which any helping spirit would think it worth while to come to him, he must, by struggle and toil and concentrated thought, acquire for himself yet another great and inexplicable power: *he must be able to see himself as a skeleton*' (Rasmussen's emphasis).[32]

A dismemberment vision seems to be the way by which the senses register the moment when a novice's mind becomes repatterned; from then on, he or she will be able to drop at will into the shamanic state of consciousness (SSC) for journeys in the spirit-worlds. In Greenland, such visions often involve a bear rushing out on an initiate to

> 'devour all your flesh and make you a skeleton, and you will die. But you will recover your flesh, you will awaken, and your clothes will come rushing to you'.

Sanimuinak, a Greenland Innu,

> 'was approached by a huge bear which bit me in the loins and then ate me. ... When it bit me in the heart, I lost consciousness, and was dead. When I came to myself again, the bear was away'.[33]

In Labrador, Torngarsoak, the Great Spirit himself, disguised as a polar bear, might eat a novice. Instead, the bear became one of Sanimuinak's guardian spirits.

In a world alive with spirits, the living had to protect themselves against malign forces. Taboos often proved effective. But where tradition failed, people relied on the wisdom of their shaman, who had to cope with evil forces by unleashing helper spirits against them.

In Inuit legend, the first shaman to journey to the Lowerworld lived at a time of famine 'around Iglulik'.[34] This stranger entered an icehouse and announced his intention to travel to the bottom of the sea in order to intercede with the Mother of the Sea Beasts. When disbelievers drew aside the hangings in front of the sleeping-shelf,

> 'he was diving down into the earth. ... How the man ever hit on this idea no one knows; he himself said that it was the spirits that had helped him: spirits he had entered into contact with out in the great solitude. Thus the first shaman appeared among men'.[35]

This was a powerful shaman: the Mother of the Sea Beasts took pity and the Iglulik people survived to tell his tale. The example of that first soul-journey has been repeated in every epoch and many cultures around the Northern Hemisphere, from one tip of the Americas to the other, and as far removed from the Arctic as the Kalahari Desert and Australia. Among the Inuit, the Netsilik woman Arnapak was so powerful that she could travel to the Lowerworld in the full light of day.

Imagine the scene of such a descent as Rasmussen describes it. Surrounded by starving people and illness, a powerful shaman prepares to make a spirit-journey to the seabed to intercede with the Great Sea Spirit, herself sick from the 'foul emanations from the sins of mankind'. With the community crowded into the snow-house the drum begins to beat its journey-power, *boom boom boom boom*, summoning the shaman's spirit-helpers to help while he transforms to the spirit-beast or bird that will guide him through his mission and safe return. Then he journeys to the seabed, his spirit-helpers battling hostile forces while the shaman tries to placate Takánakapsâluk (Sedna), assuring her that the community will mend its ways. Eventually he returns to his people with a ritual call: 'I have something to say'.

'Let us hear, let us hear', they respond.

The shaman continues in an old-fashioned language used only by spirits, 'Words will arise!'

This is the people's cue. Up goes a collective *mea culpa*, a Greek chorus of collective and personal guilt. 'It is my fault, perhaps!' Every man and woman present starts revealing wrongs they had committed, taboos they had broken. Tears and laughter flow, and the community feels better for the experience. Pressures of a dark winter recede.

In Western culture this might constitute group therapy.

'Words that we utter must be chosen with care because people hear them', said the Buddha. 'Words influence people for good or ill'.

Words have power. As healing agents, they can prove a mighty force indeed. Healers of every culture have known that words have the power to create their own reality.

As an Inuit hunter had to look over his shoulder to memorize the way home, a shaman presiding over such a community gathering had to assure himself that his soul-journey would end with his safe return. His spirits were essential to secure his return passage. Just as the first Inuit shaman was assisted by 'spirits he had entered into contact with out in the great solitude', shamans still depend upon their spirits' aid. An accomplished soul-traveler 'almost glides as if falling through a tube ... kept open for him by all the souls of his namesakes, until he returns on his way back to earth'.[36]

Note the reference to 'souls of his namesakes'. For Aua, who was named after a 'little shore-spirit',

> 'My first helping spirit was my namesake, a little aua. When it came to me, it was as if the passage and the roof of the house were lifted, and I felt such power of vision, that I could see right through the house. ... The little aua brought me all this inward light ...'[37]

Reports of power and enlightenment come from all corners of the earth. Shaman-sight gives the x-ray vision power of diagnosis, and prescriptions for healing. But power must never be abused. The spirits do not bestow it on mortals as a gift, but as a loan by which earthly shamans heal.

Among the Inuit, comfort and security grew out of a binding sense of community, of knowing that one belonged. The traditional icehouse was a hive, a crowd of busy-ness, of voices and sounds, with little privacy. Ancient hunting cultures in general, and traditional Inuit culture, foster shared community healing—catharsis, by another name.

Like many primal peoples, Inuit believe that in a distant past, humans and animals took on each other's forms. Those days are long gone. Humans no longer understand or speak animal languages, except for shamans in a shamanic state of consciousness.

Inuit tradition tells of one great shaman who was reborn as all sorts of animals, the better to experience their lives. Netsilik tradition says that this ancestor taught humans how to think like animals, as hunting peoples must. They had to invoke the spirits of animals in order to slay them. Not that a shaman was promiscuous about taking on animal form: it was the animal spirit that decided his/her altered form. If that spirit happened to be fish hawk, the shaman would be heard uttering piercing mews, for in trance states it was the helper who spoke through the human throat, not the shaman.

Tales, and Inuit carvings, describe shamans flying as birds or taking form as other beasts. For example, a Copper Eskimo shaman's head and torso turned into a muskox, standing on human legs. An Alaskan shaman appeared, before an audience, to grow feathers on his bare arms. The same phenomenon is reported from Aboriginal Australia.

Shamans routinely used false teeth and tusks in attempts to take on animal attributes. In the Arctic, masks suggested a shaman's familiar, or imbued the wearer with the living spirit of the mask. Transformation tales remind primal peoples of their bonding with the animal world, which was once the standard outlook on life. A shaman's transformation pulled him, or her, across the threshold to another, spirit-centered life and time. Does a spirit-form belong to an animal or to a human? It hardly mattered in a traditional hunting culture such as that of the Inuit. In thought—as in art—it might be both.

Shamanism flourishes in the Arctic. Spirits speak to Inuit and southerners alike in works of sculptors, artists and doll makers who have recently captured their shaman quest in works of art. Crafted in stone, skin, paper and bone, Inuit artisans recapture the spirit-world of the shamanic drum, the rhythm of healing dance, the vision of a novice shaman ripped down to his bones. Here are transformations of men and women turning to walrus, fishhawks, fish or seals. Soapstone dancers, teased from their concealing stone by sculptors' skills, hold each other by the shoulders in eternal embrace. Were we living in their spirit-world, or even in our real North, we might hear them singing legends, sucking joy from a harsh earth, turning into birds or wind, or telling us in throat music of their dream experiences and hunting tales.

An Inuit carver examining a stone does not ask 'What shall I carve?' The Inuk asks, 'What waits to come out?' Good Inuit artists may be a bit shamanic, for distinctions blur between spirit and flesh, animals, objects and man. The same lines may depict many forms: turned one way a sculpture shows Walrus, a different way, Bear. Another carving reveals Bear-Bird-Wolverine. Everything changes, yet nothing changes. Across the great sweep of the Arctic, shamanism lives.

3

Visions, Dreams, Masks and Drums
THE VIBRANT WORLD OF NORTH AMERICA

THE VISION QUEST

Turn on a radio and the ear is alive to transmitted messages that otherwise drill through buildings, air and human brains, unheard, unnoticed, unperceived. Without a receiver the message is silence. Spiritually speaking, most humans walk through life like switched-off radios. The spiritual ether lives, but many are dead to it. Those who master the art of tuning to altered states of consciousness find the spirit-world as alive with Nature's voices as a radio spectrum. The mind must be tuned—repatterned—if it is to receive. Among North American Plains peoples the accepted method is to submit a novice to a vision quest.

| Receiving the spirits

'No man begins to be until he has received his vision'

Ojibway[38]

The experience is intensely personal. If one is lucky, visions come and voices speak, leaving impressions that last a lifetime. Vision quests are traditional in the Sioux nation. Leonard Crow Dog, who served as medicine man through the 1973 siege of Wounded Knee, described a complex vision including a sequence not unlike one described by the prophet Ezekiel, in which wheels alternately formed into a fiery hoop and smaller circles. A bird spoke like a man, instructing him, while feet walked around his tiny vision pit.

| Vision quests

Brooke Medicine Eagle, a shaman of Nez Percé and Sioux ancestry, was visited by a black-haired woman in buckskin who spoke a language that penetrated Medicine Eagle's navel, not her ear. As a result she took no immediate message from this visitation. Instead, 'the words that I put to it have to be my own. I have discovered more and more of what she told me as time has gone on'.

The first step in the novice's quest for shamanic power is to seek the spirits' help. The spirits must make themselves known: one or more must join the novice as a spirit-helper. The vision quest is a time of fasting and lonely contemplation, far from the comforts of family and community, a time of waiting for first contact with the spirit world.

In the 1960s, photographer Richard Erdoes befriended a healer and medicine man of the Lakota Sioux, Lame Deer (John Fire). They eventually collaborated on a book in which the old healer related a vision that sustained him with spiritual power from the age of sixteen till the end of his days.[39]

Lame Deer's vision quest started in a sweat lodge with four medicine men. As Chest, the most experienced healer, poured water over fire-hot rocks, the boy felt as if the steam would burn the eyelids off his face. But over the hiss of steam he took strength from the words of Chest's prayer, 'Oh, holy rocks, we receive your white breath, the steam. It is the breath of life. Let this young boy inhale it. Make him strong'.

After the sweat lodge had purified him, Chest escorted Lame Deer to the top of a hill and left him alone in his vision pit for four days and nights, naked but for a blanket his grandmother had made for the occasion. Apart from his blanket, the boy took only three things into the pit: a peace pipe which had belonged to his father and grandfather, a supply of tobacco made from red willow bark, and a gourd rattle. The pipe proved most valuable, for the column of sacred smoke which rose to the spirit world brought back power to the boy in the pit. 'You feel that power as you hold your pipe; it moves from the pipe right into your body. It makes your hair stand up. That pipe is not just a thing; it is alive'.

Barely an hour elapsed between the scalding heat of purification to the moment when old Chest left Lame Deer, naked but for his blanket, in the vision pit. His skin was still tingling as night came down. As Lame Deer told Erdoes years later, the steam 'seemed to have made my brains empty'. The natural sounds of night came on, made louder by darkness. An owl hooted, mice scurried. Then:

> 'Suddenly I felt an overwhelming presence. Down there with me in my cramped hole was a big bird. The pit was only as wide as myself, and I was a skinny boy, but that huge bird was flying around me as if he had the whole sky to himself. I could hear his cries, sometimes near and sometimes far, far away. I felt feathers or a wing touching my back and head. ... Slowly I perceived that a voice was trying to tell me something. It was a bird cry, but I tell you, I began to understand some of it'.[40]

Within moments the boy heard a voice as well as the bird's call, a high-pitched sound no mortal throat could utter. Then, as if the hill and his vision pit were lifted to the orbit of the stars, he found himself looking down on the heavens with the moon close by at his left hand. A voice was telling him:

> 'You are sacrificing yourself here to be a medicine man. In time you will be one. You will teach other medicine men. We are the fowl people, the winged ones, the eagles and the owls'.

The vision-voice ordered him never to harm a fowl. In return, feathered folk would instruct him whenever he needed a helping vision. 'You will learn about herbs and roots, and you will heal people. You will ask them for nothing in return. A man's life is short', the voice concluded. 'Make yours a worthy one'.

Perhaps one who seeks a vision experiences nothing. This should not be a source of disappointment. Silence and solitude make powerful spiritual foods. Sioux lawyer and former fighter pilot Ed McGaa (Eagle Man) puts it this way:

> 'It is you and your thoughts and your prayers to the Great Spirit. ... Just you, the powers, and isolation. ... Afterward, you, the vision quester, will be better prepared to use the special gifts with which the Great Spirit has endowed you to join with those concerned ones who seek to help this planet'.[41]

DREAMERS OF DREAMS

Dream may be a more powerful form of concentration than anything the ordinary waking state of consciousness can match, and 'concentrating one's mind' on the spirits was essential if an Ojibway wished to form a bridge into their world.

> 'This is a dream I am telling you. I am walking through the bush. ... Then, suddenly ... I am moving through huge valleys, rivers and streams, and I am paddling a canoe! I am going off into the prairies, and that too has a symbolic significance. You see, I am half Ojibway and half Assiniboine, so I am in between the two. ... I look behind, and there stands a huge bear, ten or twelve feet high. I was frightened! Then out comes a Mishipashoo. It is like a serpent, but it has the features of a lynx. ... Then lots of Mishipashoo come crawling out of the water. ... A voice speaks, like vibrations in the mind, "Norval,

my son! Do you see I am only testing you to see if you are brave? That is why the Mishipashoo and the Sacred Bear are there ... All these things that you are afraid of are now down, destroyed, vanished! ... I will protect you as long as you live". So the dream was a religious experience, and it is what has given me a much stronger and stauncher belief'.[42]

Norval Morrisseau was a shaman-artist from northern Ontario whose dreams became works of art—he called them icons—helping those who see them to focus on spiritual powers. 'Whenever you are looking at my pictures, you are looking at my visions, whatever they may be'. Morrisseau's understanding of a shaman's role was to 'transmit power and the vibrating forces of the spirit', producing 'effects that are magical and miraculous'. The shaman-artist won acclaim in Canada's national press and *Time* magazine during 1962. Morrisseau was awarded the Order of Canada in 1978.

Morrisseau's worldview was Ojibway to his core: all people have personal access to power; everyone can draw on a wealth of vital cosmic energies. Everything that exists, even intangibles like folly and wisdom, have spirit powers, or *manitou*, and every manitou can be invoked. The Ojibway hunters who roamed ancestral lands in Ontario and northern Minnesota were at home among tree spirits, moving shadows and the peculiar haunting loneliness of forests everywhere. Perhaps this sense of isolation gave the Ojibway a worldview emphasizing individual as well as collective spirituality. Individual guidance came through dreams.

> Access to vital cosmic energies, manitou

Dreams, in the Ojibway world, have been extolled by professor of religion John Grim as 'the hunter's guide, the source of the warrior's strength, and the most profound revelation of wisdom'.[43] In centuries past, they were regarded as a manitou's virtual orders. French explorer Denis Roudot wrote:

'Dreams oblige [the Ojibway] to undertake wars, to make great voyages, to abandon war parties ... It is also these dreams that give them their spirit, or to use their term, their *manitou*, which they imagine takes care of them in all the acts of their lives'.[44]

Every Ojibway acted on the advice of his manitou, but few people gained sufficient revelation from the spirit world to launch them on the path to tribal sanction as a native healer.

Some did, however. Beyond guidance dreams, the Ojibway recognized a higher step, the 'authorizing dream', a psychic diploma establishing in dreams the extent of a healer's power. A dream about a horned snake or serpent, symbolizing medicine, meant that the dreamer had medical knowledge. If a Thunderbird spirit appeared in his or her dream, a healer would be granted the powers of a *nanandawi*, a sucking-doctor.

In 1937, anthropologist Ruth Landes published the tale of a young Ojibway, Sky Woman, who fled a violent home at the age of nine and lost herself in the woods until a search party found her, days later. Among her rescuers was an old woman whom Sky Woman adopted as her grandmother; the woman represented the stability and love that Sky Woman had missed. Later, when her grandmother fell sick, Sky Woman did what she could to assist her. She sent for help and then, worn out, fell asleep and dreamed that someone was handing her a doctor's rattle, saying, 'Try this on your grandmother. She might get better'. Waking, Sky Woman made a small rattle and tried a sucking cure on her old companion. Four days later the grandmother was on her feet. Help arrived to witness the miracle, and Sky Woman's healing services were in demand from that day forth. She became a famous sucking-doctor. Her dream had given her the power.

'No man begins to be until he has received his vision'.[45] That is how the first people of the Ojibway, the *Anishnabegs*, understood man's purpose in life. *Anishnabegs* were so called because they were made out of nothing, not fire, water, wind or rock. Having been created male and female, they were incomplete without the other. Togetherness gave them meaning and a soul-spirit susceptible to visions and dreams. Dreams were essential to males if they were to receive guidance and self-fulfillment. Females had less need of dreams; women, after all, had given life through the first mother, and thus were fulfilled.

Basil Johnston, a teacher of Ojibway language and mythology, relates the tale of Waubosse (White Rabbit), who chose to seek a vision. After a six-day vigil she was invited to walk the Shining Trail to the sky. There, Everlasting Standing Woman and Little Man Spirit took her to Bright Blue Sky, who told her, 'You will give new voices; you will extend the green; you will give new breath; you will give new branches'. Awaking from dream, Waubosse saw a great moon, which sang: 'You shall see far; you shall hear far; you shall hear things afar; you shall feel things not near; you shall sense things unmoved and unformed'. Only after much thought and guidance did Waubosse understand that she had been given power both to heal and to divine the future as well.

SPIRIT IN HEALTH

A healer whose trances were reinforced by an authorizing dream was drawing on enormous power. He or she was effectively empowered twice, through an authorizing dream expressed in trance. Nor was he drawing on the power of his personal spirit only, but using it to establish an intimate communication with a whole pantheon of spirit force. This channel of spiritual concentration and communication—*manitou kazo*—was the means by which the spirits brought their healing powers to bear through the person in the trance.

POWER OF WOMEN

Lucy Thompson—Talth, to her Yurok people of northern California—was born in 1853 into an aristocratic class that sent many of its daughters to undergo the rigors of training as spiritual doctors. At the age of 63, this 'full-blooded Klamath River woman', as she described herself, published *To The American Indian*, a book that attempted to rebut offensive prejudice being written about aboriginal peoples in North America.

To The American Indian described how a Yurok doctor might select one of her daughters to follow in her profession, while other girls were called to medicine by a dream. However the decision was made, their training was long and arduous. As with so many shamanic peoples, physical hardship and deprivation were the tools that reworked a novice's mind till it became sensitive to the wisdom of the spirit worlds.

Training began when the girls were taken to a purification lodge in late autumn, wearing nothing but a heavy skirt of maple bark. There they began dancing clockwise around a central fire, keeping it up for hours until they were soaked with sweat and could barely stand, at which point each girl threw her arms around the neck of a male relative who danced ahead of her until she dropped. At that point she was taken out of the sweat lodge, bathed and allowed to sleep. The effect must have been similar to that recalled by Lame Deer: the heat and steam 'made my brains empty'. An empty brain is more suggestive to images and voices from the spirit worlds.

That was just the start. These dances went on all winter until, in late spring, the girls were sent to spend summer in a mountain solitude. Only in the fall did they return to the Klamath River country to undergo the sweat lodge ritual again. It took from three to ten years before a candidate was deemed worthy to graduate, in preparation for which she was taken again to the mountains to fast, smoke sacred tobacco and pray. 'This girl is a virgin', Talth wrote, 'as perfect in stature and active in movement and health as God can make her. She can bear hardships and punishment without complaint or murmur that would make a bear whine'.

This was just as well, because now the whole community was welcomed to a grueling ceremony at which the young doctor received her final degree. Once more she danced around the fire, enduring up to four hours of heat and fatigue before two men took her by the arms and kept her dancing till she fell. 'The young doctor does not always go through this ordeal and come out safely, as sometimes she became so warm that she would never recover from the effects of the severe punishment, but this seldom happens'.

Those who survived the ordeal were proclaimed doctors with full tribal sanction. Now they were seers, using their powers of insight to scan a patient's internal organs, diagnosing causes of sickness and methods of cure, sucking pain from a client's body, and healing through the use of chanted invocations or their herbal skills.

Only after graduating were young doctors permitted to marry. Most did so, according to Talth, raising large families, 'owning the best fishing places and large tracts of land' and living to a wealthy and influential old age.

BEAST GODS: MASKS OF POWER

'The [medicine man] who was to call the buffalo rose very early ... put on a head-dress made of the head of a buffalo, and a robe, and then started out to approach the herd. ... Before long the whole herd was running at headlong speed towards the precipice ...'

Thus, G.B. Grinnell described a Blackfoot (Montana) buffalo drive in the 1870s. His account could equally well apply to a Stone Age carving of a buffalo-headed man on the wall of a French cavern, an image created more than 15,000 years before.

Did his buffalo headdress transform the shaman? Jaime de Angulo, a physician and linguist who has studied nearly a score of native tongues, described his attempt to elicit different words for 'animal' and 'man' from a native speaker of the Pit River language. Half a page of feisty dialogue later, his informant, Bill, told him he guessed something like 'world-over, all-living' would cover both animals and native peoples. The discussion became more confusing from a Western point of view when Bill went on to tell de Angulo that since everything that exists has life, the expression also took in the benches on which they sat. The upshot was that 'world-over, all-living' would work for animals and native peoples in Pit River—excluding whites, since they are '[spiritually] dead themselves'.[46]

The conclusion: primal peoples were animals in ancient times and animals were primal peoples. Everything that lived was capable of transformation. Today, that privilege is restricted to those who attain a shamanic state of consciousness. Fox, Raven, Eagle, Fish hawk, Coyote, Wolf, Dolphin, Orca (killer-whale) and Bear, particularly Bear, endowed humans with their wisdom and their power. This trait lingers in names used by the Coast Salish (Washington State and British Columbia) where a guardian spirit is known either as 'power animal' or 'the Indian', when it takes on human form.

Kootenay healers in British Columbia used grizzly bear masks to invoke the animal's hostile energy against their people's enemies, while they simultaneously danced as Bear. Tribes as diverse as the Assiniboine, Cree and Taos Pueblo people called on Bear in preparations for war. A traditional Kootenay spring ceremony reaffirmed people's friendship with Bear, wished it good luck, petitioned it for good health, and, last but not least, asked immunity from its attack. People sang their spirit guardian songs, passed the pipe, wore the masks and danced their Bear. After several nights the ceremony ended with a berry feast.

North American tribes invoked Bear's powers as a healer. Native peoples watched the animals for centuries, noticing the care with which they chose herbs to treat their own illnesses. In this way healers discovered bear bane, bearberry, barefoot, bear's wort, to name a few. At least twenty-three medicinal herbs in North America are named for their association with bears.

Well into the twentieth century primal peoples were taking on animal characteristics with the aid of dancing or masks. On the west coast, from Washington State north through British Columbia to Alaska, winter was the time of the sacred, when Pacific rains settled in and the shoreline was shrouded in fog. To this day the forests encircling coastal communities ring with the spectral sounds and echoes of animal spirits. Winter was dancing season: for the Coast Salish people of Washington State and British Columbia; for the Kwakiutl of northern Vancouver Island and the B.C. mainland. Dancers took on the character of their power animals, whether it was Bear, Whale, Kingfisher, or Orca. Dance was not intended to imitate the beast, but rather to unite man with it in spirit and in power, so that he became as one with his power animal or, as in Australia, with the animal of his totem.

Visions, dreams, masks and drums

'From the earliest times, the classic method of achieving trance was dancing. As everywhere else, ecstasy made possible both the healer's "magical flight" and the descent of a "spirit" '.[47] Eliade refers here to China, and 'everywhere else' suggests customs of Kirgiz and Siberian peoples, as well as North American, where dances were vital to initiation rites and power animal ceremonies. Salish dancers trotted like Bear or writhed like Serpent; Blackfoot or Sioux emulated Eagle and Buffalo; and dancers among many American and Asian peoples worked themselves into near-trance states by mimicking not only the movements of our brother beasts, but bird and animal calls.

Complementing the power of dance, masks represented true transformation. Once a shaman donned his mask he took its character, became its spirit-being, whether as ancestor, power animal or god. Hopi dancers in *kachina* masks took into themselves the vital sense of the spirit dwelling in the features of those peculiar abstract faces, and made them alive.

The Kwakiutl have recently revived ceremonial dancing: long-houses that once accommodated hundreds of dancers and onlookers around a central fire have been refurbished or rebuilt as the stage for *hamatsa*, celebrating a myth in which four young hunters destroyed the 'Cannibal at the north end of the world'. The Salish and Sioux are dancing again. Primal peoples—with an increasing number of urban, questing Westerners—celebrate the Beast Gods and spirit guardians, not by imitation, but through a sort of spiritual possession by consent.

| Spiritual possession by consent

That past is coming alive again.

THE SPIRIT CANOE

In the past, when a member of the Lushootseed Salish people of Puget Sound became dis-spirited—shown by a loss of health, energy or good fortune—the custom was to commission a number of shamans to journey into the spirit world to fetch back the patient's guardian spirit. Drawing themselves up in a canoe-shaped configuration with the dis-spirited person at their centre, the spirit-questers rattled, drummed and sang their way into an otherworld to retrieve a guardian or 'power animal'. The ceremony might go on for six nights, with shamans and participants resting each day. The Spirit-Canoe or Soul Recovery Ceremony was unusual in that it was one of few North American rituals where several shamans, usually jealous professional rivals, collaborated for the good of their patients and their communities at large.

Pulling together scattered and fragmentary descriptions, author Jay Miller reconstructs the Salish people's elaborate Spirit-Canoe Ceremony in his book, *Shamanic Odyssey*:

> 'Approaching a plank house while a ceremony is going on, the senses are overwhelmed by rhythmic pounding from drums, batons, and voices. Inside, the very walls and floors vibrate with the sound, fusing everything into an overwhelming reverberation. Singing and drumming constitute the main event. ... Always, there is music, with brief pauses between percussive songs.
>
> 'Such would have been the arena of the Recovery rite. People came together and beat time to each other's songs. Here, however, there was a single predominant focus: the shamans traveling to and from the land of the dead, with everyone helping them in thought, deed, song.
>
> 'The audience took its place as witness and amplifier, singing and pounding backup for the doctors ...'[48]

Entering, the shamans set up painted planks in a pattern resembling a Viking ship's shield-wall around the space marked out for the spirit-canoe.

Spirit canoe — Three-foot high cedar humanoid carvings, 'Little Earths', represented immortals whose presence gave the party sanction for their journey. By day, while the shamans slept, the Little Earths crewed the canoe. It might take as long as six nights to reach and search their destination, where they fought off evil spirits to retrieve the guardian spirit power for the patient whose body, lying in the canoe, accompanied the spirit-fetchers on their quest.

Ottawa's Museum of Civilization houses a massive carving of a fully crewed spirit canoe, sculpted by a team led by Bill Reid, whose work reflects Haida culture. Reid's spirit canoe features on Canadian twenty-dollar bills.

In 1961, anthropologist Michael Harner learned a less elaborate spirit-canoe method of retrieval from the Conibo people of the Peruvian Amazon. The Conibo shaman gets into his 'boat' and lies beside the sick or dis-spirited person. When drumming begins the healer goes into the shamanic state of consciousness (SSC), the beat of the drum being the current on which the craft floats, slowly but inexorably, towards the vortex to the otherworld. Supported by the collective will, healer and crew propel their metaphysical craft into the tunnel to a spirit world where the healer locates a power animal or guardian for the dis-spirited client. The crew goes along, but only the shaman will cross the threshold to the otherworld.

Shamans use similar methods in Indonesia, and in Siberia, where the boat is a raft. In South America and Australia, therapy groups form up as snakes rather than boats. The shape is less important than its purpose, which is to create a spiritual 'craft' of support on which a sympathetic group of mortals sets forth to obtain for one of its number a guardian-spirit from the other-world. Whether by Salish spirit-canoe, or Siberian spirit-raft, the incessant, monotonous drumming propels the travelers in accordance with lines from a *soot*, a Siberian shaman's song recorded in the 1960s by Hungarian researcher Vilmos Diószegi:

'Oh! My many-colored drum …
Like flitting clouds carry me
Through the lands of dusk
And below the leaden sky,
Sweep along like wind
Over the mountain peaks!'

The drum that is both beast and symbol of shamanism came to the attention of science in 1962 when, at a Salish Spirit Dance, Andrew Neher established that steady, monotonous drumming changes brain wave patterns.

Each beat of a drum gives back a primal, low frequency *boom* that sends a wealth of sensory information to the ear and, by that most direct of channels, deep into the nervous labyrinth that is the brain. A single *boom* is rich in sensory information; the effect of sustained drumming sets up changes in the central nervous system, stimulating areas of brain untouched by other sensory stimuli. A feature in *Newsweek* magazine described drumming as 'humanity's first big advance in medical technology, a doorway to the spirit world's healing powers'. Indigenous peoples described it as the 'heartbeat of the earth' long before our planet's resonance frequency was measured at 7.5 cycles a second, similar to that of a trance-inducing drumbeat. Psychologist and shaman Sandra Ingerman comments: 'It appears that drumming allows shamans to align their brain waves with the pulse of the earth'.

Mind-science recognizes 'rhythmic sensory stimulation' as a pathway to trance, especially when secondary rhythms reinforce the booming of a drum. Add hyperventilation and the adrenaline secretion caused by the exertion of ritual dancing, and the recipe for trance induction is complete. Montreal psychiatrist Raymond Prince describes sonic driving as a 'commonly used portal of entry' into alternative states of consciousness.

Ever since the Salish revived the Spirit Dance in the 1960s it has been powerful medicine for members who strayed into the majority world, lost their way and ended up dysfunctional in both cultures—'spirit illness' is the Salish term. The rejuvenated Spirit Dance continues to rehabilitate many of these 'dying sick', but first they have to be initiated by being ritually clubbed to death, reborn, and kept on a strict regime until they 'find their song and dance'. At that point a power animal or 'Indian Spirit' bestows the gifts of spirit-power, song, and dance. Vancouver psychiatrist Wolfgang Jilek, who has studied the reintegration of natives into their ancestral communities, comments:

> 'Initiates feel their newly acquired power when the song bursts forth from their lips and the leaping steps of their first spontaneous dance carry them through the smoke-house. To modern spirit dancers this blissful experience may appear comparable to that of altered states of consciousness induced by opiates'.

A former heroin addict turned spirit-dancer told Jilek:

> 'I was jumping three feet high and I had such a thrill, a terrific feeling as if you were floating, as if you were in the air, you really feel high. I've only had such a feeling once before in my life when I was on heroin mainlining, but then I went through hell afterwards, it was terrible—but with the spirit song's power you get this feeling without the terrible aftermath'.[49]

Vancouver gave the world the term 'skid-row'. Every winter dancing season some of the lost and lonely native people from Vancouver's skid row are 'immersed in a therapeutic ceremonial program' directed to a single end, a 'reaffirmation of the meaning of native existence'.

THE SUN DANCE RISES

The buffalo hunt was successful this year. Enough meat hangs curing on frames in the summer sun to see the community through the winds and snow of a High Plains winter. The Buffalo spirit that gave of its self so that humans might live has been asked for forgiveness. It is time to seek a general blessing from the cosmos and give thanks. Summer, when the green of fluttering cottonwoods contrasts with blanched brown grass, is the time for Sun Dance.

Catharsis, communal forgiveness, a reassertion of community sense and general healing—those values link with the ancient traditions of the

Sun Dance practised by Plains peoples such as Algonquian, Blackfoot, Shoshone and Sioux. Above all it is a profound expression of spiritual, and shamanic, power.

'More than any other ceremony or occasion, [the Sun Dance] furnished the tribes the opportunity for the expression of emotion in rhythm', wrote George Dorsey, in 1910. The Sun Dance leader will reach the chosen site long before the four-day event. He has to supervise the building of separate purification (sweat) lodges for men and women. Ceremonial tipis must be erected for dancers to dress, prepare themselves spiritually and be painted by medicine men and women with symbols, often in red ochre, the color of life-giving blood.

The Sun Dance: a four-day prayer-in-motion

Women participate fully. In fact, apart from the Sun Dance leader, a woman plays the first key role. Dressed in white buckskin she becomes Buffalo Calf Woman, who, in the early time, carried the Great Spirit's sacred pipe to the Sioux. Ever since, smoke from the pipe has carried up prayers to the realm of *Wakan Tanka*. Today, Buffalo Calf Woman leads a party into the trees, selects a cottonwood, and, apologizing to its spirit, fells it with an axe. The Sun Dance ceremony is necessary, she tells the tree, so that her people may live; life depends upon the respectful celebration of the Sun Dance.

The tree is carried, never dragged, to the middle of the dancing ground—the centre of the world—and planted in a hole above a peace pipe. Flags in red, black, yellow and white mark the four directions.

Now comes the Dance. Since early morning, male and female dancers have been purifying themselves in separate sweat lodges. As drumming begins a woman starts the dance, circling alone around the cottonwood which is become the Cosmic Tree, the axis of the world. Next come the dancers, who enter from the rising sun and circle the tree—sun wise—stopping four times in this first circuit to honor the four directions. Descendants of Buffalo Calf Woman, the women wear unadorned white. A medicine man or woman reminds them of the importance of the Sun Dance, of true living, of right thinking. The dancers offer peace pipes. Then they dance.

Drumming sets the pace: the heat, the noise of singers, dancers' whistles, the blessed torture of exertion under the Sun's heat, the ever-moving circle, onlookers around the sacred ground, and at the centre, visible from every place, the sacred axis tree.

Some dancers fall out, others fall. Many carry on, their minds made clear by rhythm, rhythm, rhythm, drumbeats and the pounding of their feet upon a sun-baked, hard-packed Turtle shell that is the outer covering of Mother Earth. Breath is racing, raucous in their throats; their heartbeats hammer in their ears. Some will find their vision in the heat and daze of day—not drawn out of their night-dark fears in a hill-top vision pit, but right here, scorched by Sun, watched by their whole community. The agony, the ecstasy, and drums, always drums. The Mother hears, doesn't she? The hunt was good. The virtuous have their reward. People will live. The Great Spirit, *Wakan Tanka*, will respond with sun and rain to raise the grass to feed the buffalo. And this din of laughter, joy, pain, sweat and tears is the prayer that will make the cycle of the seasons go around another year.

On the fourth and final day some of the men, who must have danced in a previous year to qualify, elect to be pierced through the chest so that thongs attach them like an umbilical cord to the tree that is Mother Earth. Men are pierced, never women, for they are hardened to life's pains by childbirth. They dance again, with all the others: the pain is heightened, sweating, thongs are pulling, the mind clears, thinking only of the moment, the celestial moment. Visions may come; if not, the men still do honor to themselves and their community. Rawhide thongs rip skin; men fall; medicine men and women attend, rattling, drumming, healing flesh, drawing the attention of the spirits, voicing encouragement. There is a clear parallel of intent between the torn, worn bodies of Sun Dancers and Christianity's view of the crucifixion: individual sacrifice for the good of the greater community. A pure—or a purified—life absolves a load of sins.

That was how it used to be. And, excepting that the buffalo are gone, that is how it may be, once more.

Oglala Sioux sun dancer, Eagle Man (fighter pilot turned lawyer Ed McGaa), takes up the tale at the moment when participants are free to seek their personal Sun Dance visions:

> 'The tribe's prayers are like a spiritual wind sweeping over the backs of the sun dancers and hitting the tree. The tree itself is a great absorbing funnel, taking in the prayers and sending them upward to the ultimate powers of the universe and to *Wakan Tanka* (the Great Spirit). ... It is the gathered tribe, the band, the gathered *Tiyospaye* (extended family), acknowledging the spiritual and physical relationship to all that is the *cante*, the heart of the Sun Dance'.[50]

Psychiatrist Wolfgang Jilek, contributing to a conference called 'Shamans and Endorphins' (pain-killing compounds made by the body), likened the Sioux Sun Dance to the Salish Spirit Dance in as much as both may lead to altered states of consciousness. However, to reach that point often demands fasting, thirsting, hyper-exertion, extremes of heat and cold, and drumming, drumming, drumming. All these serve to depattern personality, create it again and orient it anew. The dancer is hardened by the pain, the altered state, the vision, if it comes, and support by his or her community. And, by the celebration of this great collective force, community is strengthened, too.

EXTRACTING THE SPIRITUAL SIDE OF ILLNESS:
REMOVING HARMFUL INTRUSIONS

> 'When I take it out you can't see it. You can't see it with your bare eyes, but I see it. Whenever I send it away, I see what the disease is. When the disease comes down into a person, which the white people talk about way differently; and we Indians too, we shamans, explain it way differently. That disease that comes down into a person is dirty; I suppose that is what the white people call "germs" but we Indian doctors call it "dirty"'.[51]
> Essie Parrish, Pomo sucking doctor, California

Mrs Parrish was held in high regard. People of all races came to her for healing. As a child she had frequent visions; at eleven she dreamed her first power song; at twelve she effected her first cure. In time she was able to divine the future. Something about young Essie suggested power to those around her. When her family thought her sister would die, her great-uncle asked Essie, 'Couldn't you do something for your little sister? I say to you that you possess a prophet's body'. Having no idea what she was supposed to do, she put her right hand on her sister's body and her power song began to sing itself inside her. Within days her sister was cured. Soon after that she healed a man laid at death's door by 'double pneumonia'.

At first, Essie Parrish's power was restricted to her right palm and middle finger. 'The spirit comes down into me' to work its power, she told Robert Oswalt, in 1964. In her mid teens, 'I noticed that I had something in my throat to suck pains out with'. It took four years before the thing in her throat could bring about a sucking cure; in the meantime it constricted her throat to the point where her family called in a medical doctor who detected no visible symptom but pronounced it 'probably diphtheria'. For years Essie Parrish seemed as bewildered by her spirit-power as others were:

> 'These things seem unbelievable but I, myself, I know, because it is in me. I know what I see. *My* power is like that. You may doubt it if you don't want to believe; you don't have to believe but it is my work'.

As well as visualizing clients' diseases, she could hear them. Diseases had their own lives, Mrs Parrish said; they sounded like insects inside people's bodies. Hearing disease was like putting an ear to a beehive.

Essie Parrish's cures manifested themselves not only in physical and spiritual release for her clients, but left her with the fleshly remains of dead diseases lying in her hand for all to see. She told Oswalt,

> 'I spit out the dead disease. Then I let it fall into the palm of my hand so that many people can see it. They always see the disease that I suck out. But that is not to be touched by anyone else—it is contagious. Whoever picks the disease up, into him it would enter. ... Some diseases sit for a while—sit for a few minutes—but others are fast. Some fast diseases stay just so many minutes after being put down and then disappear'.

In time, a vision told Essie Parrish that she should reveal her power to whites as well as natives, so that everyone might benefit. As a result, her work has been documented in a film, *Sucking Doctor*

Shamans regard specific pains accompanied by high temperature—what Western physicians might call localized infections or inflammation—as manifestations of energy emanating from intrusions of harmful power. Given that bacteria and viruses may be harmful powers, medicine and shamanism thus far agree. But shamanism goes further. In modern society, stressed or angry individuals unwittingly *project* hostility into others as harmful intrusions. As anthropologist Michael Harner puts it, 'When we speak of someone "radiating hostility," it is almost a latent expression of the shamanic view'.

Intrusions, hostility

Among the Ojibway, healing shamans traditionally received their powers in dreams instructing them to practise in certain fields. Thus a shaman became a sucking-doctor, *nanandawi*, only if a vision showed him his technique.

Victor Barnouw described the experience of a Wisconsin Ojibway youth, Tom Badger, who was treated during the 1940s for severe pains down his left side. A *nanandawi*, Old Man Hay, sucked the pain out through two bones.

> 'My father beat a War Dance drum. Old Man Hay shook a rattle while he doctored me. He put a little dish next to him, with a little water in it. The two bones were lying there. ... His power was so strong that when Old Man Hay leaned over the dish, the bones stood up and moved towards his mouth. He swallowed the bones twice and coughed them up again. Then

he put the bone to my side. After he'd finished sucking, Old Man Hay drew out some stuff and spat it in a dish; it looked like blood. Old Man Hay showed it to me and to the others and then threw it into the fire. If he hadn't drawn the blood out it would have turned to pus. And sometimes, when the pus burst inside, the person dies. My father drummed all the time Old Man Hay was doctoring me. ...'[52]

Only experienced shamans should try removing power intrusions, which, from a shamanic point of view include communicable diseases. The sucking technique used in the shamanic world demands a source of spirit power or helper spirits that novices lack. Sucking can draw a client's disease into the shaman's body—Essie Parrish said they tried to hide under her tongue—from which one must know how to expel them. Extracting harmful power intrusions by sucking is difficult medicine: it is not for the untried.

BEHIND THE MASK: CONCEALING, REVEALING

In a Western sense, a mask disguises reality or conceals it. Among primal peoples a mask reveals a new reality, or creates it. When a Hopi dancer puts on a kachina mask there is no ambiguity about it: he 'becomes the kachina', a spirit messenger to his people. When he gives life to his mask—animates it—the kachina takes on a moving, breathing, mortal form, capable of stimulating laughter or terror. Without its dancer the spiritual dimension remains in hiding, unattainable to the wider community. Their masking-culture gives Hopi adults a fine awareness of a separate material and spiritual realities.

Dancers themselves offer proof: the reality created by a hideous mask comes home to its wearer when, through his eyeholes, he sees joy or fear on children's faces. That is the test of how spirits move a dancer's audience. Strip the mask off a living, mortal being, put it in a museum or a book and the impact is lost. Looking at a mask is not the point; looking through it is what brings the other reality to life.

From Hopi to Iroquois; from Arizona to New York and Ontario; from spirit masks to spirit masks and smoke ...

There were two beings at Creation, the Creator and the shaman, Hadu'i. When they met, Hadu'i made the mistake of claiming that he had created the earth. A contest followed in which the Creator moved a mountain more successfully than the shaman, who broke his nose on it. Mrs Peter Williams, an officer of the Deer Clan at Six Nations, Brantford, Ontario, related this tale to William Fenton in 1940.

'Hadu'i begged of the Master, "Will you let me live? May I continue to live on this earth?" The Creator replied, "Yes, but what relationship will you bear to these people who [will shortly] reside here on this earth?" "I will take them as my grandchildren," he said. "I have the power. I can stop the high wind storms and I can drive away disease!" [The Iroquois consider wind a vector in the spread of disease.] The Creator answered, "I will permit you to live on the earth, and I shall plant the great tobacco here, and the people shall employ that for transmitting messages [making offerings] to you, whenever they require your assistance. Furthermore, there shall be a certain way. It will come through dreams. ... Also we shall make imitations of the way you look [using masks with a broken nose]. The people shall use these likenesses to cure the sick by blowing ashes on the sick one" '.[53]

Thus began the False Face tradition of the Iroquois nations. Every spring and fall, parties of False Face maskers ran through houses with turtle rattles, blowing curative ash of sacred tobacco to scare off the spirits of disease. In addition to this, False Face healers worked with individuals in their homes, feeding the Creator's tobacco smoke to beneficial spirits and blowing sacred ash on the sick person through the mouth of the mask to transfer healing powers. As a shaman's burning candle represents a transformation from a physical to an ethereal dimension, so tobacco ash represented death, and the blowing which revived the embers stood for life. The mouth of a False Face mask was its spirit-source of words, breath, power and life.

False Face Societies have been staging a resurgence since the 1970s, when young native people began to regain their tribal heritage. In earlier times the Society's main preoccupation was public health: False Faces and other medicine societies were hard pressed to combat the epidemic diseases which struck the tribes from the time of European settlement. Cholera, typhoid and smallpox (shown on old masks as pitting) reduced native populations around Lake Ontario by almost half between 1630 and 1660. Children's diseases, influenza and tuberculosis decimated native populations well into the twentieth century. But on several occasions native people whose settlements escaped epidemics told white researchers that the medicine societies had been effective. To what extent Iroquois healers warded off even worse epidemics, only the Creator can know.

HEALING SAND

Pictures and woven blankets delude us into believing that we have seen true Navajo art. We may have seen one aspect of it, the brightly colored, rectilinear creations of stylized people, birds, corn plants, tassels and borders which an observer takes in at a glance. But sand painting designs used in the many Navajo healing ceremonies are different. To begin with they are not created as art, but as integral aids to the ritual that is healing; and each of the many healing rituals or 'ways' has its own stylized design. A particular way is carefully selected having regard to a patient's needs. Furthermore, since disease derives from a lack of harmony between the patient and the life-supporting spirits that sustain him, a first principle in Navajo healing is to establish the patient's baseline of good health within the legends of the cosmos and creation. Cure requires that a sick person be returned to a state of harmony within the web of spirits and beings that form the Navajo world. To do so a Navajo 'singer' has to re-create the patient within the subtle perfection of that world. As one key part of the healing way, this is where sand painting comes in.

Sand painting

Navajo healing designs look odd to non-Navajos. Perspective appears awkward; there seems to be no single place from which the whole can be viewed as a whole. Just as a mask's reality is gauged by others' reactions to it, so the true perspective of Navajo healing designs is only visible from the inside out, from the patient's point of view, for he and he alone will sit in the middle of the painting and study his world. Even from that perspective, the painting, like the course of life, cannot all be discerned at once. It must be assimilated by degrees. The design reflects struggles, interdependence and diversity of Navajo cosmic forces. It surrounds the patient with selected elements from the background of his tribal panorama, reorienting him, pulling him back to his place within the whole.

Beautiful as it is, when the ritual is over the painting must be erased, its colors and symbolic messages wiped into the sands whence they came. The painting has served its purpose once it has oriented the patient to the still point at the centre of his world. He sat in that world—the painting—for hours during the ritual. But, once the patient is restored to health the painting must die, for the lifeway it describes has been absorbed into the patient. A healing sand painting is as idiosyncratic as a patient's fingerprint. It can have no independent existence outside his life and his mind.

As materialists in the modern world, we tend to view our own culture objectively, as if standing apart from it. We also tend to subdivide it: religion is one thing, health another, material values a third. The accumulation of knowledge is vast; the pursuit of insight lags behind.

That is not the way of primal peoples, for whom culture, including the unity of religion and health, is the essence of being. Hopi kachina masks, Iroquoian False Faces and Navajo sand paintings illustrate an abiding principle of shamanism, namely that worlds and influences complement each other. Physical and spiritual, light and dark, *yin* and *yang*, disease and health—these are counterpoised, dependent upon each other. Health is not the exclusive product of this material world; it also dwells in an abiding spiritual sphere. True health, to be experienced, must be lived on several planes.

4

Revelations, vibrations, a matter of balance

CENTRAL AND SOUTH AMERICA

VIBRATIONS, THE STUFF OF CONSCIOUSNESS

Where most ancient cultures sought the nature of the godhead in theology, the Mayans of Yucatan discovered it in mathematics. Their Absolute Being, Hunab K'u, embodied a combination of *measure* and *movement*: measure of the soul, and movement of the energy that constitutes spirit. In this respect ancient Mayan theory is not unlike modern quantum mechanics: material form is the product of energy. Since spirit-energy vibrated in every life, a traditional Mayan knew himself to be as one with every other being. In classical times, 'you' was declared nonexistent, leaving the notion that 'you are me' and 'I am you'. Hunbatz Men, a modern authority on his people's calendars and civilization, describes people's dealings with each other and their code of ethics as being based upon 'mutual respect elevated to the category of religion, but religion in the highest scientific sense—mathematical, rather than merely metaphysical'.[54] Forces greater than man ruled Nature, balancing its forces in mathematical symmetry.

> Material form, the product of energy

Nevertheless, those forces, as well as humans and numbers, were one and the same. This bond, forged by the Absolute Being and animated by His source of spirit-energy, the sun, formed the equation that provided every answer. The cosmos vibrated with the essence of Absolute Being, whose energy infused all spirits, humans, beasts and inanimate things.

Mayan words, like those of Inuit tongues or Chinese, tend to be verbs, events caught in the happening. While the Chinese written character for 'dawn' depicts the sun rising over a tree, for example, the Mayan language takes symbolism a long step further, representing spiritual values even in the sounds of words, because sounds are life-giving vibrations. Thus the

Mayan word for shamanic awareness, ol, consists of 'O', symbolizing 'awakened consciousness', and 'L', meaning 'vibration', consciousness being the result of vibrations derived from the life-giving energy of the sun. Hunbatz Men explains that putting a 'L' at the front of *ol*, in effect wrapping consciousness in vibrations, creates *lol*, a 'flower'. That is how *lol* is shown as a pictograph in several Mayan languages.

Vibrations

'If we could see the miracle of a single flower clearly, our whole life would change' said the Buddha—speaking wistfully, perhaps.

But *lol* has other implications. Apart from 'flower' it stands for those who have returned to the essence of consciousness, the dead. *Lol* indicates that the consciousness of flowers, humans, beasts and the Milky Way continues to vibrate beyond the grave on the plane that Mayans share with the dead. *Lol* represents the cosmic consciousness of spirit, the still point, the centre.

People of many cultures instinctively speak of centering. Asked by *Newsweek* magazine about the significance of drumming, the West African drummer Babatunde Olatunji responded by bringing the palm of his hand down on his *djembe*. While its deep bass *goon* vibrations shook the room, he answered: 'Drumming helps man be at peace with himself. He can find the center'. And the scholar Mircea Eliade writes: 'The iconography of the drums is dominated by the symbolism of the ecstatic journey, that is, by journeys that imply a break-through in plane and hence a "Center of the World" '. Vibrations, the sun and a drum—and always a centre. A wealth of similar comments from cultures around the globe and across the centuries suggests that a shamanic perspective is a human being's first, instinctive point of view: this gets shouldered aside when the rational mind comes into play.

A MATTER OF BALANCE

At the other end of Mexico, high in the mountains of the Sierra Madre Occidental, a revered shaman of the Huichol people also speaks of centeredness or 'balance'. His name, Matsúwa (pulse of energy) recalls the vibrations of solar energy that are key to Mayan cosmology.) Matsúwa was about ninety when he visited California in 1977 to urge Westerners to 'find their lives' by returning to balance, a balance we were all welcome to borrow from Huichol tradition. Matsúwa reminded medical anthropologist Joan Halifax that a loss of balance in ancient times had caused a disastrous flood. (Matsúwa's reference to this flood in Huichol tradition, independent of Noah's, helps us reach a more precise definition for what Animists

Revelations, vibrations, a matter of balance

mean by 'balance'. With reference to the physical world, balance suggests the interdependence of beings and elements in a given environment; in a spiritual sense, it refers to the individual and collective human mindset needed to respect or restore such an ideal state.) Animist peoples have long understood floods to be the result of imbalance. Four thousand years ago, deforestation and subsequent drought and flood cycles helped destroy the civilization of a thousand years at Mohenjo Daro in what is now Kashmir. Deforestation and resulting floods wreak havoc in our own time in many parts of the world. Matsúwa knew this intuitively, from the spirits, as a shaman does.

After a 'sixty-four year apprenticeship' as a shaman, the ancient farmer from a mountain village had achieved an exceptional grasp of the several worlds. In a sentiment resembling Mayan philosophy, he told Halifax:

> 'We have forgotten our life source, the sun, and the sacred sea, the blessed land, the sky, and all things of nature. Unless we remember quickly what our lives are about, unless we celebrate through ceremony and prayer, we will again face destruction, but this time it will be by fire'. [55]

Isolation preserved Huichol shamanism from ravages by dominant Aztec and Spanish cultures. Huichols once hunted deer in the high Sierras; as the deer declined they took to farming, but preserved their ancient hunting beliefs, principal among them the sanctity of the hunter's fire by night and the life-giving presence of the sun by day. Matsúwa told Joan Halifax,

> 'If you have the desire to learn the path of the shaman, the Fire will teach you, the Fire, our Grandfather. You must listen to the Fire, for the Fire speaks, and the Fire teaches. And during the day you learn from the Sun. The Sun will teach you, the Sun, Our Father'.

Besides Fire and the Sun, the third member of the Huichol trinity is the sacred sacrament, peyote cactus, from which emanates the Little Deer Spirit, Káuyumari, the supreme power animal of Huichol culture. Under the influence of peyote, Káuyumari guides and teaches a shaman. Peyote-induced visions still lie at the heart of Huichol traditions.

The psychedelic peyote cactus is not a drug, as a shaman pointedly told anthropologist Peter Furst. It is a holy sacrament of Huichol belief. This cactus does not grow near Huichol villages, but 250 miles away in Wirikúta, the 'Sacred Land of Peyote'. Traditionally this land was reached after a footsore pilgrimage of many days, during which pilgrims were restricted to a rigid diet. Even without peyote, the journey itself might have been enough to induce visions. Deprivation-induced knowledge is well known to the Huichol. Matsúwa put it:

> 'Many, many times I have gone to the mountains alone. Yes, I have endured much suffering during my life. Yet to learn to see, to learn to hear, you must do this—go into the wilderness alone. For it is not I who teach you the ways of the gods. Such things are learned only in solitude'.

Word for word, Matsúwa's sentiment is that of the Inuit shaman, Igjugarjuk. As for suffering, Buddha taught that: 'All beings have suffering. Some too much, others too little'. Shamans suffer much.

In 1977, psychologist Stanley Krippner held a party in California for Matsúwa, during which the old shaman suddenly announced, 'One of my Huichol people is ill. I must return to help her immediately'. When Krippner protested that instant return was impossible, the old man said, 'You don't understand. Just leave me alone!' He turned to sit facing the wall. Half an hour later he rejoined his guests, saying, 'I have been able to help the woman who was sick. Let's get back to the party'. It was then that Krippner realized he had been present during a shaman's 'magical flight'.

REVELATIONS

Shamans who harness cosmic powers do not work with their own small energies. 'We never use the energy we are born with', warns Loren Smith, a Pomo shaman from northern California. Instead, shamans world over use the vehicle of and the medium of spirit guardians to call on mighty cosmic forces. (Sophisticated computer users will recognize this assistance from 'mighty cosmic forces' as analogous to the modern 'Cloud' in information technology.) Shamanic cosmic forces develop to the fullest among the rain forests of Central and South America.

The tropics enhance the special spiritual quality of forests. The most materialist of minds can sense a diminished divide between ordinary and shamanic reality here. Life is so rich, so concentrated. Great trees suggest an environment conducive to shape- and spirit-shifts where shamans slip-slide through this mortal life on both sides of the spiritual divide. Describing his experiences among the Desana tribe of the Upper Amazon, anthropologist Gerardo Reichel-Dolmatoff wrote: 'To the Indians this "other" dimension is just as real as that of ordinary everyday life, and for the individual to pass from one to the

Cosmic forces

Revelations, vibrations, a matter of balance

other is an experience shared by all'. Concentration, abstinence and trance have all been employed to reach this different, wonderful, horrifying world. 'But more often the perception of this dimension will be produced quite consciously by chemical means, by powerful drugs under the influence of which the mind will wander into the hidden world of animals and forest spirits, of divine beings and mythical scenes'.

Principal among the psychedelic drugs of Amazonia is *ayahuasca*[56], or *yagé*. In 1961, anthropologist Michael Harner, who had lived for a year among the Conibo people on the Ucayali River, decided to drink this shamans' 'soul vine', also known as 'little death'. Harner has been described as the Western world's leading authority on shamanism. He may have more personal experience of shamanic practices than any other Westerner. Among Harner's most formative experiences was taking *ayahuasca* prepared by his Conibo mentor, Tomás. There followed a 'supernatural carnival of demons', as he describes it in *The Way of the Shaman*: a grinning crocodilian head spewed water; strange boats formed into a Viking-like galley with a dragon-headed prow, crewed by humans with blue jays' heads, like bird-headed gods in Egyptian tombs. The most beautiful singing he had ever heard competed with the swish of oars, while 'energy-essence began to float from my chest into the boat'. Harner became aware that his brain was splitting into compartments, with the observer/commander on top, beneath which a 'numbed layer' separated the observer from the vision source. Harner was convinced that he would die. So, too, were the spirit-sources of his visions, which permitted the condemned man glimpses of otherwise forbidden things. Thus did the horror and the glory continue until his mentor, Tomás, poured an antidote down his throat.

| Ayahuasca, yagé |

Even God is not immune from suffering in his spiritual quest. Anthropologist Michael Taussig describes how the Cófan people of Colombia's Amazon explain the origin of the psychedelic, *yagé*:

> '[God] asked for some *yagé* brew, and on drinking began to tremble, vomit, weep, and shit. In the morning he declared that "it is true what these Indians say. The person who takes this suffers. But that person is distinguished. That is how one learns, through suffering" '.[57]

Emphasizing this point, a Jívaro mentor explained to Harner in 1964, 'You must suffer so that the grandfathers will take pity on you. Otherwise, the ancient specter will not come'. On this occasion Harner had presented himself at the hut of a renowned Jívaro shaman, Akachu, announcing that he had come to acquire spirit helpers, *tsentsak*. There followed a two-day forced march, purification in a cavern behind a sacred waterfall and a vision induced by a potion of *maikua*, a plant of the *datura* family. Such was the power of *maikua* that the Jívaro never took it themselves without companions to restrain them lest they ran crazed into rivers or over cliffs.

Taussig takes a good point from the Cófan tale of *yagé* enlightening God: 'Unlike that other tree of consciousness which God planted in the Garden of Eden, whose fruit Eve stole at the serpent's bidding so as to open her eyes, the vine of *yagé* brings consciousness to God himself'. Rather than precipitating the Fall of Man from Eden, the Cófans' consciousness-raising *yagé* sets up 'illumination that brings the gods to earth'.[58] Wisdom in the Animist world is not restricted to a priesthood. Wisdom is for everyone

Thus equipped with the spirit-given wisdom of one's psychedelic vision, one develops other skills. In Harner's case, he sought to acquire *tsentsak*, spirit helpers or magical darts, which are both cause and cure of illnesses. Briefly, evil forces drive their *tsentsak* into the bodies of those they wish to hurt or kill: the *tsentsak* of healing shamans must locate, diagnose, and help suck out these harmful spirits. A novice shaman swallows all manner of leaves, insects and other things in an effort to acquire a ready supply of spirit helpers. On one level, these objects are exactly what they purport to be, but in shamanic consciousness they take on awe-inspiring, powerful forms: jaguars, anacondas (whose rope-like bodies also represent the spirit of the *ayahuasca* vine), parrots, armadillos, power plants and animals of every sort. Thus fortified, a shaman goes into a psychedelic trance to diagnose his client's illness, examining all internal organs as if with x-ray sight.

At night, when the spirit world is most visible to shamanic insight, the shaman and his spirit helpers suck the offending spirit out. Pomo shaman Essie Parrish reported that her clients' diseases tried to hide under her tongue: a Jívaro shaman guards against this by keeping the appropriate *tsentsak* in his mouth to ambush the spiritual aspect of disease after he sucks it out. Between times, a shaman's *tsentsak* must be nourished: as Iroquois feed tobacco to the spirit of a false face mask, so Jívaro shamans, a continent away, drink tobacco water to feed their spirit helpers.

Revelations, vibrations, a matter of balance

Halucinogenic visions have a lasting life on paper, too. Anthropologist Reichel-Dolmatoff (1978) asked a number of Tukano Indians to draw their visions, and the results are glorious. In the 1980s, Luis Eduardo Luna, who grew up in the Colombian Amazon, befriended an experienced plant healer (*vegetalista*), Pablo Amaringo, from the Peruvian Amazon town of Pucallpa. Amaringo had been an effective healer who chose to give up his practice when the resentment of evil shamans threatened to harm his life and family. When Luna met him, Amaringo had not taken *ayahuasca* for ten years, but retained the vast fund of vision-acquired knowledge about the lives and properties of plants and animals around Pucallpa. His visions had also taught Amaringo how to paint and draw; each time he completed a painting he wrote a detailed description of the symbols and lore he had depicted. A hundred paintings, detailed notes, and five years later Amaringo gave the world an extraordinary visual glimpse into the shamanic mind-sight of a skilled Amazon healer.

As shamans in other parts of the world gain wisdom from beast or human spirit helpers, *vegetalistas* gain their knowledge of healing or harming plant properties from plant teachers themselves. The *vegetalista*, like shamans everywhere, is but the medium through which the spirit-wisdom passes—in his/her case, from a healing plant.

The insights that a *vegetalista* will gain from *ayahuasca* depend on the combination of plants in the brew. The primary ingredient, *Banisteriopsis* vine, is mixed with plants of the *Psychotria* genus. Beyond that, specific plants may be added to the brew to study their properties or because they are known to impart healing powers against specific conditions.

The process does not end there: a novice does not become a plant healer simply through visions. A plant, rock or animal only releases its healing power if a *vegetalista* has learned from those sources | *vegetalistas* their magical songs, *icaros*. Depending on its properties, each plant, animal and stone has its *icaro*. Amazon practice is similar in this respect to power songs of other primal peoples. An *icaro*, a Navajo's chant or an Inuit song all represent the flow of power and wisdom from spirit to shaman.

Noting these far-flung similarities, Luna wondered if Amaringo had unconsciously imported influences from other cultures into his work. Perhaps he had. Perhaps anthropologist Harner had, too. During his *ayahuasca* vision with the Conibo people, a gigantic crocodilian head reared up before Harner, 'whose cavernous jaws gushed a torrential flood of water'. Next day, relating his vision to American missionaries, Harner was surprised to hear his vision read back to him in passages from the *Book of Revelations.*

Which raises the larger question: to what extent did ecstasy compose all great religious tracts?

SPIRIT VERSUS SPIRIT

Far south of Amazonia, Bororo people live in a district centered on the Rio São Lourenço, five hundred miles west of Brasilia. Bororo culture is considered to have been one of the richest in South America, combining a complex social organization with an extensive pantheon of spirits and gods. Bororo cosmology is so complex that it takes two different types of shaman—one now extinct—to make it manifest. Every class of physical thing in the Bororo cosmos has a spiritual, *aroe*, a dimension. To a degree this resembles Jívaro cosmology, where spirit helpers, *tsentsak*, may be small insects or worms in ordinary reality, but take powerful forms in shamanic consciousness. Bororo spiritual discrimination is such that each person considers himself a sort of unique species that can never be reproduced. At death this unique essence continues to live in an underworld with his ancestors' *aroe*.

Aroe are spirit-selves of physical things; *bope* are spirit-essences of phenomena such as rain, heat, cold, wind, night and day. Powerful *bope* inhabit thunder and lightning. *Bope* are responsible for death and reproduction, growth and decay, not unlike fertility spirits in ancient Europe. All metamor-phosis, whether of child to adult, egg to larva, cater-pillar to butterfly, or shaman to jaguar, is controlled by *bope*.

Spirit-essences

Where *aroe* are spiritual dimensions of explicit things—including continuity *after* form in the case of the dead—*bope* are spirit essences of cycles and change. One Bororo shaman told Jon Crocker, who spent many years documenting the community's cosmos, 'Everything is on one side or another; nothing is between'.

Aroe and *bope* are complementary: *aroe* live in the underworld seldom troubling humans; *bope* inhabit middle earth and interfere.

Few peoples have such a complex social code. Marriage and clan taboos would fill an encyclopedia; adults routinely recall genealogies, including cousins' lines two centuries past, yet the Bororo have never troubled to classify illness. The reason is simple: illness results from breaking some aspect of the elaborate hunting code, for the *bope* are wildly possessive and jealous of offences to their game animals, which they call *bope ure*.

Such a society would seem to need constant ministrations by its shamans, but the Bororo are skeptical, both about their shamans' personalities and powers. A Bororo shaman, writes Crocker, 'is as much cursed as he is blessed'. The role brings power but its benefits are outweighed by liabilities. In the first place, one does not choose to be a Bororo shaman; a *bope* chooses a living body to serve as its power base. One is theoretically free to reject the call, but the jealous *bope* may make life miserable from that time forth.

Initiation takes several turns. There comes a point in a novice's life when his *bope*, having tutored him in sleep, takes possession of its shaman-body, also during sleep. At this point the novice runs through the night in wild fits till villagers hold him down and send for an experienced shaman to calm the novice's *bope*. This might go on for months. 'Some people do not survive it'. But, as Crocker discovered, no known shaman has begun his career without this kind of possession during sleep.

A shaman's *bope* may be jealous. A shaman and his family often live apart because, just as sickness may result from causing offence to *bope* game animals, a *bope* regards the person of its shaman as its own. The spirit's possessiveness extends to the shaman's goods and family. Woe betide the man who fondles a shaman's wife. Crocker describes a case in which an offender touched a woman, only to watch the offending fingers turn a gangrenous black. The offender died young.

Bope guard their own. In this respect a shaman may be 'physically polluting': even in villages filthy with refuse, a shaman's pared finger nails and hair trimmings are buried, lest others inadvertently touch them. Woe, too, to one who wakes a sleeping shaman, for when he sleeps his soul is absent, perhaps traveling on a spiritual errand. To wake a shaman suddenly is to leave his soul in limbo. To a vengeful *bope* there can be no worse offence than snatching the soul of its shaman.

Offending the *bope* invariably causes sickness, so one would think that a family's first response to sickness would be to call the shaman. But that is not so. The community flocks around, brings healthy foods, plant medicines, sympathy and good advice. A crowd of well wishers attends the sickbed. A shaman may advise, at this stage, reminding the patient's kin of their responsibilities, but does not intervene. The ways of the *bope* can never be known; no more nor the mysteries of illness. As Crocker puts it, 'Modern Bororo are sure of one thing: the shaman is their last recourse against the actions of the *bope*—but only because *some* of them work positively through him'. In other words, healing versus sickness comes down to *bope* versus *bope*.

The shaman is sent for only if sickness reaches a crucial point. He arrives at twilight with his wife who, by virtue of marriage to a shaman, imparts powers of her own. Crocker was told, 'She is almost like a shaman herself'. Before examining his patient the shaman smokes himself into a trance. Then he fumigates his patient's body with tobacco smoke, because, in trance, he may see marauding *maereboe* crawling like maggots over the sick person's flesh. At last, between blowing and rubbing the patient's flesh with tobacco smoke, he begins sucking until the pathogen's physical malady comes out.

Usually the healing *bope* acts through the shaman to extract a beetle, *erubo bope*, 'medicine of the *bope*'. Beetles, mantises, mucus and pus: hostile *maereboe* use all sorts of weapons as darts in their struggle against Bororo shamans' *bope*-souls and their familiars. Others may see what the shaman extracts, but the patient never gets a look at the pathogen. Instead the shaman rubs it, crushed, into the patient's head. Here is an extension of ancient shamanic belief. That which one suffers can also make one strong. (Reasoning of this sort led in time to a triumph of modern medicine, vaccination.)

Even Bororo who are skeptical about the extraction of the beetle—'It was in his mouth all the time'—have no doubts about the efficacy of the cure, reasoning that the combination of tobacco smoke and sucking drove the offending spirits into the beetle.

'So the devils besought him, saying, If thou cast us out,
suffer us to go away into the herd of swine.
And he said unto them, Go.
And when they were come out,
they went into the herd of swine'.

MATTHEW 8:31-32

A shaman is routinely enlisted to help in the hunt. Most directly he assists is a time-honored tradition of shamanism everywhere: his familiar directs hunters to places where game will be found. 'In such and such a place there is a tapir. Surround him. He will run here, or there, or perhaps double back on his tracks. If you do not kill this one, you will not kill any in this hunt'. These words may be familiar. They recall the ancient Siberian hunters' invocation to the Lord of the Wild Game—made through a shaman—requesting that the supreme spirit might lead elk to their snares.

Since *bope* are responsible for transformation, it is no surprise that shamans transform themselves to power animals such as Jaguar, Alligator or Rattlesnake. Or can they? No shaman whom Crocker met claimed such a power, though other Bororo firmly believed it to be so. Like the flight of disease into the beetle, this may be another example of ordinary people putting more faith in shamanic powers than shamans do. In other words, Man may be imperfect, but the ways of the spirits, our understanding of them, and our belief in their power—this is real!

Perhaps Bororo shamans are valued more for their ability to transcend time in visions and to predict the future. A shaman who dreams that a neighbor will fall and break a leg will warn that person to avoid the location, and he will. The Bororo are great believers in shamanic healing via dream-discovered prophylaxis. Epidemics are visualized as dark clouds rolling towards a village, which the shaman and his spirit helpers attack with fans, dispersing it before it arrives.

> Dream-revealed prophylaxis

One thing Bororo shamans have not been able to disperse is the encroachment of modern life. Reduced by war and disease, Crocker notes a 'collective solidarity' against the foreign society (modern Brazil). The core of an ancient people is tenaciously clinging to its culture, relearning it as if culture itself were a prophylactic dream announced by a waking shaman. Perhaps one day the shamans will be able to stand at the approaches to their villages and fan the dark clouds away. With the aid of the *bope*, of course.

THE MIND CONQUERS MUCH

Shamanism at opposite ends of the Americas seems oddly symmetrical. The strange spirits that haunt the Inuits' Arctic cosmos appear as similar manifestations among the Ona people of wind-whipped Tierra del Fuego. Perhaps extremes of climate produce extremes in visions. The winters, the darkness, the hunger, the tensions of hunting the fleet-footed, red-wooled guanaco. And always the wind.

E. Lucas Bridges describes the terrible spirit-visions of the Ona: a horned man 'as gray in appearance as his lurking place'; two cruel sisters, one from the clouds and another from the region's red clay; a creature from the grey rocks 'whose only garment was a whitish piece of parchment-like skin over his face and head'—and so on.

Born in 1874, Bridges was the son of a clergyman who had set up a mission four years earlier. This later became South America's southernmost town, Ushuaia. Bridges spoke the Ona tongue and spent years among them, becoming a member of the men's society. A skeptic, Bridges dismissed Ona medicine men as 'humbugs' before describing a classic scene of shamanic extraction that might have taken place anywhere in the world:

> 'Gazing intently at the spot where the [patient's] pain was situated, the doctor would allow a look of horror to come over his face. Evidently he could see something invisible to the rest of us. ... With his hands he might try to gather the malign presence into one part of the patient's body—generally the chest—where he would then apply his mouth and suck violently. ... At other times the *joon* would draw away from his patient with the pretense of holding something in his mouth with his hands. Then, always facing away from the encampment, he would ... fling this invisible object to the ground and stamp fiercely upon it. Occasionally a little mud, some flint or even a tiny, very young mouse might be produced as the cause of the patient's indisposition'.[59]

Bridges once asked the great *joon* Houshken to display his magical powers. Houshken brought forth something that seemed to be 'a piece of semi-transparent dough or elastic; whatever it was it seemed alive, revolving at great speed, while Houshken, apparently from muscular tension, trembled violently'. Bridges took pains to admit that he could offer no physical explanation for this, which was witnessed by some thirty other people.

> 'The natives believed this to be a malignant spirit belonging to, or possibly part of the *joon* [Houshken] from whom it emanated. It might take physical form, as we had just witnessed, or be totally invisible. It had the power to introduce insects, tiny mice, mud, sharp flints or even a jellyfish or baby octopus, into the anatomy of those who had incurred its master's displeasure. I have seen a strong man shudder involuntarily at the thought of this horror and its evil potentialities'.

Bridges' final comment may say more about its author than his subject. 'Although every magician must have known himself to be a fraud and a trickster, he always believed in and greatly feared the supernatural abilities of other medicine-men'.

Distraction lands us in another part of the Americas. In 2008, Charles Langley published a book with a wonderfully nineteenth century title, *Meeting the Medicine Men: An Englishman's travels among the Navajo*. Unintentionally, Langley links the mental worlds of our *joon*, Houshken, with continuing practice among the Navajo. He writes:

Revelations, vibrations, a matter of balance

'Parts of quantum physics defy common sense. On the other hand common sense tells us the earth is flat and the sun goes round it. Common sense also tells us that a Navajo Medicine Man cannot speak to the spirit of a long dead snake or make a baby well by looking in a fire. At least, that's what it tells most white men, but it tells most Navajos completely the opposite. Common sense apart, reason suggests the quantum world appears so strange because we do not have the full picture. It is the large chunks of the picture that are missing, the parts completely unknown to us, that make the sub-atomic world look so crazy.

'Was it not reasonable to suppose that [the Navajo Medicine Man] Blue Horse's world might look crazy to me because I did not know enough about it …

'Perhaps the ability to cure was once innate in us, but in [the modern world] we have lost the ability …'

This leads us to quantum physics, later. For now …

Whether a healer is a doctor or a shaman, the passage of centuries has shown that a major part of healing can be found in a patient's belief—in the powers and persona of his culturally sanctioned physician. 'All that we are is the result of what we have thought. The mind is everything. What we think, we become', said the Buddha.

This chapter's subhead is 'A Matter of Balance'. That is one truth of the human condition: the mind conquers much, if not all.

~ *The mind conquers much, if not all* ~

5

From the recesses of time
Europe: fertility and redemption

Fifty thousand years ago, glacial ice covered everything north of a ragged line extending from eastern Siberia to south central France. Over the next 35,000 years the ice retreated, leaving plants and animals free to probe northwards, challenging the glacial front. Some of the oldest known *objets d'art* have been found in settlements associated with this line. They are 'Venus' figurines, small carvings in bone or ivory of women, large-breasted, big buttocked, and pregnant. The Venuses are distended caricatures of femaleness. If one can draw a conclusion it is that fecundity, not sex, was humanity's first great obsession.

Between fifteen and thirty thousand years ago artists began depicting animals of the hunt in caverns of southern France, notably Dordogne. The collages painted on walls at the vast, many-chambered grotto at Lascaux are undoubtedly religious art, and fertility is still the driving force. But this time the paintings invoke fertility for beasts of the chase, not humans. May the hunt prosper! May beast spirits thrive! Such cave art was surely as sacred to the prevailing beliefs of the Stone Age men and women who created it as the later expression of Christian passion that built medieval cathedrals. But there is a significant difference: Christianity puts Man at the centre; even God takes human, male, form. In the sacred cave art of the French Stone Age it is animal life that prevails, dominating the scene. Man is present as hunter, and, in the case of a human with a bird-topped pole, as shaman.

Three hundred kilometers to the south may be the oldest known depiction of a shaman, cut in the wall of the cavern *Les Trois Frères*, sixty feet below ground in the Pyrenees. Wearing deer antlers, the ancient 'Sorcerer of *Les Trois Frères*' appears to preside over a collage comprising several hundred animals of the chase. Hidden among these beasts, a bison-headed man either uses a bow or strikes a drum (reminding one of the Copper Eskimo shaman with the musk-ox head). But it is the sorcerer/shaman who commands attention. His bones, symbolic x-rays,

From the recesses of time

At first, ABBÉ HENRI BREUIL called this image the 'Sorcerer' of *Les Trois Frères* cave. He later revised his opinion, referring to the presiding 'god' or 'spirit' of the cave. The Sorcerer might have mediated between the fertility of game animals and a sustainable hunt. The many creatures on the limestone walls are in profile, incised by shallow lines cut with flint points. Only the Sorcerer is painted directly onto rock. He alone looks out at his grotto and his herds, observing the observer. Depicted when glaciers covered northern Europe, the artist endowed his guardian spirit (or power being) with x-ray characteristics still found in modern Ojibway and Aboriginal art. The Sorcerer's figure includes aspects of deer, wolf, bear, lion, wildcat, horse and human. The transformation theme is consistent with shape-shifting, which modern Inuit artists present. This key theme in Animist societies, that 'all is one', passed into Taoism and Buddhism, where separateness is illusion and every entity expresses aspects of a single consciousness.

The drawing by Abbé Breuil is in the public domain.

are as visible as his flesh. The style is common to this day in the art of primal peoples. Among hundreds of creatures in the cavern sanctuary, only the shaman is highlighted with rich black paint to show his bones.

The x-ray shaman of *Les Trois Frères* began looking down on his animals more than fifteen thousand years ago, staring out through the solid rock walls of his cave, forward to our present time, and past us, too. Beneath his deer antlers he has ears like a wolf; his face is maned like a lion; his paws are a bear's or a wild cat's; his tail is that of a horse; his testes are placed like a cat's; his penis hangs down like a man's. To a shaman, forms are interchangeable.

There is a parallel between shamanic spirit-journeys to the Lower World and the very physical presence of these first depicted shamans in the grottoes of Lascaux and *Les Trois Frères*. The shaman of Lascaux rests at the bottom of a deep shaft isolated from the main cave complex, while the struggle to reach the wizard's lair at *Les Trois Frères* will repel anyone who feels uncomfortable in the confined space of caves. After climbing through a hole in limestone at the surface and negotiating a series of narrow passages linking cathedral-sized galleries replete with stalactites, the first explorers confronted their greatest challenge, the tunnel-passage to the shaman's cave. Count Bégouën, on whose estate the cave was found, described his first visit to the wizard's grotto:

> 'The tunnel is not much broader than my shoulders, nor higher. I can hear the others before me groaning and see how very slowly their lamps push on. With our arms pressed close to our sides we wriggle forward on our stomachs, like snakes. The passage, in places, is hardly a foot [30cm] high, so that you have to lay your face right on the earth. I felt as though I were creeping through a coffin. You cannot lift your head; you cannot breathe ... And so, yard by yard, one struggles on: some forty-odd yards [37m] in all. ... I hear the others groaning, my own heart is pounding, and it is difficult to breathe. It is terrible to have the roof so close to one's head. And it is very hard: I bump it, time and again. Will this thing never end? Then, suddenly, we are through, and everybody breathes. It is like a redemption'.[60]

The count's choice of word—redemption—aptly described his release from physical pain and panic that must have gripped everyone who made those first quests to the rediscovered cave. It is to discover redemption for themselves, and others, that shamans have trained and endured the rigors of cold, fasting, suffering, near madness and solitude through more millennia than we can surmise.

From the recesses of time

It is surely no coincidence that the shaman-crypts at Lascaux and *Les Trois Frères* are where they are, in silent coffin-wombs far from main cave chambers in locations both physically and mentally challenging to reach or escape from.

Imagine the trials of a novice lowered into the crypt at Lascaux or, at *Les Trois Frères*, required to crawl one hundred and twenty feet along a tunnel no wider or higher than his straining body, perhaps to be abandoned for days in the absolute, timeless dark and silence of the Lower World. Around him the black velvet of eternal night, the cave silent but for dripping stalactites creating the impression of things moving in the dark. More terrifying than sounds in silence, the novice would be stripped of any measure of passing time and left only with a horrible, overwhelming sense of oppressive place. Madness might come as a relief. Who could doubt that a first spirit-helper must come before long?

It is conjecture to suggest that these two Old Stone Age shaman-crypts were used for the initiation of novices. But we do know that most footprints found in these caves were made by adolescents. 'One fact is very striking', writes André Leroi-Gourhan. 'Practically all known footprints were made by young people'.[61] To this day caves play an important role in the initiation of Australian shamans (notably in the Northern Territory), in Chile, in southern Africa and North America. To imagine Stone Age crypts as ancient vision pits links a well established practice with a continuum of shamanic traditions surmounting oceans of water and oceans of time.

MANDALAS AND MAZES
HOMES FOR THE MYSTERIES, A-MAZE-MENT FOR ALL

It needs no great leap of imagination to advance from hunting peoples invoking animal spirits in natural shrines to later cultures creating symbolic and literal grottoes—mandalas and mazes—in which to enshrine the Mysteries.

Skeletal visions deriving from soul-flight journeys—the exposed ribs, the bony hands—suggest the hoops and concentric circles or geometric tracery that frame and support a shaman's tunnel to and from the Lowerworld. For this reason shamanic art sometimes reflects concentric themes, crafted to imitate the perspective of rushing through a tunnel. Some Inuit shaman masks are cut in concentric designs, and Siberian shamans embroider the tunnel motif on their garments. At its most elaborate, shamanic art represents this 'Hole of the Spirits' as a mandala, a traditional form with roots in a time when shamanic precepts were absorbed into Buddhist and Taoist thought.

Whatever its pattern, the effect of a mandala is to lock the rush of dynamic creation into an instant of time. A mandala is a freeze-frame of evolving cosmos, a tunnel to eternity along which a soul-flight traveler speeds. Or does the tunnel itself rush past a static traveler, presenting other worlds? On one hand the rigid fourfold symmetry of a mandala's geometry represents the tunnel, the ribs of the earth and the journey; on the other it allows sacred art to incorporate all the elements of earth and cosmos—flowers, birds, weather, the spirit world—those ghost-forms which each soul-flight traveler will meet.

<small>Mandalas, effects of</small>

A novice's mind must be disoriented and reoriented before he can become an adept who can drop at will into a shamanic state of consciousness to journey in and out of otherworlds. Psychiatrist Charles Tart describes the process as a destabilizing and repatterning of brain and mind—and the artistic conventions of mandalas suggest this effect. If one stands close and stares unblinking at an elaborate mandala for long enough one's eyes interpret the design as an out-rushing visual chaos through which the viewer is drawn in and sucked along the central tube. Now blink, look again, and the thing becomes a perfectly ordered symmetry, perfect in detail, a static whole: mobile/static; chaotic/ordered; fractured/intact.

Keep the dynamic image of a mandala in mind as Rasmussen describes the soul-flight journey of an Inuit *angakoq*. Imagine staring into its design; then, on cue, blinking to arrest the visual *trompe-l'œil*:

> '[D]ifficulties and dangers attend the journey of an ordinary shaman. But for the very greatest, a way opens right from the house whence they invoke their helping spirits; a road down through the earth ... or down through the sea ... and by this route [*Stare at the mandala*] the shaman is led down without encountering any difficulty. He almost glides as if falling through a tube so fitted to his body that he can [*Blink*] check his progress by pressing against the sides, and need not actually fall down with a rush. [*Stare*] This tube is kept open for him by all the souls of his namesakes, until he returns on his way back to earth'.[62]

At its best the art of the mandala illustrates a shaman's power of soul-flight between worlds. As art, its uncompromising symmetry of design represents victory by spiritual discipline over a jumbled chaos of primordial powers. Here is a shaman's mind-force, assailed at first by an on-rush of specters, then standing four-square as it reworks them, forging an ordered sense from the apparent random madness of a spirit world set up behind the false front of our own.

If we take another step, a mandala becomes a maze.

Mazes have represented the dark, chaotic forces of a frightening world since European prehistory. Like life itself, a maze is a matter of checks, disappointments, retreat, entrapment and advance. Within the same maze each human experience will be unique. But a maze once trodden and remembered represents, no longer chaos, but the ordered symmetry of a reworked mind advancing from the 'I' state to the Inner Self—in shamanic terms, reborn. In ancient religions the maze seems to suggest the powerful hold of the tomb. But, once threaded and escaped the conquered maze spells reincarnation. Here is death and rebirth, retold in ancient European stones. Stylized mazes, which may have been cut by Phoenician sea traders four thousand years ago, have been found near European coasts as far north as the Baltic Sea.

| Mazes

Thirty-five hundred years ago the influence of Minoan Crete was at its height in the eastern Mediterranean. Nowhere was maze-lore more sophisticated, suggesting that the principles on which it was based were older by a substantial order of time. The Minotaur, the bull-man lurking in the Mycenæan labyrinth, recalls another minotaur carved more than ten thousand years earlier on a cave wall at the end of a panic-making tunnel-maze—the bison-headed hunter concealed in the collage of animals at *Les Trois Frères*.

Another image from Minoan Crete rears up. An enduring symbol from that ancient island-world is the double-headed axe, the *labrys*, a form discovered between the horns of a bull at Mycenae and cut on menhirs at Stonehenge. Modified to a figure of eight, the blades still stand for centering or infinity: ∞. The wanderer is doomed to return by the same, inevitable route along the edges of the blades. British novelist John Fowles points out that with *labrys* comes *labyrinth* and *labor*, a word we retain most poignantly in the final course of childbirth. We slip through the tunnel into life, into light; we slip through the shamanic tunnel to an altered state of life, into enlightenment. The struggle to run one's course through life is the most enduring symbolism of the European grotto-womb or of the Mycenae labyrinth.

SPIRIT IN HEALTH

OF SOUL-FLIGHT AND BROOMSTICKS / FREYJA RIDES

The New Stone Age brought more than agriculture to southern England. It also enhanced respect for the dead, who lie in communal graves called long barrows running tens, even hundreds, of meters in length. These earthen mounds are often located on high ridges, as if their builders intended them to be seen from afar. Or perhaps high ground allowed for easy escape of souls to the sky. Neolithic long barrows dot the uplands to this day.

In time, long barrows gave way to Bronze Age round barrows, the graves of tribal dignitaries. By 3,500 years ago society had advanced to a point where it could channel vast energies building structures such as Stonehenge, Silbury Hill, Avebury and the stone rows of Brittany. These, and other monuments, seem to address the sky-god, the Sun, the maleness of things.

But these great works were hardly completed before the social fabric dissolved, leaving southern England in a sort of prehistoric dark age. The change coincided with a time when many north European peoples stopped burying their dead in barrows and started cremating them. Earth to earth gave way to ashes to ashes. The change infers a shift to a collective belief that a soul could escape its corpse more readily by burning than by burial, especially if birds or their wings were interred with the ashes. Soul flight, at least for the dead, found new importance.

In Denmark the change to cremation followed the arrival of an Earth Mother whose prototype was already honored in the Middle East. Before this goddess reached Denmark around 3,500 BC, Danish tribes had offered all votive gifts to male spirits. Once the Earth Mother joined the Danish pantheon, however, the nature of offerings began to change. For several centuries gifts intended for a female deity—loom bobbins, cooking pots and jewelry—made up about half of the total. By 500 BC, over ninety percent were for the Earth Mother. Her local name was Nerthus, and she was a sympathetic and powerful figure whose images show her extending one hand in welcome or assistance while the other holds a coiled snake, the timeless symbol of the healing arts. Sympathetic or not, women were slow to follow the goddess's lead and take over the healing profession. About thirty graves older than 500 BC have been found to contain shamanic medicine boxes designed to be worn on belts. Pebbles, crystals, a snake's tail and animal bones are obvious aids to spiritual healing, marking the graves as

> Gods, male or female? Time and the context decide.

shamans', all male. Then the pattern changes: after 500 BCE archaeologists find similar medicine bundles in graves interred with women. Gradually healing, as well as the godhead, became a female preserve.

Then the Danish climate began to change for the worse. Summers grew shorter and colder; crops failed. A high proportion of Denmark's people migrated. A general exodus from northern Europe created population pressures and warfare elsewhere: the Celts of southern England dug in, building hilltop fortresses of earthen banks and ditches to keep a flood of invaders from overrunning their lands. The power of Nerthus, the Earth Mother who had served Danish tribes for a thousand years, was inadequate to stave off disaster. The Danes turned to male deities, Odin and Thor, the Norse gods of war.

When Christianity came to Denmark more than a thousand years later, Christ was forced to share the pantheon with the male Norse gods. Some surviving coins bear the cross of Jesus combined with Thor's hammer. By then the climate had improved to a point where pollen analysis shows that the eleventh century (1000-1100 AD) was warmer than average. Once more Earth was cherishing her human children. The Earth Mother returned.

We owe what we know of the goddess's resurrection to an Icelander, Snorri Sturluson, whose *Prose Edda* (c. 1220) describes how the Earth Mother found a new lease on life as Freyja—for whom Friday is named. According to Sturluson, Freyja was the last Norse god: Christ had vanquished the others. Far from being vanquished, twelfth century paintings of Freyja riding her shaman-staff (the medieval witch's broomstick), and her familiar, a cat, adorn Schleswig cathedral. Freyja became the matriarch of better times whose coterie of female spirits, the Vanir, presided over agriculture, fertility and childbirth. Female shamans channeled the powers of these spirits through a type of shamanism called *Seidhr*, in which prolonged chanting induced their souls to journey. It is not clear whether shamans' souls or their animal helpers journeyed during trance, but in a shaman's world it hardly matters. Perhaps, like Freyja herself, they rode their power animals. Female shamans practising *seidhr* were reputed to be reliable seers and healers into the late Middle Ages.

CONSTRUCTIVE SCHISM / GREECE

Around the time that proto-Danes were celebrating the brief ascendancy of female spirits and entrusting women with shamanic powers, Hellenes were struggling to resolve a titanic culture clash. In Greece, invaders from the north confronted an established civilization nurtured by the Mother Goddess. The newcomers spoke a new language, Greek, and worshipped an extended family of alien gods. The product of this uneasy merger, Classical Greece, never did resolve its schism fully.

The old (Mycenaean) culture took spiritual strength from *mythos*, a concept encompassing imagination and 'all that cannot be subject to verification, but contains its truth in itself or ... in powers of persuasion arising out of its own beauty'.[63] In short, Animist visions. But the new, thrusting northerners operated on the principle of *logos*, meaning 'reasoning' or 'logic'. Herein lay 'everything that can be stated in rational terms, all that attains to objective truth, and appears the same to all minds'.[64]

Mythos & logos

The older culture maintained its ancient spiritual traditions, exemplified by Orpheus, who traveled in the underworld, and whose power of song could move mountains and trees. Fighting a rearguard action against change, a later Orphic cult preserved a literature documenting Animism's decline.

The invading culture introduced the precision of mathematics (Thales, Pythagoras, Euclid, Archimedes). Subjected to the new disciplines of number, angle and shape, notions about matter effectively 'froze'. Physical objects came to be seen as solid, unchanging, and therefore inanimate. This concept of immutability had not shackled the human mind before. Certainly not the minds of Animists. From this point, 'reality' in European thought slowly becomes synonymous with 'solid, concrete form'.

Small wonder that protagonists in dialogues of Plato (427-347 BCE) often mirror the *mythos/logos* split. The philosopher himself was concerned to explore 'ideas of being'. The debate 'what came first, mind or matter?' starts from this point. And Socrates would 'search for clarity and definition through rational argument coupled with the sound of an inner voice, the depths of a trance, and divine revelation in terms of the obscure and profound symbols of religious myth'.[65]

The brash new world of mathematical *logos* came empowered by the equally brash new pantheon of the northerners' gods and goddesses, led by Zeus. The playwright Æschylus (*Prometheus Bound*, c. 488 BCE) documents the 'struggle between a harsh, young and angry Zeus' and the 'defiant

From the recesses of time

determination of a glorious and philanthropic Prometheus' who, shaman-like, sacrifices himself to defend mankind.

Here, Prometheus lists the gifts he has given to humans, for which Zeus makes him suffer:

> 'Listen to the troubles that there were among mortals and how I gave them sense and mind ... They had eyes to look, but looked in vain, and ears to hear, but did not hear ... I first harnessed animals ... [and] discovered the seamen's vessels which with wings of sail are beaten by the waves. Such are the contrivances I, poor wretch, have found for mortals. ... Through lack of medicines they wasted away until I showed them the mixing of soothing remedies ... I set forth the many ways of the prophetic art ... All arts come to mortals from Prometheus'.

Not the least of the gifts Prometheus stole from on high to give to mankind—for which Zeus punished him—was that of fire. 'High-thundering Zeus was stung to the depths of his being ... as he saw among men the gleam of fire'.[66]

Both Hesiod (*Theogony*, c. 776 BCE) and Æschylus were spiritual conservatives. They harked back to the old world of shape-shifting shamans, heroes and prophetic dreams. Both describe the primary god of the new order, Zeus, as an oppressor; both celebrate the fire-bringer Prometheus as an ancient saviour of mankind.

Indeed, even after the new deities were firmly enthroned on Olympus, writers still subjected them to transformations based on cultural memories drawn from the older, Animist world. This passage from Homer's *Odyssey* equally well describes an Inuit *angakoq's* journey to the seabed to visit Sedna, Mother of the Sea Beasts.

> 'Eidothea dived down into the vast cavern of the sea and brought out of the depths four skins of seals ... for she was planning to trick her father ... [She threw a seal skin over each of us]. ... At midday the Old Man came forth from the deep ... we rushed upon him with a shout ... but the Old Man did not forget his devious arts. First he became a thickly maned lion, and then a serpent, a leopard and a great boar. And he became liquid water and a tree with lofty branches. But we held on with steadfast spirits'.[67]

Metamorphoses, the 'Book of Transformations', by the Roman writer Ovid (c. 9 AD), is a fifteen-volume compilation of transformations drawn from Greek literature. Even the new gods were not immune from old shamanic transformations. Ovid describes how the supreme deity himself took on mortality.

> 'Reports of the wickedness of the age had reached my ears; wishing to find them false I slipped down from high Olympus and I, a god, roamed the earth in the form of a man'.[68]

The gods of ancient Greece had originally personified Nature's powers: wind, water, earthquake, storm, and rain. Later, as mankind ceased to personify these phenomena, the divinities developed independent personalities. Belief divorced Nature. So it went: from the Hellenes, to Greece, to Rome; from Homer and Hesiod, to Ovid. But much that was ancient survived. Divinity mixed with mortality; divinity put on mortality. Spirits and shamans lost out.

THE WEB OF WYRD

Far to the north, in Iron Age Britain, the coming of Celts (6th to 3rd centuries BCE) and the later Anglo-Saxons (5th to 7th century AD) may have bolstered shamanism, a powerful influence in the Nature religions of both peoples. Psychologist Brian Bates has spent years reconstructing Celtic shamanism and Anglo-Saxon 'Wyrd' as it was practised in the British Isles during the first Christian millennium. Our modern 'weird' derives from that Anglo-Saxon word for a mysterious or inexplicable spiritual frce.

Wyrd evolved from the Anglo-Saxon belief that two vast regions of fire and ice reacted at the beginning of time to create an all-encompassing mist imbued with the essence of spirituality and life-giving force. This 'mist of knowledge' is eternal, outside space and time, accessible only to those who attain the shaman state.

Anglo-Saxons: fire and ice

Brian Bates points out that, apart from the all-encompassing mist, the cosmos of wyrd manifests itself as a web of fibers connecting every thing that is. Just as sub-atomic neutrino particles pervade the cosmos of modern physicists, the world of Anglo-Saxon shamans was alive with webs of fibers flowing through and connecting everything. As a spider feels the vibrations of events taking place on her web, so the slightest influence at one part of the Anglo-Saxon cosmic web was instantly felt through the rest. An Anglo-Saxon shaman trying to discover the nature of forces at work in his client would visualize the pattern of fibers passing through his body.

Curvilinear lines of Celtic and Anglo-Saxon art preserve this web-like cosmic view. The fluid lines of Celtic art travel from one design to another, uniting the whole. Anglo-Saxon craftsmen's lines neither start nor stop. Lacking ends, they merge. Artisans created intricate knots, designs without endings, celebrating the joy of eternal continuity. Insofar as Celtic and Anglo-Saxon craftsmen were interpreting their own cosmology, the influences they suggest are threefold: everything is interconnected; that which is real is eternal; and all forms that exist may evolve from a web or a line.

Such a cosmos resembles the Chinese belief that creation is the product of a web without a weaver; and the original force fields of fire and ice suggest the hot/cold, male/female, wet/dry, earth/air influence of *yin* and *yang*.

Bates had his first direct experience of cosmic threads when he went walking in an English wood. Feeling a pulsing around his navel he became sick. Then hundreds of lines of light from all directions passed through his body. 'They seemed like warm fibers supporting me, and I felt as if I were walking on air', he told an interviewer. Later, Bates and other British shamans discovered that they could work with the fibers to centre clients' life forces.

Anglo-Saxon shamans considered that the path of each life followed a pattern woven into the design on a goddess's loom. Accordingly, Bates speaks of clients wishing to change aspects of their lives as trying to alter their 'life design'. A person's original life path and pattern, whatever it be, exists on the loom; though it can be changed it must be done in harmony with the original design.

| Life design

Other techniques of offering modern shamanic therapy involve getting people to write about or draw their animal dreams. Then guardian animals are introduced. Bates' work is based on years of researching old texts, including *Lacnunga* (i.e. *Leechbook*, a collection of remedies or cures), a thousand year old manuscript in the British Library (MS Harley 585). *Lacnunga* was once the spell book of an Anglo-Saxon shaman. As in many shamanic cultures, healings often began with a shaman drumming or chanting into trance in order that the spirits might teach the nature of diagnosis and cure. Then, incantations brought spirit forces to the patient's aid from the web of wyrd, inducing images within the body/mind that might effect that cure. *Lacnunga* also provides incantations to be followed in pursuit of lost souls. As late as the tenth century the importance of shamanic healing was such that one surviving manuscript describes a woman shaman traveling with an entourage of thirty chanters, men and women, and perhaps drummers as well.

Christian missionaries had to work hard to overcome Nature religions during the first millennium. Winfred (St Boniface) was martyred in Frisia for attempting to cut down an oak tree sacred to the pagan gods. St Patrick did the same in Ireland but survived. An English law passed by King Canute in 1018 banned the worship of 'heathen gods, the sun, the moon, fire, rivers, fountains, rocks and trees'. Meanwhile, across the North Sea, Danes were turning back to Freyja and her female spirits of the earth.

Anglo-Saxon shamanic training depended on gender. Men and women enjoyed equal respect, though women had the edge in matters of childbirth and prophecy. However, as Christianity made inroads, missionaries persuaded kings to replace their male shamanic counselors with monks. Since the Church could not bring itself to believe that women might hold positions of authority, female shamans were largely ignored. As a result, shamanism fell from being a court-centered spirituality to being a grass-roots peasant culture of healing, relying on herbal cures and the 'superstitions' of 'old wives'. (The history of shamanism in Korea is not dissimilar.) Not until the Middle Ages did the Church turn its vicious attentions to rooting out and destroying female 'witches'.

OF WIZARDS AND WITCHES: WALES

> 'I am prepared to sing the madness of the prophetic bard'
> The opening line of the twelfth century
> *The Life of Merlin*

The bardic tradition of Celtic Wales created a literary tradition based in large measure on shamanic lore. The *Mabinogion* is a medieval collection of Welsh legends, some dating from the seventh and eighth centuries. Many involve Pwyll, Prince of Dyved, who was reputed to be a better than average soul-flier (like another Welsh shaman-king, Bladud, the founder of the healing baths at Bath).

One day, embarking on a vision quest, Pwyll sat on a high mound that had a reputation that no one could 'go thence, without ... seeing a wonder'. As he sat there 'a lady, on a pure white horse of large size, with a garment of shining gold around her' rode past, her horse seeming to move 'at a slow and even pace'. Though her horse never quickened its pace, Pwyll could never catch up. Days elapsed, the lady trotting past while Pwyll exhausted his fastest steeds in an effort to overtake. 'Of a truth,' said he, 'there must be some illusion here'. Ultimately the lady responded to Pwyll's hail, confiding: 'My chief quest was to seek thee'.[69] It seems that Pwyll, setting out on a vision quest,

Vision quests, illusions

found that the lady of his vision was seeking a helper spirit of her own. Shaman, meet shaman.

The next account, also from Wales, combines mythic traditions with the sort of initial shamanic crisis that scripture and legend have reported since the dawn of human time:

> '[He] did not cease to pour out laments, and he strewed dust on his hair and rent his garments, and prostrate on the ground rolled now hither and now thither. He had now lamented for three whole days and had refused food, so great was the grief that consumed him. Then ... new fury seized him and he fled to the woods. ... He lived on the roots of grasses ... hidden like a wild animal he remained buried in the woods, found by no one and forgetful of himself and of his kindred.
>
> '[After a season, he] became mindful of himself, and he recalled what he used to be, and he wondered at his madness and he hated it. His former mind returned and his sense came back to him, and [he left the woods] to the city of the king. ... But when [he] saw such great crowds of men present he was not able to endure them; he went mad again, and, filled anew with fury, he wanted to go to the woods ...
>
> 'Finally since the king could not retain the sad man by any gifts, he ordered him to be bound with a strong chain lest, if free, he might seek the deserted groves. The prophet, when he felt the chains around him ... fell to grieving and remained sad and silent ...'[70]

Here is Europe's great shaman, Merlin, cast as mad hero; he is a seer fleeing to the woods, a recurring trait among prophets since Moses descended Mount Sinai with Ten Commandments. Merlin's downfall and later redemption is typical of 'god-triumphant' myths. A passage in *The Life of Merlin* links four elements: a king enthroned; a wild man, Merlin, bound before him; a woman, Ganieda, the king's consort and Merlin's sister; and an effeminate boy (disguised by order of the queen).

R.J. Stewart explains:

> 'The king represents justice or rule; the prophet represents the wild powers of nature and the unpredictable raw energies of life; the boy represents the many aspects of human incarnation; the queen represents the goddess who directs all the drama from her originative position of power'.[71]

Like Prometheus, son of a Titan, Merlin was a man of foresight and vision tamed by the civilizing forces represented here by the king. And, though she stands in the shadow of her king, Mother Earth (Ganieda) still has authority.

Had Merlin lived a thousand years later he would not merely have been bound, but burned at the stake by the Church. In 1488 Pope Innocent VIII issued a bull calling on Christian nations to rescue the Church from the black arts of Satan. Similar bulls from Popes Alexander VI (1494), Leo XI (1521) and Adrian VI (1522) launched Christian Europe on an orgy of hangings, burnings and drownings that would last the better part of two centuries. By the nineteenth century the only overt shamans in Europe survived in distant Lapland, which the *Oxford Dictionary* defines, in part, as: 'formerly, the fabled home of witches and magicians, who had power to send winds and tempests'. Why 'formerly' in that definition? Because nineteenth century Lutherans staked Sami (Lapp) shamans out on frozen lakes to die.

Fire and ice! Those elements connect the dawn of Anglo-Saxon cosmology with the ritual murders of European shamans at the end. What next? Celtic and Anglo-Saxon craftsmen who took such care to integrate every aspect of their work into designs revealing no visible ends would say: There must be a 'next', a starting again. Some ancient Animist traditions never died. Lads still wear antlers at modern village fairs, like the ancient Stone Age shaman in the grotto at *Les Trois Frères*. Men run before bulls in Pamplona; May Queens and Green Men are chosen on May Day; and the world axis tree, disguised as maypoles, is coming back. Meanwhile a new sensitivity to the cries of Mother Earth, be she called Gaia or Environment, is making her children aware once more of old Nature-based beliefs.

AMAZEMENT AGAIN

Which returns us to labyrinths—not the one at Mycenae but rather to the craze for mazes that stimulated Elizabethans to build them at great houses like the Palace of Hampton Court. The best and brightest brains of that age, and ours, possessed a spirit-sense willing and eager to express a/maze/ment at the wonder of the magic, hidden world. *A Midsummer Night's Dream* and *The Tempest* are awash in maze-lore set for the ears of courtly audiences. As *The Tempest* draws to a close, Gonzalo offers this fearful plea:

> 'All torment, trouble, wonder, and a-Mazement
> Inhabits here: some heavenly power guide us
> Out of this fearful country!'

From the recesses of time

A hundred lines later he can thank Ferdinand and Miranda for releasing them all from the miserable thrall-maze of plot, adding:

> 'Look down, you gods,
> And on this couple drop a blessed crown;
> For it is you that have chalk'd forth the way
> Which brought us hither!'

The maze-like complexity of modern living combines with the threats we pose to our living envelope to draw human attention to ancient Earth-based Animist beliefs. After centuries of taking things apart, science is beginning to discover the interconnectedness of things once more. Animists and their shamans never knew anything else. Though battered and torn, the light-borne fibers in the Anglo-Saxon web of wyrd are being patched and repaired.

A MODERN PERPECTIVE:
DO GODS COME DOWN? DO SPIRITS INTERCEDE?

In 1985, the Canadian Broadcasting Corporation's *the fifth estate* television series broadcast the story of New York theatrical producer Jack Garfein. A television team accompanied Garfein to Auschwitz. He had been sent there in 1944 as an underweight thirteen-year-old, with his mother and sister. On arrival his mother had shoved him away from her, roughly pushing him into the men's line, correctly suspecting (as he discovered only after the camp was liberated) that males had a better chance of survival. CBC filmed the following dialogue at the place where Josef Mengele separated those who would live from those who would die. This excerpt is from the broadcast transcript of *the fifth estate*, courtesy of CBC:

> GARFEIN: 'I looked up at [Mengele] ... He said to me, "How old are you?" I said, "I'm sixteen". There was a kind of pause there. And an old man behind me suddenly stuck his head out and said, "Your Excellency, he and I are great mosaic artists. We are world famous". I didn't know what mosaic artist meant ... I never saw this old man, didn't know about him. And Mengele went like this [*pointed to the labor camp*] for both of us. So the old man started. I started after the old man ... I said to the old man, "Why did you say that? You know I don't do that!" And he ... The old man started to run away'.
>
> REPORTER: 'Did anybody really believe you were sixteen?'

GARFEIN: 'I think that pause [by Mengele] is what made the old man say that we're world-famous mosaic artists. That made [Mengele] switch'.

REPORTER: 'It would be that split second that he had gone that way with his thumb'.

GARFEIN: 'Yeah. You know, when I read the *Iliad* in school when I came to America, I said: Greek mythology? That's true, that gods come down and … I had this god come down in the guise of an old man, because I never saw that old man again'.

6

Heal till it hurts
SOUTHERN AFRICA
MAGICAL PEOPLE, THE BUSHMEN

The Bushmen peoples of southern Africa were 'just always there'. That is the verdict of time. It is also the verdict of each and every origin-myth told by the many black races living south of a line across Africa from the Okovango River to the Zambezi.

'He came from nowhere! He was like the tortoise, yellow-throated lizard and springbuck—just always there!' With these words an 'old father' of the Hottentot race—themselves the first black immigrants to southern Africa—described the Bushmen's origins to an insistent little boy, Laurens van der Post. Whether they are Herero, Ovambo, Bechuana, Basuto, Zulu or another of the powerful warrior Bantu tribes, their oral history is always the same. They, the black peoples, migrated from the north in the early time. But the Bushmen, the short, olive-skinned hunters of southern Africa, like the rocks, like the trees, like the colored earth into which they could instantly melt away—the Bushmen had always been there.

Recently, three research groups were able to combine findings confirming that, indeed 'the Bushmen had always been there'. Research results show that all non-Africans descend from a single human migration out of Africa between 50 and 80 thousand years ago (y/a). Before that, the San/Khoisan (Bushman) people of southern Africa began to split from other human races around 200,000 y/a, becoming 'isolated' around 100,000 y/a.[72] The San people are indeed very special.

Van der Post was born in 1906 on his parents' farm near the Great (Orange) River 'in the heart of what for thousands of years had been great Bushman country'. The Orange River defines the border between the Republic of South Africa and what is now Namibia. South of the river the map still identifies Great Bushman Land and Little Bushman Land, but the true Bushmen are nowhere to be found. Pushed south by advancing black peoples, then shoved north from the Cape after the first Dutch settlers landed in 1652, Bushmen were killed by many other peoples. By the early years of the twentieth century survivors had fled to refuge in the Kalahari, one of the most inhospitable environments on earth. When van der Post was eight years old he wrote this declaration in his diary: 'I have decided today that when I am grown-up I am going into the Kalahari Desert to seek out the Bushman'. More than forty years would pass before he could fulfill his promise, recording his search for the Bushman in a documentary for the BBC and two books, *The Lost World of the Kalahari*, and *The Heart of the Hunter*.

Five thousand miles to the north and just months before van der Post wrote his boyhood declaration, three small boys—brothers—had discovered a cave on their father's property in the south of France. The cave was *Les Trois Frères*. The balance of probability suggests that its walls were painted 15,000 to 20,000 years earlier by a race of hunters likely related to the relict modern Bushman population of the Kalahari, whom van der Post would one day set out to find.

The Bushman differs from other races physiologically. In the heart of the black continent, his skin is Mediterranean olive. High cheekbones emphasize eyes that are neither African nor European, but curiously Asian. Tens of thousands of years of adaptation to the hunter's life of feast or famine have marked his body: a good hunting season distends his belly until men as well as women look heavily pregnant; and his buttocks function like a camel's hump or the tail of a fat-tailed sheep, swelling with fats and carbohydrates to sustain him through the hungry times—the six month Kalahari drought each year.

Nor is that all. Pure Bushman males are born and go through life with a semi-erect penis; females are born with a flap of skin, the *tablier égyptien*, screening their genitals.[73] These physiological details connect the Bushman to the ancient Mediterranean rim rather than Africa: the *tablier* was a feature of Egyptian women of the Second Dynasty, according to anatomical descriptions of that period; the semi-erect penis which features in Old Stone Age European cave art has been widely interpreted as a physiological response to shamanic trance, but it may also represent a Bushman-related people who lived and hunted in southern France and the Iberian peninsula fifteen to twenty thousand years ago.

Around 450 BC, Herodotus, the 'Father of History', wrote about a 'little people of adroit bow and arrow hunters' in what is now southern Libya. That might put a race of North African Bushman in position to have created the paintings and carvings of game animals on the rocks of Tibesti, a high plateau in what is now the virtually lifeless center of the Sahara. These putative connections to the shamanic peoples of Stone Age

Europe explain why the relict Bushman of the Kalahari and its littoral is the most truly shamanic in Africa. His antecedence, unchanged until the destruction of his people in the last three centuries, belongs to the rich diorama of Stone Age Europe and Africa. He enjoyed a wealth of game and fortune that he was careful to depict as sacred art in the caves of Spain, France, and on the walls of cliffs in northwestern Botswana at Tsodilo, the Slippery Hills.

By the standards of any other people on earth, Bushmen take next to nothing from the material world. A loin cloth, a robe of skin, a spear, a bow with poison for arrows, a stamping-block made out of ironwood, with which women crush seeds and sun-dried meat. Hides tanned with extracts from bulbs provide shelters; ostrich eggs hold water and give women the raw material from which they make beads.

What Bushmen do possess are skills and knowledge of the earth, its wisdom and its gifts. They can spin rope thin enough to snare a lizard or thick enough to hang a carcass in a tree; extract water from seemingly dry sand; mix different poisons for different types of game; run twenty miles in summer heat to bring down fleet-footed game; track the spoor of a wounded beast among several hundred in a herd.

The Stone Age artists working far from daylight in European caves rendered the lines and actions of animals intuitively. Similarly, Bushmen take from the hardships of life a mental form of the earth and its species that is as much intuitive as learned. They are as one with the spirit sense of creature, plant and stars. As van der Post expresses it in *The Lost World of the Kalahari*:

> 'He seemed to know what it actually felt like to be an elephant, a lion, an antelope, a steenbuck, a lizard, a striped mouse, mantis, baobab tree, yellow-crested cobra, or starry-eyed amaryllis, to mention only a few ... It seemed to me that his world was one without secrets between one form of being and another ... He was back in the moment which our European fairy-tale books described as the time when birds, beasts, plants, trees and men shared a common tongue, and the whole world, night and day, resounded like the surf of a coral sea with universal conversation'.

Nothing belonged to the Bushman; rather he belonged, as his survivors still belong, to the earth and Creation, wholeheartedly and without reservation. This emerges in his rock paintings. They are stylistically and thematically similar to the best of French and Iberian cave art. Here are animals of the chase, lovingly rendered, hunted by giants—for the diminutive Bushman was sensitive only in the matter of his size, overcompensating for his stature in his art—rendered in Africa and Europe in similar colors; signed, too, with hand prints smeared in pigment and held against the rock.

Although the artistic tradition of Bushmen in Africa did not survive to the twentieth century, it was still a living tradition in the mid-nineteenth, when more than one extermination commando of European settlers reported killing warriors with ten or more little pots of paint slung on a cord at their waists. This aspect of their culture was still remembered by old people in the 1950s; when van der Post showed copies of Bushman rock art to an elderly couple living in the heart of the Kalahari, they wept at the recognition.

The oldest rock art, whether in Europe or Africa, shows animals alone: man is absent. He enters the scene later, first as fellow creature, then as hunter, but always as an integral part of the natural landscape and the spirit forms, which the physical world revealed.

Art and the spirits combined to threaten danger when van der Post led his 1958 expedition into the sacred summits of the Tsodilo hills.[74] Walls lining the narrow path to the summit were richly decorated with rock paintings, some clearly very old: at one level the face of a rhinoceros stared out at them; at another, a tortoise; next, animals *en masse*; just below the summit a whole herd awaited weary pilgrims. In southern Africa (as well as Australia) many paintings show evidence of having been repainted, renewing the magic of the image on the rock.

The rock paintings were not the only show of spirit-power that the Tsodilo Hills imposed on van der Post and his party. Some weeks before, on the western edge of the great Okovango swamp, he had engaged the services of Samutchoso, a healer and a seer, to lead his party into the Tsodilo Hills. Samutchoso (whose appropriately shamanic name translates as 'He who was left after reaping') attached one strict condition of employment: he would lead the expedition into the hills only if no life was taken on the way to the sacred site. Samutchoso explained that if any game were shot *en route* to the sacred hills the spirits of those hills would be grievously offended, perhaps to the point of killing the offenders. Van der Post agreed to this condition, but, distracted by other business, forgot to pass the order to his companions who, traveling in another Land Rover, shot a wart hog and a steenbuck for meat.

Subsequent events at Tsodilo proved extraordinary. On its first morning bees attacked the expedition—not one swarm, but seemingly dozens. Later that day they discovered a massive rock painting of an eland bull framed by a mother giraffe and her calf. Three times they tried to film the scene for their BBC-commissioned documentary, and three times the magazine jammed, unprecedented in the experience of cameraman Duncan Abraham. While Abraham struggled with his equipment, the others found a veritable 'Louvre of the desert filled with treasure'. Advancing past this to the sacred summit, Samutchoso was going down on his knees to pray when a force hurled him backwards, denying his petition to pray.

The second and third days were a replay of the first: bees attacked at dawn, the camera died repeatedly and the tape recorder failed. Samutchoso went into a trance to consult the spirits, which confirmed that they were angered by the arrival of a party with blood on its hands. That night, van der Post, a bush-hardened settler and soldier, wrote a letter of apology 'To the Spirits, The Tsodilo Hills. ...' The next morning he and Samutchoso buried the letter, signed by everyone in the party, beneath the rock paintings of the eland and the two giraffes. No bees attacked that day. Samutchoso consulted the spirits to be told that the humans were forgiven. Thereafter the expedition turned from disaster to success.

> 'The spirits of the hills are not what they were. Ten years ago they would have killed you'

As van der Post describes it, events at Tsodilo read like trials from the *Odyssey* rather than an expedition of desert-hardened veterans filming for television in the late 1950s. Even so, Samutchoso told van der Post later: 'The spirits of the hills are not what they were. Ten years ago they would have killed you'—but they still exert and loan their powers to the few who can understand.

Bushmen did not restrict themselves to expressing the spirit world in painting. There was music, song, and a dance for everything. 'He danced birth', writes van der Post, 'he danced adolescence; he danced his marriage and many another event of life and spirit ...'

In the late 1970s, Harvard psychologist Richard Katz lived with Bushmen—the !Kung—to study the ritual of healing, specifically the healing dance. As with the Salish and the Sioux, healing in the broadest sense involves not just individuals, but the community as a whole; and it works at spiritual and psychological as well as at physical levels. Roughly every quarter of the moon, the !Kung hold a healing dance, the rhythm provided by clapping women sitting around the fire while the men, and some women, dance. Katz calculated that about half the men, and one woman in ten, claim some measure of healing powers. Excitement grows as the dance proceeds,

> Healing dance

sweat pours out and the spirit rises, creating in the dancers a healing energy known among the !Kung as *n/um*. Only when they are possessed of sufficient *n/um* can the healers transform into an altered state of consciousness, *!kia*, during which they heal all those who sit around the healing dance.

> 'Being at a dance makes our hearts happy'
> Told to Richard Katz

Healing energy, *n/um*, emanates from the pit of the stomach and the base of the spine, rising, rising, reaching to the skull—then bursts forth as the healing trance-state, *!kia*. An experienced healer, Kinachau, told Katz:

> 'You dance, dance, dance. Then *n/um* lifts you up in your belly and in your back, and then you start to shiver. [*N/um*] makes you tremble, it's hot. ... When you get into *!kia* you're looking around because you see everything, because you see what's troubling everybody ... [and] *n/um* enters every part of your body right to the tip of your feet and even your hair'.[75]

This *!kia* state inspires cures, permits the healing dancers to diagnose internal maladies by using their powers of 'seeing properly' or 'eye-insides' (cf. Australian Aborigines' 'strong eye'). *N/um*, and the resulting *!kia*, allows a healer to argue with the spirits that cause sickness by struggling to seize men's souls.

Healing, and trance states

But *n/um* is a mighty force; a healer must learn to control it or be overwhelmed by it. '*N/um* explodes', says one healer, 'and throws me up in the air and I enter heaven and then fall down'. Fierce discipline must harness *n/um*, before a novice healer can 'see properly'. An experienced healer, !Wi, drew Katz's attention to the behavior of a younger man, Dau, at the healing dance:

> '[Dau's] eyes are rolling all over the place. If your eyes are rolling you can't stare at sickness. You have to be *absolutely steady* to see sickness, steady eyes, no shivering and shaking, absolutely steady ... with a steady gaze ... you need direct looking. Your thoughts don't whirl, the fire doesn't float above you, when you are seeing properly'.[76]

This *!kia* is powerful spiritual territory. As in other shamanic cultures, spirit-death and rebirth precede the power derived in altered states. !Wi told Katz:

> 'In *!kia* your heart stops, you're dead, your thoughts are nothing, you breathe with difficulty. You see things, *n/um* things; you see

Heal till it hurts

spirits killing people, you smell burning, rotten flesh; then you heal, you pull sickness out. You heal, heal, heal ... Then you live'.[77]

There is also the laying on of hands. As healers impart the power of their *n/um* to others, so their hands draw sickness out. The same word describes the action of laying on hands and drawing out disease; they are not different acts, they are one and the same thing.

Men and women of the Bushman culture travel different spiritual paths to their initiation. The quest for males is long and arduous, beginning in their teens, culminating in proficiency, if they are lucky, from their twenties to their forties. It is easier for the ten percent of women who become healers, but, although it may take women only a matter of days to receive the energy of *n/um*, it never comes to fruition during their reproductive years. The power of *n/um* can damage a fetus or a nursing child.

> Shamans and endorphins

Katz presented his work with the !Kung at a 1980 conference entitled 'Shamans and Endorphins' in Montreal, speculating upon 'a role for endorphins', the natural painkillers created by the body, resulting from the healing dance.[78]

If there ever was an 'original' human condition, it may have resembled the society of the Bushman, the !Kung, for whom sharing is everything, and the sense of community is the highest order of moral life. Healing a person involves spreading healing through the whole community. 'Medicine' in the Bushman sense involves the social health of his community as a whole.

7

Bring All Things Into Being
Balga Ma Ni!—Bring All Things into Being!
The Walbiri Language, Central Australia

In the beginning the earth was without form, and void. That is the biblical tradition. In the beginning there was only a flat and featureless plain, and an absence of conscious mind. That is the Aboriginal tradition.

And God said: Let there be light …

At which point, in Australia, the Sky Heroes came forth from the upper and lower worlds to pronounce *tjukurpa*, the Time of the Dreaming, Creation, even the Big Bang. It was the moment from which chaos was dispelled and the cosmos took form.

The Sky Heroes, Lightning Man and the Rainbow Serpent among them, imposed land- and mind-scapes on the consciousness of living things, which themselves took on newly invented form and being.

The Guardian, 22 September 2016, couched the arrival in Australia of humans and Sky Heroes in modern terms:

> 'The first major DNA study of Aboriginal Australians has confirmed that they are the "direct descendants" of Australia's earliest settlers and are *the planet's most ancient living culture*, dating back about 50,000 years'.[79] (*Emphasis added*)

At the time of first European settlement, Australia was home to many distinct peoples. The Aboriginal race reached Australia fifty thousand years ago; and *tjukurpa*, which translates inadequately into Dreamtime or the Dreaming, is at the root of Aboriginal culture.

Let the Dreaming be the spiritual springboard on which we embark.

When the Sky Heroes had done the work of the Primordial Event, they disappeared, leaving the marks of their struggles and their passing on the land in the forms of Australia's topography. '*Tjukurpa* is existence itself, in the past, present and future. It is also the explanation of existence, and it is the law that governs behavior'. The speaker is Burnam Burnam, of the *Wurundjeri* people, explaining the essence of being to Jungian analyst

Bring all things into being!

Jan Clanton-Collins.[80] They met as keynote speakers at the Australian Transpersonal Conference, in Brisbane (1986). Two years later, Burnam Burnam enhanced his reputation as a powerful advocate for his people when he planted the Aboriginal flag outside the Houses of Parliament in London, claiming Britain for the Aborigines.

Burnam Burnam's reference to *tjukurpa* as 'existence itself, in the past, present and future' raises an echo from Evelyne Lot-Falk's analysis of Siberian shamanism: *the past infuses the present, and the future overtakes the present in a constant beginning-again (Chapter 2).* The only remarkable thing about this similarity is that Animist principles all over the world have been consistent through many millennia

In Australia, creation did not stop when the Sky People and the Spirit People (*Mimi* folk) disappeared. In Aboriginal culture, *tjukurpa* is existence itself in every form and through all time. It is the root of being. It embodies the first creation and a timeless, eternal coming-to-be 'alongside present events', as Burnam Burnam puts it. *Tjukurpa* expresses itself in three ways:

> *Tjukurpa* is existence itself, in every time and form. It is the root of being.

• First, as the land, the continent's rocks and hills, its water-worn gullies, dry creeks and vast arid plains. *Tjukurpa* is the jagged stone beneath our feet, the scent of eucalyptus;

• Second, *tjukurpa* is 'people and their actions in hunting, marrying, ceremony and daily life';

• Third, *tjukurpa* gives Aboriginal peoples a 'charter for living, drawn from the actions of the [*tjukurpa*] beings themselves'. For at least 50,000 years the ancient tales of deeds and misdeeds have taught Aborigines the rights and wrongs of 'being in the world and living with each other'.

Thus, *tjukurpa* explains not only the fact of existence but, since it acts through all time, it underlies inter-reactions among existing things. That which governs inter-reactions is in effect natural law, a prescription for living. *Tjukurpa* is much more than a creation myth. It codifies the lore that regulates behavior, making it the basis of a social code fifty times older than *Magna Carta*. In *tjukurpa*, lore is law.

In order to re-create events that took/take place in *tjukurpa*, an Aborigine embarks on a Dream Journey. (Nineteenth century graziers and stockmen coined the pejorative term 'walkabout'.) A Dream Journey is a pilgrimage whereby an Aborigine becomes a 'socially responsible' human being by

> Dream Journeys

learning the 'song lines' of his or her *tjukurpa*, song lines which link people and sites across Australia. To travel one's path is to learn. Dream Journeys were vital in a material sense, too. Hunter-gatherers migrated with the seasons in search of food and water. Dream Journeys taught the practical arts of survival.

Poet and novelist James Cowan describes the two-fold practical and spiritual reasons for Dream Journeys taken by Toby Gangele and his family, of the Mirrar Kunjai:mi people. Their territory, encompassing large tracts of tropical bush and swamp in Arnhem Land, Northern Territory, is subject to six seasons a year. As food sources move with the seasons, so do the humans.

> 'During this time, of course, Toby Gangele and his family would have travelled over a region of approximately 1000 square miles looking for sustenance in a time-honored way. The route that they had taken would vary little, if at all, from that covered by their ancestors for perhaps thousands of years ...
>
> The seasonal cycle is a practical reason for making a Dream Journey. Toby Gangele and his relatives are ... also well aware of another reason for making the journey; a reason integrally associated with their spiritual life. For the land they cross is a part of themselves. The Dream Journey on the ritual level is a way of renewing contact with themselves, since they and the land are inseparable. It is at this point that the Aborigine enters into a Dream world where the land is transformed into a metaphysical landscape saturated with significations'.[81]

A Dream Journey, then, may act on several levels: it has a practical purpose; it represents a physical event, a voyage of recreation, rediscovery or re-acquaintance; and it may induce an altered state of consciousness. That which the traveler desires most is a return to the source of the Dreaming: and that source is the wellspring of eternal cosmic power. Here is a realm through which one's little self is lost in the discovery of an infinitely greater mental being, revealing to one's mind the cosmos, unthought, just being. All life, all rocks, stars, seas and the sweep of the vast air well up from within oneself to furnish the worldscapes without. Here dwells *tjukurpa*, the Dreaming.

To that end, generation upon generation of Aboriginal novices has subjected itself to rigorous training (in some communities, but again, not in all). If they are successful, they will receive a measure of the Sky Heroes' cosmic power. The essences of spirits—Sky Heroes, Lightning Man, the

Bring all things into being!

Rainbow Serpent, *Mimi* people—these endow man and Nature with mortal life and the knowledge of being.

Aboriginal spirituality must be among the most 'democratic' or 'anarchic' in all humanity. It recognizes that all human spirits are in constant touch with the spiritual cosmos, though in the ordinary state of consciousness one may be unaware of such links to the divine. Aboriginal society needs no hierarchy of priests to bind flesh to spirit, earth to cosmos, red rocks to sky. All communion is possible through shamanic techniques of ecstasy, and anyone can be his or her own shaman, given sufficient desire.

But there are limits. To heal others, one needs the sanction of the spirits and one's own community. Trained healers, Aboriginal 'clever-men' who have won the privilege of entry to the spirit-worlds of Then and Now, can diagnose with the power of the 'Inner Eye', heal the sick, journey to retrieve lost souls. These are they whom pioneering Australian anthropologist A.P. Elkin termed 'Men of High Degree'.

CULTURAL FAITH

This book began by relating an incident that took place in 1935: white doctors' medicine had proved ineffective for many Aboriginal patients until their own clever men extracted offending objects and threw them away. Faith between healer and healed at such times—cultural faith—counts for much.

Nineteenth century anthropological studies unwittingly tell modern readers more about the mindset of Victorian authors than about the cultures they describe. Anglican clergyman J.G. Wood was as condescending towards Aborigines as to other 'uncivilized races'. But he *does* concede one point. Regarding clever men's curative powers: 'Sundry superstitious rites are employed ... and the remedy is efficacious ... in consequence of enlisting the imagination of the sufferer'.[82]

| 'Imagination of the sufferer' |

How does 'imagination of the sufferer' respond to 'superstitious rites', thereby effecting cure?

An Aboriginal man of high degree heals through the training and inspiration derived from two sources: his craft's spirit-heroes, familiars and guardian spirits; and the long line of ancestral healers going back to, and drawing their past and present powers from, ancient and modern creation—*tjukurpa*, the Dreaming. 'I see the world as it should be, as it was and is'.

That was the concept of Aboriginal spirit-life explored and described by Elkin from an anthropologist's point of view. Elkin reported the supernatural and the marvelous. His description of Aboriginal doctors as 'Men of High Degree' strikes many Western health care workers as overstated. 'Anything seems more marvelous when the explanation is not available. Some of the most reliable observers tend to dwell on supposedly supernatural powers, such as telepathy and divination', writes psychiatrist John Cawte.[83] Health care workers' experiences in Aboriginal communities are more down to earth: they have to cope when indigenous healing fails.

And indigenous healing has failed. Has it failed because the web of spiritual and social life supporting and supported by the oldest and most consistent human social system—the one instilled by *tjukurpa*—has collapsed beneath white settlers' assaults? Aborigines' faith in their traditional model is disintegrating, taking with it a belief in the efficacy of native healing and undermining the authority of clever men. A human rights report released in May 1997 attacked white Australia's approach to its indigenous peoples as 'genocidal policies'. The same week found the head of the Australian Medical Association describing the disparity between white and Aboriginal death rates as 'an absolute national disgrace. It is the worst health status of any group on this planet, as far as we can find'.

The Medical Journal of Australia describes psychiatrist John Cawte as having 'an extraordinary passion for the human condition that made him an innovator in the field of transcultural psychiatry'. Dr Cawte spent much of his own time working with remote Aboriginal communities, the result of a childhood in which he watched first-hand the losing struggle of Aborigines to cope with social change. Cawte has tried to identify and correct the most abrasive sources of culture shock that continue to wear down Aboriginal self-esteem. Though he has much respect for his indigenous colleagues, his down-to-earth approach is that of a clinician, far removed from Elkin's reportage on the spiritual aspects of the Aboriginal world.

Cawte states that any study of Aboriginal medicine must include the social context in which it is practised: the medicine of Aboriginal clever men is indissoluble from hopes, aspirations and social setting of its patients and practitioners. His book title, *Medicine Is the Law*, sums up his thesis well.

Clever-men treat, patients depend. For as long as humans have lived in Australia, aboriginal doctors in small, tightly knit communities have used their power to induce a degree of social conformity. The unity of medicine and the law is clear from the 'extent of common ground shared by the

Bring all things into being!

procedures for preserving health and the procedures for controlling social behaviors'. As Cawte puts it: 'conform, lest you become ill'.

No one now living can list the diseases afflicting Aboriginals before British settlers changed the rules, importing tuberculosis and other ills for which clever men have no cures: Neither did Western medicine until recently.

In other respects Aboriginal doctors have been millennia ahead of their Western counterparts. Presented with a paralyzed arm, a Western doctor looks for a physiological cause. Not so the native doctor, who examines his patient's injury with regard to what we might call its psychosomatic origins. Cawte, drawing on his experience with the Walbiri people, explains: a Walbiri man believes he has an invisible twin watching over him (a concept not unlike medieval Christianity's guardian angel or the Sioux' *nagi*). If he falls ill, it may be because his spirit-brother, his *millelba*, made him sick because he broke a law. The paralyzed arm, then, is a 'spiritual projection of what a medico-legal mind might call conscience or a religious mind might call the soul'. This concept, ancient in the Aboriginal world, entered Western medicine after Josef Breuer and Sigmund Freud published *Studies on Hysteria*, in 1895.

'Conform, lest you become ill'

If the traditional clever man of former times was more Freud than physician, to what did he attribute the diseases parading before him? His prescriptions invariably depended on the social context as well as on the malady itself. Was the patient suffering from a foreign object 'sung' into his body by an enemy's sorcery? Was the patient possessed by evil spirits or by devilish animals? Had tribal elders or the patient's *millelba* inflicted disease upon him by way of punishment or warning? In the last instance, the clever man might let justice take its course. Cawte reports a case of a man who, wanting to make a boomerang, cut down a tree growing in another's territory. His own *millelba* 'sang his shoulder sore'.

Who, in an Aboriginal context, becomes a native doctor? Mystics and rogues, certainly. But Western observers describe their 'common character' as altruistic mediators. The great majority of native doctors just want to help.

Helping demands special powers: shamanic journeys to other-worlds; the cloak of invisibility; x-ray vision for detecting malign spirits and foreign objects in the body. (An x-ray vision informs Aboriginal art.) Here are components of shamanism we met north of the Arctic Circle: telepathy, knowledge of distant happenings, surgery without incision, the repair or renewal of body parts. To Western health workers the whole package smacks of 'magic'. *The Oxford Dictionary* defines it: 'the pretended art of influencing the course of events by compelling the agency of spiritual beings, or by bringing into operation some occult controlling principle of nature; sorcery; witchcraft'.

But that is not how native doctors work. Having lived with them in many parts of Australia, Cawte comments, 'A doctor with a solid reputation does not need to exploit magic, and does not do so'. As for levitation, invisibility and other phenomena that Westerners lump together as magic, Cawte reports that his native colleagues make no pretence that soul-flight involves travel in the flesh. Theirs are *spiritual* journeys across space and time.

But sleight of hand is another matter. If it will effect a cure, clever men are not averse to a little trickery. The Walbiri doctor Barney Tjangala gave an 'impressive' demonstration by sucking bad blood from Cawte's arm. Though the skin was never punctured, Tjangala spat out several gobbets of bright blood. Then, at Cawte's request, 'Barney revealed the small flake of stone in his mouth that had been pressed by his tongue to cut his palate'. On another occasion Cawte watched a clever man roll a ball of mucus that he then 'removed' from his patient as if it were a hostile object. It was, Cawte writes, 'an impressive performance. A sophisticated Aborigine who watched it said: "Of course you don't believe it. But you know what: That man get better. You know why: Make 'im glad, eat 'im tucker straight away. From his heart he feel glad and get better" '.[84]

Neither native healer was a fraud. Freud, perhaps. In common with their colleagues in the Western world, a clever man knows that about half of all ills will heal without intervention. If a patient transfers trust and faith to a healer, and that moves the healing process along, so much the better. Suffice to say here that the very act of laying on hands provides a powerful springboard to self-healing and regeneration.

KOOMPARTOO / A FRESH START

Apart from his role as emissary for Australian shamanism, Burnam Burnam, author of A Traveller's Guide to Aboriginal Australia, is widely known for advocating koompartoo—a fresh start. (In 1988, two hundred years after a British fleet established the first colonial settlement in Australia, Burnum Burnam stood on a rock at the foot of the white cliffs of Dover, annexing England 'on behalf of the Aboriginal Crown' and promising to bring the British 'good manners, refinement and an opportunity to make a koompartoo—a fresh start'.)[85]

Bring all things into being!

Koompartoo forms Burnam Burnam's personal vision of hope that all races in his homeland will come together to realize a common respect for 'the earth our mother'. This tale begins in Australia but, as we shall see, the power of the Outback is extending its lure beyond that country's burning rocks and ochre soil. Aboriginal spirituality is slowly but surely elbowing a place for itself in the halls of government.

But first, we return to the past, the present and the future: we visit again the Dreaming.

During *tjukurpa*, humans, plants, animals, and Sky Heroes criss-crossed the land creating and destroying, fighting, sculpting the earth's every feature. *Tjukurpa* gave birth and gives birth to Uluru (Ayer's Rock), as well as to the infinite world of lesser forms. To express the concept clearly to a Western mind, it might be helpful to think of *tjukurpa* as a moving picture without end, each frame replenishing the instant of 'now' by replacing the frame that came before. *Tjukurpa*—ongoing creation—is an elastic thought; it never stops.

The Dreaming

The beings of *tjukurpa* were, and are, travelers, whose journeys, struggles and deeds the Aboriginal people celebrate in stories, dances and songs. The paths of *tjukurpa* criss-cross the earth and the Upper- and Lowerworlds as well. Burnam Burnam knows of at least twelve song traditions extolling the sacred *tjukurpa* sites around Uluru. But nothing about *tjukurpa* is static in time or place, and these traveling tales of Sky Heroes and the Rainbow Serpent reach out to link sacred sites with far-flung settlements across the continent.

This is where Aboriginal cultural tradition incorporates 'medicine' in its broadest sense of meaning, because to live on the land and follow the beasts of the hunt through the seasons is to follow the paths of *tjukurpa* in the literal sense. Thus an indelible link is forged among sacred sites, people, other beings and the ongoing, unfolding process of creation. To sing the songs, to dance the dances in the traditional Aboriginal world is to know where one is going. *Tjukurpa* is a map of life without a map, a confident bearing without a compass, a star to guide one safely forward when the night is overcast. To follow *tjukurpa* is medicine for living, adherence to natural law.

Humans see similar images through similar eyes, but not all humans perceive what they see in similar ways. To a European a pile of boulders is a pile of boulders. To an Aborigine it may represent sacred beings celebrating *tjukurpa*. Boulders as parallel lives, boulders as markers of future and past, boulders as gravestones, for even in death each one of us becomes a part of the trail of *tjukurpa*, a part of our being.

SPIRIT IN HEALTH

Aboriginal culture conceals from outsiders an extraordinary wealth of oral literature and tradition. Why *conceals*? Because, for Aborigines, *tjukurpa* works its will 'alongside present events', meaning that our real-time, material world tunes out *tjukurpa*'s frequency. In that respect it would seem to mirror the larger world's experience with 'dark energy'. Here are two functions in the cosmos that are active and present, but they both go undetected. As Cawte puts it, Aboriginal culture 'achieved an ecological relevance and a practical sustenance rarely attained' within the belief systems of primal peoples. As the industrial world struggles against environmental degradation, an understanding of *tjukurpa* has much to offer in giving us *koompartoo*—a fresh start.

TJUKURPA AS AN INSTRUMENT OF CHANGE

Tjukurpa guided Aboriginal peoples successfully for fifty thousand years. Then came British invaders, importing material values and cultural death. Aborigines may have numbered half a million when Captain Cook landed in 1770. Within generations that figure had dropped to fifty thousand. The Aboriginal law of the spirit, the indigenous lore of survival in vast open spaces, had nothing to teach about coping with grasping settlers and their statutes of ownership and property. Nothing in the concept of *tjukurpa* paved the way for change.

The Aborigines' disastrous clash with Western values was recent, and sudden. Worldwide, Animist cultures have tumbled before the march of materialism and jealous gods since ancient Hellenes explained their downfall in the myth of Prometheus' fall. Then, some twenty-six hundred years ago, Confucius, Lao Tsu, Homer and the Buddha put their indelible stamps on human culture. Two thousand years ago the ghosts of the Greek pantheon mixed with Roman law, Midrashic interpretation of Jewish prophecies and Egyptian Gnosticism. As Christianity, this jealous new religion would sweep away the cultural beliefs of one third of humankind. Then came Islam. So it goes.

The Dreaming is dreaming again.	But ancient cultural beliefs are like old shamans, tough, resilient under pressure and persecution, enduring till a better day. Old methods of ecstasy and strategies for survival in harsh times have never been

totally swept away. Not completely. The shock of the new defiles the old, scatters the old, takes strength from the old, absorbs the old—but never wholly destroys it.

So it is with *tjukurpa*. The Dreaming is starting to press its way forward again. And not just in Australia. Unrecognized, it is sapping bastions of

Bring all things into being!

modern material culture in other parts of the world. The Dreaming is dreaming again. *Tjukurpa* is stirring in unlikely places.

In the 1960s, Aborigines at Yirrkala in Australia's Northern Territory took legal action against a syndicate intent on mining their traditional lands. Central to the case was land ownership, as defined by Australia's Anglo-Saxon laws of property. The concept that land can be owned is not merely alien to traditional Aboriginal thinking; it is abhorrent, offensive. Burnam Burnam points out that his people's eternal relationship with the earth is reflected in the phrase 'the earth our mother'. As Mother, the earth is not a tradeable commodity.

Finding for the mining syndicate, the judge summed up:

> 'The evidence seems to me to show that the aboriginals have a more cogent feeling of obligation to the land than of ownership to it. It is dangerous to attempt to express a matter so subtle and difficult by a mere aphorism, but it seems easier, on the evidence, to say that the clan belongs to the land than that the land belongs to the clan'.[86]

True enough. Traditionally, the only objects an Aborigine claims to *own* in the English sense of the word are his or her dreams.

Mr. Justice Richard Blackburn's judicial statement on *tjukurpa*, sympathetic but unhelpful in the short term, took on life of its own. (Burnam Burnam called the decision 'ludicrous but highly spiritual'.) Animists could have told the learned judge that words, poems and songs are powerful tools for creating the reality they express. Blackburn's comment had the effect of breathing life into a struggle for the magical land of Australia. After that finding, the campaign for the re-enchantment of the continent found wings.[87]

The Aboriginal concept of 'the earth our mother' is a birth certificate, a baptismal certificate, a rite of passage, a contract for life, the deed and the keys to a home and a death certificate rolled into one. Burnam | The feminine essence, *tjukurpa*, stirs in the land

Burnam predicted that white Australians would one day wake spiritually to the fact that they, too, belong to the earth, and not the other way around. The old paternalist gods are dying; the feminine essence, *tjukurpa*, stirs again in the land. Burnam Burnam added: 'Aboriginal Australia was, and remains, a female energy-point in the universe. She is the mother from whom beings are born'.

She is also the mother from whom an apology was born. In 2008, Prime Minister Kevin Rudd rose in the Australian Parliament to apologize to the country's Aboriginal peoples:

'The time has now come for the nation to turn a new page in Australia's history by righting the wrongs of the past and so moving forward with confidence to the future. We apologise for the laws and policies of successive Parliaments and governments that have inflicted profound grief, suffering and loss on these our fellow Australians …

'For the future we take heart; resolving that this new page in the history of our great continent can now be written. We today take this first step by acknowledging the past and laying claim to a future that embraces all Australians'.

As Walbiri people say: '*Balga ma ni!*' Bring all things into being! Indeed, the ancient ways persist, returning with vigour. In December 2016, Jessica Wynne Lockhart ran this feature: 'Indigenous experiences pull visitors to Australia'. Its subhead ran, 'A trip reveals the people's connection to the land they use for food and medicine'.

In her story, Lockhart and others 'traipse single-file through the world's oldest living rainforest … until our guide, Tom Creek, suddenly stops.

'He calls, in the tongue of the Kuku Yalanji people, "*Yuda binga binga ngayu jenan oondool yali jilbanga.*" The dense tree canopy nearly swallows Tom Creek's voice, but he seems satisfied his message has been received.

' "I'm letting the spirit world know that we're here and why," he explains. … The Yalanji still actively practise these traditions today—and it's these authentic experiences visitors to Australia are increasingly seeking out.'[88]

Lockhart uses the words 'authentic' and 'seeking out'. Spirits and their human adherents have been authentic through untold generations. That continues, today.

8

Where the spirits never died
SOUTHEAST ASIA

INCENSE AS ANTIDOTE, DIAGNOSIS AS CURE: HONG KONG

The fan in the second-floor window doesn't help. It shoves hot, humid air through the tiny apartment, air laden with a mixture of odors as characteristic as a finger print: cooking oil and soy, fish, frying vegetables and the exhaust from motor scooters jostling along the narrow street below. Direct sunlight strikes into this part of the alley for perhaps three hours a day, but the upper hemispheres of the red Chinese lanterns across the street are sunburned to orange, their tops baked brown with dust.

Seen from the dim room, the man of the house sitting outside on his narrow balcony is a bright silhouette, framed by a window, just a head over shoulders supporting straps of an undershirt. The silhouette shifts from time to time to light a cigarette or turn the pages of a newspaper.

The object of our quest is the woman, shaded in the relative darkness of the room. Between a marked overbite and a hairline set back from a prominent forehead, her eyes are dark and restless. Nothing in her outward appearance suggests the seer, probing as deftly into the minds of ancestors as into the lives of the living. Her shrine is carefully placed. Smoke-blackened and decorated with red paper, its carved wood facade faces neither window nor door directly, lest spirit energy drain away.

She looks older than her mid-thirties, but Hong Kong is a pressure-cooker. She coughs a lot, but not from smoking. She may have poor health because she is a spirit-medium; or she may be a spirit-medium because she has poor health. In matters spiritual, effect and cause intertwine. Counting her age from conception, she says that when she was sixteen she ran a high fever for almost a week. Afterwards, what began as delirium became an active, life-long converse with the spirits.

> To be chosen by the spirits is no privilege

In that respect the induction of many spirit-mediums in South China is not unlike that of Siberian shamans. Crisis. Sickness. Transformation. In Hong Kong, to be chosen by the spirits is no privilege. Far from it. More like a life-long sentence of indentured servitude. And 'life-long' may be a poor choice of words because the women chosen for this task do not, on the whole, live long lives. The spirits seem to select those with a delicate constitution. Why? Who knows? It is not sufficient to note that *yin* represents the broken line in divination hexagrams. Here again, cause and effect are opposing mirrors, reflecting the craft of the wounded healer.

The spirit-medium was still living with her parents when her struggles with spirits began. A friend of her mother's, desperate with fear, came to confide that her young son had been taken violently ill after a school trip into the hills. It came on suddenly, she said. Just like that! As the spirit-medium tells it, she was listening to the woman when, seized with a vision, she slumped onto a chair and started chattering about gravestones. (Old family graves and shrines dot the hills overlooking Hong Kong. High places commanding a southern aspect are considered auspicious).

The mother ran home, questioned her son and discovered that he had indeed wandered away from his class and thrown pebbles at an old stone pillar. At that point the young spirit-medium's first healing began. Burning incense at the cardinal points around the boy to repel further assault by offended spirits, she prescribed an offering of rice and dried fish to appease the guardian of the shrine. The boy was soon up and about.

Incense played a major role in this woman's practice. In much of Asia, incense is to hostile spirit energies what antibiotics are to bacterial pathogens. It serves to repel. In addition, burning incense carries messages into the ether, into the spirit realms beyond.

The case of the boy and the gravestone shows an act of reprisal by an external spirit, but I am reminded of an incident reported from Australia, where a man cut a tree growing in another's territory, whereon his own spirit-guardian, his *millelba*, 'sang his shoulder sore' by way of warning.

One had the sense that spirit-work for the woman in this Hong Kong alley was an extension of housework, of living. She cooked, she washed, she met with patients, listened, probed the spirits and prescribed. She would have preferred that the spirits had looked elsewhere but, so be it, this was her lot.

The tale of the boy and the grave was straightforward, a spiritual case to the core. The spirits had revealed the diagnosis to the young healer right away. Before she had become involved, in fact. Most cases were harder to crack. Typical were wasting conditions which Chinese or Western medicine failed to address. Here the spirit-medium had to become part analyst and part detective, questioning her patient minutely, talking to the family, retracing their actions again and again to establish, first, if and how the spirits had been slighted; second, what corrective to apply.

One difficult case involved a businessman, a wholesaler who sold watches and small electronic appliances to retailers. He had been employed by another man in the same business before leaving to set up his own company. Within months his health began to slide. Something resembling chronic fatigue syndrome set in. The spirit-medium questioned her evasive patient closely, finally establishing that he had left his former employer with the other man's client-list. The former boss had called upon the spirits for redress.

Responding, the spirit-medium asked her patient to write a fulsome letter of apology to his previous employer and to give her a hand-written copy of the stolen client-list—no small task considering the number of names. Adding incense, she burned both documents on her altar, relaying her client's promise to cease and desist. The human principles never spoke to each other and the addressee never read the letter of apology. The whole transaction took place in the spirit realm. The wholesaler's business went bad for a while, but his health was restored.

You always find the source of trouble close to home, the spirit-medium explains. One way or another. That's where you look for the cause.

Will she always do the spirits' work?

She would like to retire some day, to enjoy life in the here and now. Spirit-work leaves her exhausted. But she can't just stop. She sighs. When she does, the spirits make her sick.

A TRADITION OF HEALING DANCE: KOREA

There is nothing reticent about Hi-ah Park. Ask a search engine to find her and back come references in English and German, on-line stories and billboards for her appearances as a Korean ecstatic ritual dancer and shaman. She has been the subject of feature articles and interviews, too.

Hi-ah Park is a widely known ambassador for a tradition in Korean shamanism whose roots stretch back to the Neolithic, five thousand years ago. Enshrined as the state 'religion' two thousand years ago, shamanism was as much a part of Korean life as breathing. But cultural imports from all-powerful China gradually buried shamanic traditions under the teachings of Confucius, Buddha and the Tao. More recently, Christianity swept through Korea. But shamanism survives as the spiritual discipline of the countryside.

As in Hong Kong, so in Korea. Interviewed, Park replied, 'I didn't choose to be a *mudang*. The spirits chose me'. *Mudang* has come to refer to female shamans simply because the great majority of Korean shamans are women. It was not always so. Male shamans—*paksu*—used to share the calling. But, as Korea became a male-dominated Confucian society, a female backlash held onto shamanism as a powerful folk-religion. It became, in effect, a spiritual discipline for the gender of the under-caste. Few men are registered *paksu* in what is now South Korea, compared to seventy thousand *mudang*, women.

That figure may link to a view expressed in Korea that feminine intuition gives women more finely tuned and open channels to the spirits, to the gods. Before the ancient Chinese word *yin* was applied to the feminine essence, it meant 'sunless' or 'dark': a mountain's north slope was *yin*, the sunny south side, *yang*. *Yin* ruled winter, waned in summer, and so on. In time, as women excelled in navigating the dark, pathless worlds of the spirits, the term came to embody their feminine spiritual skills. (This theme opens *Chapter 11*.)

Apart from that, generations of Korean women have enjoyed a second, unsought and dubious 'advantage'. Men, not women, had the benefit of formal education through much of Korea's history. This had the effect of severing men from their innate spirituality, preserving the connection in women. Park told Nina Otis Haft: 'I had to unlearn twenty years of education before I was ready for initiation [as a shaman]'.[89] Learning blunts wisdom. It can be a poor substitute for the intuitive self.

'Learning blunts wisdom'

We met this before: the initial sickness, loneliness, night sweats and nightmares, a desire to abandon the affairs of life and flee. Park suffered more than her fair share of initiatory illness, *sinbyong*. She had moved to the United States before *sinbyong* set in. The spirits kept calling, but for years she failed to recognize the illness as a call, let alone heed it. As she recalls her bouts of illness and anxiety, one recalls the sufferings of the great British shaman, Merlin. It was not until Park returned to Korea after fifteen years abroad that she was finally initiated as a shaman.

It was during the initiation ceremony that her godmother hid her bells and fan and asked her to find them. When Park stopped to let her conscious mind concentrate on the task, her godmother teased her: 'Too many years at university!' meaning that Park's intellect had smothered the all-knowing intuitive self. Park then dropped into ecstatic trance and, as a seer, found her bells and fan.

'Ecstatic trance' here suggests both loss *and* abandon (in the sense of freedom from constraint or convention), because a shaman who drops into ecstasy does so to seek spiritual solutions, freed from the weight of the world's here-and-now, relieved of the fetters of sequence, the prison of place. These are necessary losses, excess baggage on shamanic journeys. | Ecstatic trance, Ecstatic dance

Beyond the ordinary, the realm of the seer reveals causes of illness and torment, spirit helpers, power animals and pieces of soul. But reaching the wisdom beyond may cost a novice years of discomfort and trauma.

Ecstasy, Park says, is like 'seeing and hearing with the heart' unaffected by constraints of sensory inputs from ears and eyes. In the Korean *mudang* tradition, ritual dance and ceremony is the vehicle to ecstasy.

Park spoke of the 'clown quality' she manifests during her ritual dances. Was that something like the Trickster of Europe, Africa and the Americas? She replied, 'There is definitely the trickster quality, but it's more than that. The clown transcends all dualities. If he's sad or if he has joy, you cannot pinpoint that; the clown is funny, but at the same time serious'. The | The Trickster returns

clown has a profound value in shamanic work. Since the clown enables a shaman to transcend the dualities, he—the clown is *yang* by convention—represents what Park calls 'the highest quality of shamanic work'. That is because a shaman must travel through risky spiritual dimensions in search of healing. As the shaman does so, the clown character absorbs opposing forces, neutralizing them, protecting a shaman who ventures into perilous states.

In the spring of 1991, the Women's Alliance invited Park to perform a ritual ceremony in the San Francisco Bay Area. Before the ceremony, a woman | Possession by the warrior spirit

in the audience told Park that she hoped to cure her breast cancer. During the ceremony, Park, 'possessed by the warrior spirit', pulled the woman out of the audience and danced on her chest. 'Evidently, when a shaman enters an ecstatic state, you generate a radiation kind of heat. It's not coming from the shaman. The shaman's ability is to be the medium transmitting that energy through the feet. I was dancing on her chest for half an hour'.

'A full half hour?'

'Yes, I danced. Almost three hundred women [in the audience] were terrified, but nobody moved. They were all supportive. They all beheld that moment, you know. It was a very powerful evening'.

And then?

'The woman completely surrendered to the spirit'.

A week later the woman reported that three doctors subsequently found her free of cancer. Park offers no explanation, 'no proof', as she puts it. Why should she? Medical literature abounds in cases of spontaneous remission that offer no rational explanation.

In retrospect the incident reminds Park of the Hindu god Shiva, who is often displayed dancing with fire beneath his feet. Shiva the Destroyer? 'Yes, in that sense I was the destroyer, purifying [the woman's] negative emotions. She was completely surrendered to it'.

Western minds tend to define 'the Destroyer' as negative. But in Asia the Destroyer destroys that which is negative. Park cites another figure, more familiar to North Americans: the Rainbow Warrior. 'When I was personifying or embodying the rainbow warrior I was the destroyer of that negative emotion. The reason modern medicine's powerful drugs have side effects is that they might work on a patient's body but they cannot cure the emotion. When disease stems from a psychosomatic background you need somebody who can change the frequency of that emotion. Ritual healing is possible because the shaman's job is to change the frequency of that emotion. When emotions are negative, frequency is a door [to disease]. That's why people get sick. Purification is the main issue in ritual ceremony because it can change the frequency'.

> Negative emotion

'Restoring the appropriate frequency returns a body to harmony?'

'Right'.

This reminds one of the important part played by frequencies and waveforms in the Mayan healing tradition (*Chapter 4*) and in the Himalayas (*the next section*). Hi-ah Park's thoughts draw us back to the start of the book. There, we found Aboriginal Australians and Algonquians—amongst others—recognizing a spiritual component in maladies that Europeans consider to be purely physical: appendicitis, for example. For many primal peoples, surgical intervention in the modern conventional sense is not enough.

Where the spirits never died

Park sums up: 'Psychic surgery' was effective only because the patient herself was ready and willing to transform herself. Park is suspicious of those who claim to heal others. She says that a shaman's task is to transform a patient's attitude. If it can be made to feel trust, free of fear, then the organism that is us can heal itself. The cancer-sufferer in Park's audience had given herself wholly to the 'primal spirit', being ready to confront her own 'dark side'. 'I don't mean cutting into the person', Park told Nina Otis Haft, explaining the term 'psychic surgery'. 'My surgery involves cutting through the fear, stitching up the psychic tears in the fabric of mind, body, and spirit'.

| Transforming attitude |

We have found that Aboriginal doctors are experts on the psychosomatic origins of disease: that Jívaro shamans use spirit helpers or magical darts (*tsentsak*) to locate, diagnose and extract the harmful spirits of disease; that an Inuit or Yakut shaman's healing power derives from spirits via the booming, driving rhythm of his drum; that Celtic and Anglo-Saxon shamans drew forth healing spirits from the web of wyrd. Weird indeed, and very wonderful.

After speaking to Hi-ah Park, we can add ecstatic dance to our list. The spirits diagnose, the spirits prescribe, and the spirits heal. Remission takes many forms in many places.

WISDOM LIKE A MOUNTAIN: THE HIMALAYAS

Wisdom descends from lofty summits where spiritual beings dwell. At the same time, the human spirit strives to ascend the peaks toward spiritual perfection. That thought from the Venerable Nandisvara Nayake Thero[90] says much about the approaches to spiritual life as it is lived in the valleys and passes of the Himalayas.

Some years ago I worked on a film shot in Nepal, a film for which I wrote the narrative script. *Solitary Journey* recorded interviews with Dawa Tenzing, the second Sherpa on that fabled first ascent of Chomo Lungma (Goddess Mother of the World), 'the mountain that the foreigners call Everest'.

Born in 1903, Dawa Tenzing was nearly eighty-five when he entrusted his thoughts to a camera. As a boy he had worked on tea plantations near Darjeeling before enlisting as one of the first Sherpas to climb with European mountaineers. Speaking thirty-five years after he played a major role in the first, celebrated ascent in 1953, he was still puzzled. In translation he said: 'The foreigners came to climb, to conquer, as they put it, Everest. But we Sherpas do not come. We *are* these mountains. How do we gain by conquering these mountains when we know that they are us? Chomo Lungma is not a trial for conquest. She is at the centre of our hearts'.

In ancient times the lands of the high Himalayas might have served as a better archetype for shamanism than Siberia. But inroads by Buddhism, Taoism and a leavening of Buddhist Tantrism created in the Himalayan highlands a spiritual world of intricate and overlapping layers. Even native scholars have difficulty separating the shamanic spiritual methods of the old 'nameless religion' and *Bon* from later influences. The Buddhism of Tibet, *Mahayana*, translates to 'Great Vehicle', but many of the wheels on that vehicle to spiritual release were old before Siddhartha, the Gautama Buddha, began his ministry a little over 2,500 years ago. The ancient pre-Buddhist 'nameless religion' was, and remains, a product of its land. In this vast space the raw forces of Nature cannot but dwarf the most brazen human ego. One stands on a ridge in air so thin that it hardly supports bird flight, staring up at mountains that rise from an unmeasured drop at one's feet. Here is stillness as profound as meditation, a silence that can press oppressively upon the ear. Updraughts carry fragrant reminders from verdant, wooded valleys far below. And voices. Voices of specks toiling miles away carry to the ear; but echoes die, damped and muted in thin air.

The ancient 'nameless religion'

Dawa Tenzing again: 'Among these mountains the effort is great and the reward meager. Here, each small joy that breaks the hardship will be cherished like a jewel. We have to overcome the terrors of the outer world by finding a tranquility within'. Dawa spoke while medals awarded during the reigns of three British monarchs gleamed on his chest, medals awarded for Dawa's services to climbing parties. To the end of his days the old man regularly walked more than twenty rugged kilometers into Kathmandu, and back. He died in 1988, weeks after filming his interviews.

The miracle is that we thrive ...

If one fails to find God or the gods among these peaks, at least one discovers what it is to be a microbe among the jagged teeth of an immense and temperamental beast: for now the beast stirs. Darkness falls, or wind comes up and sudden storms attack the unwary with gobbets of air seemingly solid as millstones. Even in repose these mountains resonate power, but at times of tempest all the forces in the cosmos seem to hurl themselves against these peaks. Once aroused, the winds shriek as conflicting currents chatter off icy walls like ghosts, until the weight of sound grabs at one's very being.

Where the spirits never died

While tranquility lasts here, treasure it; for storm, earthquake and avalanche can carry off whole slopes with the villages upon them. A gentle stream of melt-water trickling across a mountain track can, without warning, become a rushing torrent discharging rain and rocks from higher slopes.

Not surprising then that, since the beginning of human time, this vastness of rock, thin soil and surging air should dominate the lives of its inhabitants. Nature in the raw was everything, although Her forces *per se* were considered neither good nor evil. They were powers beyond human control, potentials that appropriate responses might adjust by tweaking Nature herself, just a little. Appropriate gifts, deeds or devotions might shorten the long odds stacked against mortality.

Shrines or cairns mark dangerous ways through high passes or across exposed cliffs. Each traveler adds a rock to the pile—light-colored stones are more auspicious. Worldwide, shamans concern themselves with safe passages into, through, and out of spirit worlds. By contrast, early shamanism in the Himalayas had much to do with procuring safe passage for mortal lives through the here and now.

Without doubt the ancient spirituality of the Himalayan highlands sprang from shamans' struggles to improve the odds of villagers and villages against a hostile world. In time, shamans gained competence in handling external threats. Thubten Jigme Norbu explains in *Tibet* [91] that adept shamans moved on after that to harness the spirit-powers they had previously fought, drawing them into their service. | Converting hostile spirits

Centuries passed. Around the year 750 in the Roman calendar, a miracle was seen to unfold on the surface of the River Indus. A swollen lotus bud opened to reveal a boy sitting among its petals. Lopon Rinpoche[92] grew up to become the great teacher who brought Buddhism to Tibet. From a shamanic point of view it is more important to note that he is credited with taming the hostile spirits among Tibet's legions of demons and ghosts. He harnessed their formerly hostile powers in support of human life, rather than in opposition. | Taming the spirits

Lopon Rinpoche's Tibetan ministry began in spectacular fashion. All attempts to build a temple at Samye had failed. Demons shook the ground as soon as stones were laid, so that the newly built walls kept falling down. But the Master exorcised the ghosts and the temple rose to lasting glory.

For almost half a century Lopon Rinpoche traveled Tibet, exorcising demons by turning their powers to serve the people. In effect, he applied Buddhist teaching to shamanic beliefs. At root, Buddhism encourages moderation in all things, knowing that the pendulum of human emotions must inevitably swing in an opposite direction. Mood swings threaten balance. Slow the pendulum, and one is closer to attaining proportion and balance in all aspects of life.

Faced with a populace for whom demonic evil was as real as rock, Lopon Rinpoche made no attempt to deny its force. Rather, he preached that what we conceive as evil is the counterweight to what we hold to be good. Confront the one in tranquility to attain the other. Evil can be mirrored, its fangs drawn, its power converted for the good of all.

Confronting evil to attain good

In this context, Thubten Jigme Norbu points out that the ferocious demons depicted on Tibetan prayer flags do not represent evil or hostility; rather, they depict spirits whose powers have been turned to serve mankind. The hostile masks represent powerful allies.

Which begs the question: do spirits and demons exist? Are they real? Buddhist literature on the subject fills libraries. In Western culture, Homeric literature is replete with instances of gods taking earthly form to meddle in human affairs. Queen Elizabeth I's courtiers, notably John Dee, debated the subject fueled by Animist aspects in plays by Shakespeare and others. Waking in a sweat from a nightmare involves wiping real sweat and dispelling real fear. If a mind creates a demon—or an insuperable obstacle—then the demon or obstacle is real in the life-map of that mind. This passage from the play *Dark Sovereign* addresses the age-old question in Renaissance English:

> 'The mind doth make the fact, for good or ill.
> If I fear of murder in a dream,
> though the murderers be phantom,
> yet the dream is made on them is real.'

The dream exists, and the person 'possessed' will modify his or her behavior accordingly.

In much the same way, each of us places different values on inputs from what appears to be a similar external world. A pilot parachuting into a rain forest might starve or be poisoned, whereas a Jívaro tribesman would be at home in a supportive web of medicine, shelter and food. That extreme example illustrates a point: any given external world reflects the product of each participant's senses, life experience, training and personal neuroses. The same environment empowers or defeats different people differently. We all look into the profound heart of the same jewel—through different facets.

Where the spirits never died

That is not to deny the mundane existence of rock, air, water, heat and cold. It means that where we find Animists chanting or drumming their world into being each day, it truly is *their* world they seek to create, a world governed by *their* spirit allies. It is not the world that the collective 'us' experiences.

So far, most Buddhists would agree. But now we reach a point of departure for many followers of the Gautama Buddha's 'Middle Way'. Given sufficient spiritual power, is it possible to import mental images into the physical world and endow them with material forms? Conversely, can material objects be made to evaporate into realms of pure spirit?

Lopon Rinpoche's long ministry in Tibet was spent among people who fearfully believed that demons took material form at will. Acting on the principle 'fight spirit with spirit and form with form' the Master became adept at creating images with which to fight images. On one plane this is not as esoteric as it sounds: we will meet the phenomenon of using imaginary helpers later, in the context of modern conventional medicine (*Chapter 10*).

| Tantricism

Lopon Rinpoche was adept at a spiritual discipline widely practised in northern India during his life, a discipline older than Buddhism by many centuries. 'Tantricism is a belief in the powers of nature that can produce life and death in all beings and things', Thubten Jigme Norbu tells us in *Tibet*.[93]

But before discussing the tantric projection of mental imagery into the physical world we have to examine its opposite, its non-image. In general terms, Buddhists hope to escape from the cycle of mortal suffering by attaining salvation in the 'Absolute' (sometimes called the Emptiness), an entity/non-entity that can be revealed only through meditation. A mind attaining the Absolute through meditation has learned to filter out the chaff of object- and pattern-cluttered conscious thought, banishing the brain-busy ego to focus far beyond, finding enlightenment in the Emptiness.

'Until you give up the notion that something is going to happen, nothing is going to happen'.
Sakyong Mipham Rinpoche on meditation.[94]

Something odd is working here. A concept—even one as profound as the Absolute—is defined by comparison with its complement. Heat has no meaning without the comparative concept of cold; stars seen in the blackness of space represent both light set against darkness and matter poised in the void. Thus the Absolute (the Emptiness) can have no meaning without its complement, the world of phenomena, concepts, things—a world that takes its own definition from comparison with the Emptiness.

Since one complement requires the other if it is to be valid, it follows that meditation itself recreates the co-dependence between the Emptiness of the Absolute and the world of phenomena, things. An eminent scholar of Tibet, R.A. Stein,[95] writes that meditation 'allows a kind of experimental demonstration, a living experience, not only of supreme Reality, Emptiness,—the Absolute—but also of the nature of phenomenal existence which is only the latter's mental creation'. This 'happens to have a side-effect ... a sort of by-product, viz. supernatural powers'. In short, an adept can introduce images into the physical world. 'They are not essential', Stein adds, 'but the saint may make use of them to convert people with miracles ... and in general to "benefit beings" '. Thubten Jigme Norbu tells us, 'Tantricists consciously use imagery, mental and physical. ... In his trance-like state, these symbols become realities to the practitioner. He may be content to leave it at that, but if there is need, he can transfer the images from the mental world to the physical world'. In this way, Lopon Rinpoche is credited with bringing water from a rock (*à la* Moses) for thirsty horses, and stopping the sun.

It is often through the medium of sound that Lopon Rinpoche's successors effect their mental/material transformations. Tantric shamans effect healings through the transformative sonic energy of awareness-spells (*ngak*), better known as mantras. British-born Ngakpa Chogyam Rinpoche told *Shaman's Drum* magazine[96] that male and female practitioners of *ngak* became known as *ngakpa* and *ngakma*, 'visionary Tantric practitioners, or Tantric shamans'. 'Through their magical use of mantra and vision, sound and light, they have the power to influence external conditions for the benefit of others'.

Tantricism borrows heavily from yoga, which itself demands intense self-discipline. But 'tantricism goes far beyond yoga'. Thubten Jigme Norbu describes it as the 'most severe self-discipline ever demanded of man in spiritual endeavor'. One power borrowed from yogic technique is that of altering wavelengths. As the human ear is sensitive only to certain wavelengths of sound, so 'matter is only visible or tangible within a certain range of wavelengths'. The power to materialize or de-materialize spirits or objects may be an adept-induced perceptual shift.

Ngakpa Chogyam explains that an awareness-spell (mantra) is 'a method of resonating with the raw energy of *Being* through sound'. In the Tantric tradition, this resonance is transmitted directly, from teacher to pupil. 'In order to transmit an awareness-spell, you [the master] really must have experienced the power of that mantra'. Ngakpa Chogyam means by that that one must have activated its power 'through giving voice to it yourself'. The only awareness-spells that he himself transmits to his pupils are those he has sung one hundred thousand times for each syllable in the relevant mantra. The power of an awareness-spell becomes 'tangible' only through intense and lengthy practice.

As an aid to healing, Ngakpa Chogyam explains that a likely first step would find him entering into vision via an awareness-spell, then merging with and 'being "born" out of space in the form of an Awareness Being'. In that state, 'I'd emanate a radiance that would dissolve obstacles, and then I'd transform the disturbance through a series of visionary processes until it relaxed into its natural condition'. (We recall two comments by Hi-ah Park: 'radiation kind of heat' and 'change the frequency'.)

'Radiation' and 'frequency' are terms describing energy transfer generally associated with physics. But, as Ngakpa Chogyam puts it: 'To a Tantric practitioner, everything is energy and—because energy arises spontaneously from primal spaciousness and is unrestricted—everything can be transformed or transmuted'. As tantrism, so physics.

Spirits at work in modern healing

9

The healing shaman
SHAMANS, DOCTORS AND DISEASE

WHAT'S IN A NAME?

In 1950, a nineteen-year-old Ojibway named Norval Morrisseau drank a poisoned herbal potion. Although he was admitted to hospital and treated with all the resources of modern medicine, Morrisseau wasted away in ten days to skin and bones. Then a medicine-woman attempted to suck the hostile 'objects' or 'medicine' from his body. But when even Indian medicine failed Morrisseau, who is himself a shaman, the sucking-doctor resorted to the Ojibway equivalent of administering extreme unction: she changed his name. She gave him a name of such power that he not only recovered but felt empowered for life. For more than fifty years, Morrisseau, an internationally acclaimed painter and founder of the Woodland Indian School of Artists, signed his work with the name of a sacred metal combined with the most powerful spirit in the Ojibway pantheon—Copper Thunderbird. (Six large panels by Morrisseau at the Art Gallery of Ontario illustrate 'Man Changing into Thunderbird', 1977.)

For much of Morrisseau's far from easy life, he was among the finest aboriginal artists in North America. As a shaman he traveled, spiritually: 'I go to the inner places. I go to the source. I even dare to say, I go to the house of invention where all the inventors of mankind have been'.[97] We heard these notes before, notably from the Caribou Inuit shaman, Igjugarjuk, and the Mexican shaman, Matsúwa.

SHAMANS AS PSYCHOTHERAPISTS

A paradox underlies much of modern medicine. Even as Western science makes remarkable strides in treating physical disease, more and more people are reaching to retrieve ancient healing wisdoms from a shamanic past. And many *physical* maladies are found to have *psychological* origins. The wellbeing of a body may be rooted in the wellbeing of its mind.

This book began with the seventeenth century account given by a Jesuit missionary, Father Paul LeJeune, who reported that shamans believed much disease to be a product of 'the mind of the patient himself, which desires something …' Two and a half centuries would pass before Sigmund Freud exposed the same subconscious desires in Europeans.

Psychiatrist E. Fuller Torrey pricked professional bubbles in the 1970s and '80s with his thesis that shamans with drums and shamans with medical degrees, while differing in approach, get similar results from their treatments of psychological disease. Even his title, *Witchdoctors and Psychiatrists*, was provocative.[98] To achieve success, clients' expectations and healers' approaches must be rooted in their cultural background and hopes, not in 'magic' *versus* 'science'. It makes no sense to tell a Third World peasant that his phobia springs from fear of failure; nor would a Western psychotherapist blame a patient's anxiety attacks on possession by evil spirits.

A cultural gulf divides ways in which primal and Western people perceive the nature of healing, healers and disease. But the starting point in all cultures is similar. Both the shaman and the doctor start by diagnosing their client's psychological distress—giving it a culturally valid name. That way they think they know what they are dealing with. So, to his relief, does the client. As the saying goes: 'Better the devil you know than the devil you don't'.

> 'The shaman provides the sick woman with a language by means of which unexpressed, and otherwise inexpressible, psychic states can be immediately expressed. And it is the transition to this verbal expression … which induces the release of the psychological process; that is, the reorganization in a favorable direction of the process to which the sick woman is subjected' [99]

Anthropologist Claude Lévi-Strauss explains that giving a name to what is intangible makes disease tangible, makes it susceptible to treatment in the cultural framework that nurtured it. Much healing lies in shared communication. Diagnosis—giving disease a name—is central to successful psychotherapy in any culture. Lévi-Strauss's phrase 'reorganization in a favorable direction' suggests beneficial repatterning of a patient's mind similar to what some novice shamans undergo.

> 'The way that can be spoken of
> is not the constant way;
> The name that can be named
> is not the constant name'.

The healing shaman

These opening lines of the *Tao Te Ching*—Taoism was profoundly influenced by the 'old religion', shamanism—suggest that there are many ways of reaching the same end. A Western physician seeks to name his patient's disease in a mass of objective clinical facts, drawing his diagnosis out of his culture-based learning about organs, functions and a web of complex biochemical relationships. A shaman seeks his diagnosis of a disease in the possible loss of power animals or a guardian spirit, the loss of a soul, taboo violation, the intrusion of a hostile object or spirit. To heal his client he delves into a web of spirituous relationships.

Another difference is that the shaman fetches diagnosis and healing from a spirit world at psychic cost to himself. He and his spirit helpers journey to dark worlds, wrestle with hostile forces, extract healing wisdom, seek power animals, bring the healing back and fix it in his client's body or his head.

DISEASE IS WHAT YOU THINK IT IS

Luisah Teish, a priestess of Oshun in the Yoruba Lucumi tradition, poses the following cross-cultural situation.[100] A West African woman goes to the river to fetch water. As she kneels on the bank a falling branch kills her. A European coroner finds a verdict of accidental death from a specific physical cause. Her fellow villagers take it further, asking, 'Why was she fetching water at that time, under that tree? Why did the tree shed its branch just then?' Before the woman can be laid to rest an oracle must discover whether it was her time to die, or whether an external force moved against her. If so, why? What had she done to offend the tree or the spirit whose agent it became?

Anthropologist Carlos Castaneda once attempted to fit his understanding of Yaqui mental illness into Western categories. He failed. He started again along Yaqui lines, reaching what he called 'an intricate, logical, and internally consistent set of theories'.[101] The phrase 'internally consistent' means that, for diagnosis and healing of any disease to succeed, its *naming* has to fall within the culture of the healer and the client. Lévi-Strauss noted similar finesse in many tribal belief systems; B.L. Fontana called a disease theory of the Piman people of Arizona 'as subtle and as sophisticated as any other such theory'.

Where personal privacy is rare, collective therapy can work wonders against psychosomatic diseases. The Bushman (!Kung or San) people make a practice of holding a healing dance about once a week (*Chapter 6*). In the following passage, *n/um* is an energy said to reside in the pit of the stomach. It intensifies as the dance progresses, eventually 'boiling' until it results in *!kia*, an 'enhanced consciousness'.

> 'In *!kia* you see the *n/um* rising in other healers. You see the singing and the *n/um*, and you pick it up. ... As a healer in *!kia*, you see everybody. You see that the insides of well people are fine. You see the insides of the one the spirits are trying to kill and you go there. Then you see the spirits and drive them away'.[102]

!Kia heightens emotions: it is during this enhanced consciousness that !Kung healers perform their cures. Everybody gets some healing at the healing dance. As the experienced healer, Kinachau, told Richard Katz, it 'boils' from the healers to the healed.[103]

Among the Inuit, too, a sharing culture helps foster shared healing—catharsis, by another name. Earlier in this book we met the powerful Netsilik shaman Arnapak restoring her people's morale through collective catharsis.

Shamans long ago discovered that if a client, or a community, is burdened by too much of a particular emotion, such as fear, the excess can be confronted and thrown off in the *shamanic* state of consciousness. The new equilibrium transfers itself to the *ordinary* state of consciousness, bringing therapeutic relief to the client or the community as a whole.

Whether they be !Kung, Inuit, or Plains Indians at a Medicine Wheel, skillful shamans can evoke from people in close communities a powerful sense of openness, group feeling and relief. And what works on the individual also works on the clan. In Western parlance this is called Group Therapy.

The story of the Onondaga shaman/warrior/chief Ta-da-da-ho is often told in words and sculpture to show how psychotherapy can work in primal cultures. Ta-da-da-ho was a rebel, a powerful figure whose support had to be won over if the tribes were to come together in a peaceful Confederacy. Once again the power of words was brought to bear as Hiawatha, in speech and song, managed to convince the rebellious chief of the benefits of the Confederacy. Ta-da-da-ho's aggression and rebellious behavior is represented in story and carving as a nest of writhing snakes that slowly transform to the sweet, well ordered benefits of a peaceful, fertile earth.

WESTERN HEALING NEEDS HEALING

A ruptured appendix requires the skill of a surgeon; a broken leg demands to be set; and nobody, least of all an accomplished shaman, would deny the heroic role that Western medicine has played in the past century and a half. However, we must still resolve two basic questions: Which diseases demand physical medicine? What sorts of diseases lurk deep in the mind? The answer looks cut and dried, but really it is not.

People in the West have been subjected to a forty-year campaign alerting them to risks likely to cause coronary atherosclerosis, resulting in a fatal or debilitating heart attack. Smoking, high blood cholesterol and high blood pressure are the major risk factors. Certain foods should be avoided (taboo), others preferred. The chain of biochemical events leading from life-style to coronary atherosclerosis has been scientifically proven. No disease could be more purely *physical* with respect to its demonstrated causes and their effect. And yet a majority of people who suffer a first heart attack in North America do not fit any major risk group. A 1972 study showed that the best predictor of coronary artery disease was job satisfaction, with 'overall happiness' running close behind. In short, the precursors to that most physical outcome, a first heart attack, were the person's self-perceived standing with respect to his family or community, his level of satisfaction, and his sense of self-worth. The life of the body was determined by the quality of life in the mind.

Dr Larry Dossey, former medical chief of staff at a Dallas hospital, marshaled those facts in an attempt to draw doctors' attention to the values that shamanic qualities could offer modern medicine. Dossey's argument was that it is difficult to be an effective healer without putting part of oneself in one's work: a doctor who remains aloof cannot easily improve a patient's mental attitude. Yet Western medicine cultivates a deliberate remoteness that views illness as a thing distinct from the mind-frame of the body/spirit burdened by it—and utterly removed from that of the professional attempting to heal it. Even the Association of American Medical Colleges has expressed doubts about whether it is training physicians to be adequate healers.[104] As Dossey puts it: 'The modern [physician] lives in a dispassionate, mechanical world, the shaman in an enchanted one'.[105]

No shaman worthy of the name would attempt to address his client's disease without involving his own inner self in the process. He must. That is what soul-flight is about. That is the end to which the quest for power is directed. An eagle spirit warned Leonard Crow Dog: 'I give you a power, not to use for yourself, but for your people. It does not belong to you. It belongs to the common folks'.[106]

Study after study makes the point that successful psychotherapy in Western terms has less to do with therapists' formal training than with the way they empathize with patients or clients. Researchers have identified three personal qualities in a good therapist—true empathy, warmth without being possessive, and sincerity. These are essential to giving effective psychotherapy. According to E. Fuller Torrey, therapists possessing these qualities consistently get better therapeutic results than those who do not.

Native healers in Puerto Rico develop such empathy with their clients that they come close to identifying with their patient's illness. The best native healers in India have been described as 'somewhat like a hemodialysing machine' in that they ingest their clients' troubled thoughts, digest them, and return them to the patient purified. Good shamans may be imbued not only with spirit helpers, but with their clients' psyches, too.

A physician injects drugs; a shaman blows a guardian spirit into a client's chest. A physician gives his patient verbal comfort where he can; a shaman fetches up a power animal and whispers its name to his client's ear. A physician removes damaged tissue; a shaman extracts harmful intrusions. Given the mind-born basis of much physical illness, those parallels may be more real than contrived. And yet, where a Western physician is trained to be coldly objective and 'never take his patients home', the shaman must journey for his, fighting the good fight against demon spirits of disease, even absorbing his client's illness for a time before he can expel it from his body/mind. To be a good healer may hurt. It is worth repeating a !Kung healer-in-training's comment to Richard Katz: 'We !Kung seek *n/um* even though it's painful because we can help people. If someone is very sick and almost dead, with *n/um* we can bring them back to life. So we seek *n/um*'.

'Hippocrates first banished spirits from the healing arts.
For the past 2,500 years the faithful have struggled
to force them back in'.
Margarite Fernández Olmos and Lizabeth Paravisini-Gebert
Creole Religions of the Caribbean

It is not realistic to suggest that Western healing professionals should 'go native' with rattles, drums, and spirit-masks. However, 'native' means that which is born in a place, in a tribe, in a body, in a soul. And soul is as native to a warm, living body as breath. To import 'soul' into Western medicine is not to add something new, but to replace something that was lost long ago.

'LORD, HEAR MY PRAYER'

A pioneering minority of Western medicine's more courageous practitioners is indeed rediscovering the value of 'soul'—if not yet spirits. Many physicians in Britain and other countries have long welcomed the assistance of healers; but the conservatism of the medical profession in the United States has kept alternative healers at bay. Nevertheless, more and more bold souls are risking the derision of their peers to call on spiritual powers in assisting their patients.

Among medical pioneers, Harvard University cardiologist Dr Herbert Benson is well known for researching the healing aspects of what he calls 'the relaxation response'. The phrase describes patients' physiological responses to meditative techniques, of which yoga is one. Put bluntly, Benson is convinced that belief in God (broadly defined) conveys real health benefits.

> 'DOES PRAYER HAVE THE POWER TO HEAL?'
> *The New York Times*, September 12, 1997

Dr Dale Matthews (Georgetown University School of Medicine) is an evangelical Christian who studied forty people suffering from rheumatoid arthritis. At the start of the study, all forty were treated with prayer at a hands-on, faith healing session. Unseen, unknown people then prayed for twenty out of those forty patients every day for six months: the other twenty received no additional prayers. A third, control group received no prayer or faith-healing ministration of any kind. His results appeared 'extremely promising'. 'Maybe at some point we'll discover that there's some sort of energy field at work here', he told the *New York Times*.[107] 'But I don't think we're ever going to figure it out—and I'm not sure we want to'.

'A MERRY HEART DOETH GOOD LIKE A MEDICINE'

That line from the Book of Proverbs (17:22) may be the oldest recorded prescription stating that spiritual contentment is essential to good health. Similar sentiments run right through history. Hippocrates devoted a section to spiritual happiness and good health. So did Galen, the second century surgeon. When plague broke out in the year 169, Emperor Marcus Aurelius commanded Galen to come to Rome: for a while he served as court physician. These, and others, made similar comments through the centuries. They have been shown to be correct.

'A young man asked his shaman, "Why do I get so confused?"

The shaman replied, "Each person has two wolves inside them. One wolf feeds on anger and envy; the other feeds on serenity, love and happiness."

"Which wolf wins?" the young man asked.

"The one you feed" replied the shaman'.

A Cherokee aphorism

T- and B-cells are vital to the human immune system. A study group of men whose wives died of breast cancer showed that, for months after their bereavement, the husband's T- and B-cells stopped working, seriously depleting the immune system. Study after study has shown that mental health, or the lack of it, directly affects the immune system.

Norman Cousins was a senior lecturer at the School of Medicine, University of California, Los Angeles. For many years he edited *The Saturday Review*. His article, *Anatomy of an Illness*, published in the *New England Journal of Medicine*,[108] later became the first chapter of his best-selling book by that name. Years earlier, Cousins had been diagnosed with ankylosing spondylitis, a condition which left him, in the opinion of one specialist, with one chance in five hundred of recovering. Among other things, the connective tissue binding his spine was disintegrating. Apart from taking large amounts of injected vitamin C, Cousins learned by experience that ten minutes of laughter was worth two hours of deep and pain-free sleep. By watching reel after reel of *Candid Camera* and Marx Brothers movies Cousins laughed himself to sleep, retrieved his own soul, and his life.

> 'I have learned never to underestimate the capacity of the human mind and body to regenerate—even when the prospects seem most wretched. The lifeforce may be the least-understood force on earth'.

Norman Cousins

It is this sort of catastrophic disaster in a life—serious illness, grief for a spouse, loss of a career—for which shamans journey to restore spirits to dis-spirited persons and to retrieve their clients' lost souls. Soul loss, in a shamanic context, is described by psychologist Jeanne Achterberg as 'injury to the inviolate core which is the essence of a person's being'.[109]

The Western psyche has a lot of catching up to do. Soul was a problem for the medieval Church, which devised three levels of entitlement: plants enjoyed a vegetative soul; animals were endowed with sensitive souls;

humans were gifted with rational or reasonable souls. Since its origins the Christian Church has fought for the redemption of *soul* while dismissing *body* as a diseased, wretched and lustful impediment to spiritual attainment. (Bernard of Clairvaux was a leading exponent of that viewpoint.)

Meanwhile, Western Medicine evolved, attempting to redress the balance by learning to treat the diseases of body with no consideration of soul. (In large measure this was a self-protective strategy to avoid incurring the wrath of the Church.) Then it was soul's turn to be forgotten. Western Medicine is, by its very nature and ambition, dis-spirited. Given the opportunity, shamanism will help Western Medicine recover its soul.

10

Healing

THE NEED TO BELIEVE

Navajo medicine man Denet Tsosi told psychoanalyst Donald Sandner, 'Sometimes Navajo people need treatment in a hospital. In your practice of medicine you operate, you cut him with a knife. When he comes back he feels he should have a Life Way [ceremony] to heal the wound'. Another Navajo medicine man, Natani Tso, told Sandner about a woman who had a gall bladder operation, still felt unwell afterwards, but recovered following a Blessing Way ceremony.[110]

Years before those interviews, the University of Wisconsin's Dr Guenther Risse noted that white doctors on Navajo reservations were well aware of the shaman's power, recognizing that recovery from operations was often faster if the patient had been visited by a medicine man before surgery.

Then there is the tale with which this book began. Australian Aboriginal patients failed to heal until clever men sucked spirit-objects from their bodies that white doctors had missed.

CRISIS OR OPPORTUNITY: IT'S HOW YOU SEE IT

Western medicine is in crisis. Having criticized doctors for being remote, we now have to take into account that they are also overworked. State-financed health systems are over-used and under-funded, while the free enterprise United States' system is still plagued by insurance and medical costs rising faster than the population's ability to pay.

And yet a great burden of disease is born in the mind and could be treated, in the first instance, outside of hospitals and doctors' offices.

As progressive health care administrators in many parts of the world recognize the vital role of traditional healing for primal peoples, the old ways—often in association with Western medicine—are making significant advances in modern cultures.

Shamanic healing makes no claim to be a substitute for essential surgery, nor does it claim to replace much that is positive in modern medicine. Shamanism does not seek to challenge science, although the sciences could benefit from studying shamanic traditions objectively, rather than dismissing them as superstitions. Modern medicine could also benefit from the humane values of shamanism, which has proven effective in widely diffuse cultures over tens of thousands of years.

In many ways medical science and shamanism are complementary. A resolute minority of Western doctors acknowledges this.

Dr Michael Gelfand had much contact with Shona medicine men, *ngangas*, in the course of his long career in what is now Zimbabwe. In the 1960s, Gelfand took *ngangas*' patients into hospital and referred his Shona patients to *ngangas*. The Shona had faith in the skill of white doctors. However, they believed their skills worked better with white patients, just as *ngangas*' skills worked for Shonas, not whites. That cultural bias is as true of Western patients and Western doctors as of Shonas, Aborigines or Navajos. It marks the point where cross-cultural name-calling begins: Magic! Superstition! Witchcraft! Quack!

The oldest traditions of shamanism and the most progressive aspects of the New Medicine share common ground in at least three respects: visualization techniques; a placebo effect independent of cultural bias; and a variety of methods for stimulating the human body to produce its own natural painkillers, endorphins.

VISUALIZATION

In a previous chapter, a shaman of the Caribou Inuit, Igjugarjuk, described how he cured a man who was 'so wasted that he could no longer swallow food'. Igjugarjuk prescribed a community song-feast while he himself went out, 'thinking uninterruptedly of the sick man and wishing him health'.

That case took place in the Barren Lands, west of Hudson Bay. More than superficial similarities link it with a pioneering example of a Western physician telling a patient to visualize cancer as a foreign body, and his radiation therapy as its healing agent. In 1971 a sixty-one-year-old man came to the University of Oregon Medical School with a throat cancer so severe that he could barely swallow. His weight had dropped from 130 pounds to 98, and doctors debated whether to treat him, given that therapy might make the patient more miserable without shrinking the tumor.[111]

Oncologist Carl Simonton instructed the patient to set aside times each day when he would instruct his body's muscle groups to relax, starting at his head. When he had attained this relaxation he was told to picture himself in a pleasant, quiet place. Then he was to 'imagine his cancer vividly in whatever form it seemed to take'. When the patient had fixed his target, the cancer, firmly in his mind's eye, Simonton told him to bombard it with 'millions of tiny bullets of energy' representing the radiation therapy he was receiving. Finally, the patient was asked to visualize his body's white blood cells swarming all over the cancer cells, devouring them or flushing them away. After two months of radiation therapy and visualization the patient showed no sign of cancer. Buoyed by his success, the same man went on to score another, more limited, triumph over arthritis.

Shamans have been assisting clients and communities to achieve this healing success since the Stone Age, setting loose their spirit-helpers to attack hostile forces or fetch clients' power animals or souls. Blowing a power animal into a client's body is a first step to empowering him to do the task himself.

In the conservative world of American medicine, Simonton was taking a considerable professional risk by heading in a direction opposed to the conventional wisdom of the day. The index of Simonton's 1978 book, *Getting Well Again*, co-authored with his psychotherapist wife, Stephanie Matthews-Simonson and James Creighton, contains no index references to shamans or medicine men. Acknowledging the connection would have been too controversial, too 'unscientific' for North American doctors to accept. More years would pass before North American medicine was ready to recognize the phoenix-like rebirth of ancient ways. But *Getting Well Again* does give one strong clue to the intellectual connections between visualization in cancer therapy and primal healing. Dr Jeanne Achterberg's name is prominent in the Simontons' acknowledgments: she assisted in making a list of effective images for cancer patients to visualize. Seven years later, in 1985, Achterberg, a research psychologist, published *Imagery in Healing: Shamanism and Modern Medicine*, making the connection explicit.

The term biofeedback describes a body's responses to disciplined and conscious mental control, and biofeedback studies have shown for a long time that people can influence such things as their heart rate and blood pressure. Visual imagery—imagining whatever has to be controlled

Healing: the need to believe

in a physical form—plays a principal role in many biofeedback control techniques.

For example, one of the Simontons' patients was able to beat back cancer when he visualized his white cells as an army of bright knights with sharp lances and fine horses. But on two occasions his visions betrayed him: his knights turned dark; their lances bent like wet spaghetti; their steeds turned to dogs. Both times his cancer returned. It became apparent that the images reflected the actual passage of events in his life: bright knights or dark; contentment or stress; remission or cancer. His visions accurately reflected his general mental state, and his health responded accordingly.

We may have passed that stage. On August 4 2008, the *Toronto Star* reported conclusions of a study based on a video game designed for young cancer patients. The *Star* headline, 'Videogame nanobot helps kids blast at their cancer' continued: 'A study, published today in the journal *Pediatrics*, found that [the game, *Re-Mission*] can help them battle their disease'. Affirming more trials are needed, the study's co-author, Dr Steve Cole, commented: 'Visualizing the battle helped give [teenage cancer patients] a sense of power and control over cancer. That helps them to be the victor instead of the victim of cancer'.

Remember the Cherokee shaman's tale? Each of us hosts two wolves. Which wolf do you feed? (*Chapter 9*). That which is new is also ancient.

THE HEALING PLACEBO: A NEED TO BELIEVE

In Latin, *placebo* means 'I shall please'. In its generally accepted sense a placebo is an imitation medicine, often a sugar pill packaged, presented and prescribed as if it were an active drug. For almost fifty years the lowly placebo has been studied in order to discover why a non-drug should produce measurable therapeutic effects on people suffering from a wide range of physical ills. These non-drugs have been shown to alter body chemistry, even to mobilize the immune system against disease. Researcher Dr Arthur Shapiro found that placebos had 'profound effects on organic illness, including incurable malignancies'.[112]

Medical researchers do not agree that a placebo's power stems from the 'infinite capacity of the human mind for self-deception'. The positive view is not that a placebo fools the body, but that it works in the mind, translating the will to recover into belief that stimulates physical healing responses—and, incidentally, proving there is no clear-cut separation between body and mind. It may be that a placebo triggers the endocrine system, in particular the adrenal glands. On the other hand it will do nothing at all if the patient knows that it is 'only' a placebo. This point speaks volumes about the interdependence of body/mind. The power of hope ('A merry heart ...' in the Book of Proverbs) can channel the body's fight into making vital physiological changes ('... doeth good like a medicine'). And it does.

General practitioners and shamans know that about half their patients would get well without intervention. Some studies show that up to nine cases in ten fall within the body's curative powers. In most of these, giving a placebo becomes the first link in a chain of events: the doctor or the shaman gives a prescription; the client's faith in the healer transforms into faith in the cure; the body, taking its cue from the mind, kicks its immunological and healing systems into gear; and the client is healed because the human body is its own best healer, given its mind's encouragement.

'Each patient carries his doctor inside him'

'And Jesus said unto the centurion, Go thy way; and as thou hast believed, so be it done unto thee. And his servant was healed in the selfsame hour.'

MATTHEW 9:13

Norman Cousins, whose *Anatomy of an Illness* has helped reshape the way in which Western doctors and psychotherapists view physical ailments, visited Dr Albert Schweitzer at his Lambarene hospital in Gabon, West Africa. One morning Schweitzer took his guest to a clearing to meet *'un de mes collègues'*, an elderly witch doctor. Cousins and Schweitzer watched while the healer gave herbs to some of his clients and told them how to prepare them. A second group received chanted invocations by way of psychotherapy. The old man directed a third group, those in need of surgery, to Dr Schweitzer.

Later, when Cousins expressed skepticism about the witch doctor's effectiveness, Schweitzer replied by divulging a secret known to healers in all cultures. 'The witch doctor succeeds for the same reason all the rest of us succeed. Each patient carries his own doctor inside him. They come to us not knowing that truth. We are at our best when we give the doctor who resides within each patient a chance to go to work'.

Cousins concluded: 'The placebo is the doctor who resides within'. Currently we seem to be making strides in bringing that placebo up to date:

'The optimist is right. The pessimist is right. ... Each is right from his own particular point of view, and this point of view is the determining factor in the life of each. It determines as to whether it is a life of power or of impotence, of peace or of pain, of success or of failure'.

Those words launch *In Tune with the Infinite*, Ralph Waldo Trine's 1908 classic. A bestseller through much of the twentieth century, it is still in print. Lest one imagine that optimism or pessimism is a fixed, congenital condition, like eye color, the first decade of the new millennium has taught us that a human brain can re-program itself as late as old age.[113] In the decade following the centennial of Trine's book, banishing pessimism has received much attention. For example, Eckhart Tolle's *The Power of Now* was also popular. It explains practical Zen to Westerners.

SHAMANS AND ENDORPHINS: NATURE'S PAIN KILLERS

Endorphins are morphine-like substances produced in many animals' bodies, including humans'. Endorphins kill pain. The body also produces valium-like tranquilizers to ease life's stresses. Raymond Prince, Professor of Psychiatry at McGill University, chaired a conference called *Shamans and Endorphins* (1982). Prince's introduction reads: 'This improbable juxtaposition of an archaic healing system and a rapidly advancing new field in neurochemistry probably requires a word of explanation'.[114]

Prince's 'word of explanation' referred to the fact that healers, whatever their cultures and techniques, can produce pain relief, euphoria, shamanic ecstasy, altered states of consciousness, amnesia, and the ability to reduce anxiety. In convening *Shamans and Endorphins*, it occurred to Prince to ask how much of healers' therapeutic powers were the result of persuading their clients' bodies to manufacture morphine and valium-like substances.

Researchers who have studied the Salish Spirit Dance and the Plains Indians' Sun Dance confirm what native people have known all along: rhythmic sensory stimulation—drumming—does prevent pain signals from reaching many areas in the brain. It also seems to exert a direct effect on the central nervous system as a whole.

> 'No man, however highly civilised, can listen for very long to African drumming, or Indian chanting, or Welsh hymn-singing, and retain intact his critical and self-conscious personality ...

> If exposed long enough to the tom-toms and the singing, every one of our philosophers would end by capering and howling with the savages'.
>
> Aldous Huxley, 1961 [115]

In North America, Guardian Spirit ceremonies survive among Pacific Coast Salish peoples of British Columbia and Washington State. For centuries, Winter Spirit Dancers have quested for personal visions, through which successful dancers would obtain a degree of supernatural power. To reach that goal demanded endurance, fasting and discomforts, until successful initiates found 'their song and dance' and were visited by the 'Indian Spirit' or a 'Power Animal' bringing them the gift of spirit power. And who could fail to receive a vision when the power in the dance embraces all?

Then there was the ancient Sun Dance practised by Plains peoples such as the Algonquian, Blackfoot, Sioux and Shoshone. Along with the Salish Winter Dance, the Sun Dance—*Wiwanyag Wachipi*—expresses shamanic power by which a participant hopes to draw on otherworld influences to mediate with spirits and help suffering people. Before the four day ceremony, a woman, representing Buffalo Calf Woman, apologizes to a cottonwood tree for taking its life, explaining that her people need to set it up at the centre of the Sun Dance circle, a ceremony which is 'highly important, for by doing it, the people will live'.[116]

Participants in both Salish Spirit Dancing and the Sun Dance prepare for the task by fasting and thirsting, strenuous motion, exposure to heat and to cold—and the drums, always the drums, hour upon hour.

In conclusions to his Montreal conference *Shamans and Endorphins*, Raymond Prince suggests that drum and dance type ecstasy may reward participants with both a hypnotic pain relief and an endorphin pain relief, a 'biological mechanism providing a base for the psychological "faith" mechanism'.[117] Here again, body is inexorably linked to mind.

TRICKS OF THE TRADE: A LITTLE SLEIGHT OF HAND

'During our stay at South Hampton Island I was witness to...a case where a Shaman named Saraq went out to fight against evil spirits, but I discovered that he had taken some Caribou blood with him beforehand and rubbed himself with this without being discovered by anyone else. When he came in he stated that the shaman who had been out with him had been unable to hold the evil spirit, but he, Saraq, had grasped it and stabbed it, inflicting a deep wound. ... All believed his report, all believed that he had driven the evil spirit which had been troubling the village, and no one was afraid any longer'.[118]

That was Knud Rasmussen's experience in the 1920s. Then there is the 1951 tale of the renowned Iban (North Borneo) healer, Manang Bungai, who took on himself to slay an evil spirit blamed for the death of a baby girl. Alone in a dark room the *manang* summoned the demon. After a noisy scuffle Bungai emerged with a bloody spear, claiming to have mortally wounded the spirit. Never mind that anthropologist Derek Freeman subsequently discovered that the blood was a monkey's. The encounter convinced the majority of Iban people present that the threat was gone and that justice had been done.[119]

Lest any be tempted to dismiss such people as primitive tricksters and charlatans, one should remember that St George, a well-known slayer of evil spirits, remains the patron saint of England. And who was St George? A pagan shaman-hero, a slayer of dragons, sanctified by the Church in order to import his legendary power and prowess into the mysteries of early Christianity. In medieval Europe the image of St George slaying his dragon evoked the power of the shaman-hero's fight against hostile spirits and the forces of evil. Only a shaman could banish such enemies to outer darkness. And what spirits does the dragon represent? Plague, pestilence, war, famine, death in childbirth, a cold and miserable world. Medieval Europe must have seemed ruled by such demons. St George's cross, a long step removed from Christ's, forms one element in the flag representing the British Union, the Union Jack. As Shakespeare puts it in his best shamanic voice: 'Follow your spirit; and, upon this charge cry "God for Harry! England and Saint George!" ' The Church sanctified St George and others like him in order to inherit their powers, showing more than a little Christian sleight of hand.

In summary, we have an Inuit shaman's 'fight against evil spirits', an Iban *manang's* scuffle with an evil spirit, and St George warring with the dragons of medieval Europe. From a substantive and spiritual point of view their missions are not dissimilar. Any perceived difference is merely a matter of iconography, and of cultural preference and bias.

THE TRICKSTER IN HEALING AND MYTH

Since the distant world of the Old Stone Age, a principal, universal and enduring motivator in story and legend has been an ambiguous, cruel/kind, wise character usually known as the Trickster, but also as Harlequin,

Joker or Punch. In West Africa the Trickster, Elegba, is one of seven major Powers. He controls the *da*, the energy of creation; as a communicator between humans and gods he supervises *nommo*, the power of invocation. The Trickster represents primordial disorder and chaos—at least, when his antics are set down in stories told by settled farming folk: here is Prometheus again! But Prometheus also gave us culture, and with help from the Trickster brought us fire. His Nordic equivalent is Loki, whose very nature is said to be fire.

To the people of Haida Gwaii (British Columbia's Queen Charlotte Islands) Raven, as Trickster, assisted the first humans into being. When a primordial flood receded, Raven caught sight of a giant clamshell partly buried in sand. The tiny humans inside cowered from Raven's shadow, but he, with his Trickster tongue, cajoled them to emerge in the bright new world—this world. Out came the Haida people, the first human beings.

Joseph Campbell describes Trickster as a 'super-shaman'.[120] In North American cultures the fire bringer is an animal: Coyote to Thompson River Indians of British Columbia; Raven to the Chilcotin and Haida people further north; Rabbit to the Creek people of Georgia and Alabama.

The Trickster travels among us wearing many masks. In Genesis he took the form of a serpent stealing knowledge from God to empower the first humans, Adam and Eve. To the Plains Indians of North America he lurks in the skin of wily Coyote. In the Eastern Woodland tradition he is Rabbit or Hare, taken up and adopted by black slaves in tales of the legendary Br'er Rabbit. In Sioux he is *heyoka*, the upside-down man, the clown. Trickster is Raven on the Pacific coast or in the sub-Arctic, Reynard or Fox in Europe, and also Crow. As Punch, Joker or Harlequin he became the jester of kings' courts who later took his place on the theatrical stage. But the central point in all these legends is that the fire-bringer has to seize the precious 'element' by trickery and deceit from the jealous spirit-guardians of sacred fire. And often the fire-bringer, the Trickster, sacrifices his life to the human cause.

Fire means more than oxidation by which man learned to cook and heat his dwelling. Fire remains the symbol of magic and religious power. A body possessed by the sacred is said to radiate heat. This explains the radiant energy emitted by those in the blissful state of Enlightenment, whether shamanic or religious. A frequent attribute of shamans is said to be 'mastery of fire'. (Which reminds one of a term for Bushman healers: 'They are called *n/um k"ausi*—masters of *n/um* or simply healers'.[121])

Healing: the need to believe

The fire stolen by the Trickster from the gods for our use represented not only heat, but also 'sacred power', medicinal power. In diverse cultures all over the globe—'wherever shamanism has left its mark'[122] a Trickster-equivalent in one form or another somehow manages, at great personal risk, to steal precious powers from spirits or gods in order to empower humans. For people through most of human history the sheer business of daily survival must have seemed like a struggle to glean scraps from the spiritual rulers of the world. So, in the legends of many peoples, this strange Trickster figure sacrifices himself to bring us the Divine.

> 'If boiling *n/um* is so painful, so feared, how can the !Kung accept it, or 'drink' it? Their motivation is clear. Despite the pain, they seek boiling *n/um* so they can heal'.
>
> Richard Katz[123]

Hermes (Greek) or Mercury (Roman) personified Trickster in classical Europe. The gods' messenger was said to carry his staff of healing—the entwined snakes, caduceus—to and from the underworld. Hermes escorted souls to the underworld; he also caused them to be born again. So Hermes the Trickster is both taker and giver. Joseph Campbell calls him: 'the generator both of new lives and of the New Life', another hint at the importance of death-in-life experienced by novice shamans.

It is no accident that the capricious Trickster plays a major role in the healing arts. Inuit or Iban shamans playing tricks with caribou or monkey blood effectively calm fears and restore emotional stability to their communities. Animal blood as placebo? A Trickster as placebo? It hardly matters. Among primal or modern humans, the effect may be the same. When communities support their shamans, belief systems kick in and take over, reinforcing a shaman's authority and overcoming fear. Confidence between healer and healed is paramount.

THE NEW/OLD WORLD AWAITS

Biologist Lyall Watson was traveling along the Amazon in the 1970s when one of his boatmen collapsed from fever induced by an abscessed tooth. Electrician's pliers failed to pull the tooth, so the crew put in at the cabin of a local healer who reached into the man's mouth and 'lifted out the offending molar as though it had been lying loose there under the tongue'. Then the healer set about removing the pain, making the client sit with his mouth open while he himself began to chant. Within moments a column of army ants sallied from the client's mouth—'an ordered column of ants, marching two and three abreast'. Watson estimated that a hundred ants marched down the boatman's body and into the grass. Then everyone laughed and the boatman felt fine. Watson remained mystified till someone explained that in the local language the word for ants and pain was one and the same.

One caution: Watson himself was mystifying. His obituary by William Grimes in the *New York Times* (July 21, 2008) points out that Watson explored the 'soft edges of science', while chafing 'at the limitations of traditional science'.

'Probability arises from the mind'
Karl Marbe,
mathematician and philosopher

In a 1992 CBC Radio broadcast, anthropologist Marie-Françoise Guedon described her contact with a shaman in Alaska's Copper River country:

'The Dené people tend to enter into what I would call "awake dreaming". A shaman on the Copper River has a guardian spirit which gave him a knife; his power was the knife. It meant that he had the gift to heal cuts, so, if someone came to him with a wound, the shaman would start by putting his knife on the wound, creating a link between the wound and the knife. Then he would go into his dream state, and, in his dream, blunt the knife. So there couldn't be any cut since the knife couldn't cut. By blunting the knife he would communicate to the client's body, to the client's wound, that it was impossible for the wound to be there, and then the shaman would come out of trance and the wound would be gone'.[124]

Australian researchers A.P. Elkin, R.M. Berndt, Catherine Berndt and others report case after case in which the power, *miwi*, of Aboriginal clever men influences the actions of others, locally or far off. Clever men have healed or killed by suggestion. With the aid of a pointing stick, *ngathungi*, they have influenced the actions of others long distances away. In effect, Australian clever men, along with their fellows in many parts of the world, routinely transfer their thoughts into their clients or communities and bring them to act accordingly. Perhaps this 'pointing the bone' encapsulates much that worldwide shamanism, or African magic, represents: the force of Inspired Mind acting, usually benignly, for the good of other souls.

Healing: the need to believe

From a lifetime's experience, Elkin writes a summary of Australian native doctors which surely applies to shamans in the larger world:

> '[They] are men of high degree; that is, men who have taken a degree in the secret life beyond that taken by most adult males—a step which implies discipline, mental training, courage and perseverance. Secondly, they are men of respected, and often of outstanding personality; thirdly, they are of immense social significance, the psychological health of the group largely depending on faith in their powers; fourthly, the various psychic powers attributed to them must not be too readily dismissed as mere primitive magic and "make-believe," for many of them have specialized in the working of the human mind, and in the influence of mind on body and of mind on mind; fifthly, the ritual of "death and rising" by which they receive their powers includes and causes a deep psychological experience; and lastly, that as long as they observe the customary discipline of their "order," this experience continues to be a source of faith to themselves and their fellows. In brief, Aboriginal men of high degree are a channel of life'.[125]

By now, shamans' explorations in the Mind should cause no surprise. The Dené shaman who seals cuts with a blunt knife is returning the subject full circle to mathematics and quantum physics. Mathematician Sir James Jeans, thus:

> 'The concepts which now prove to be fundamental to our understanding of nature ... seem to my mind to be structures of pure thought, incapable of realization in any sense which would be described as material ... As the beginning of the road by which we explore nature is mental, the chances are that the end also will be mental'.[126]

Or, to reprise Sir Arthur Eddington, 'To put the conclusion crudely— the stuff of the world is mind-stuff'. Substance is energy, and energy is Mind. Small wonder, then, that Mind is capable of anything, including healing.

11

The twenty-first century
THE TWENTY-FIRST CENTURY MUST BE FEMALE

THE FEMININE TOUCH: WOMEN AS SHAMANS

The Realm of the Spirits is *yin*, and so is Woman. Who better to explore the *yin* of the threefold spirit worlds than the *yin* of the human condition? Appropriately, in many parts of Asia, the work of spirit mediums falls to women. That is the positive way to look at things. But in a cosmos of polar complements, the negative aspect also rears its head.

To outsiders, Chinese culture appears obsessed with the need to enforce a clean divorce between the living and the dead. Many Chinese festivals serve the purpose of keeping the spirits happy, appeasing them—anything to stop ghosts from tripping around in the lives of the living! The Hungry Ghost Festival is, in effect, a month-long emergency clinic set up to care for the spirits of those who died without families to serve their needs. People give food and comfort-goods to hungry ghosts; street performers entertain them. The intention is to send orphaned spirits contented to the world beyond. But, in spite of such solicitude, someone has to be on call to cope with angry ghosts. That is the work of spirit mediums: and who better to cope with yet another dismal domestic chore than a female spirit medium, a woman?

Women's work! The human condition presents the abiding question: do women take on key responsibilities because they are better suited; because they are more competent or clever; or because males of the tribe are conserving their superior strength against that certain moment when they will have to spring to their feet and slay a mastodon? As ever in matters of *yin* and *yang*, grains of truth lie scattered everywhere.

Women's spiritual and emotional receptors and responses are different. According to British research announced in 1997, Nature, not nurture, is responsible. Dr David Skuse and his colleagues[127] found a specific gene that switches on feminine intuition 'long before birth', making females more sensitive and responsive to their surroundings. By contrast, 'the same mechanism switches off in boy babies after conception, leaving them to grow up awkward, gauche and insensitive'. Skuse goes on, 'What we might call feminine intuition—the ability to suss out a social situation by observing nuances of expression in voice and so on—is a set of skills of genetic origin which has nothing at all to do with hormones, as far as we know'. In short, females enter this world equipped with potential for social skills. Males have to learn them.

<blockquote>Male, female: different social attributes</blockquote>

Lest this go to women's heads, they should recall what all good Taoists know: a little bit of *yang* resides in *yin*, and *yin* in *yang*. A female's talent for social deftness and intuition stems from switched-on genes carried on a chromosome she inherits from her father. Male fetuses inherit similar genes from their mothers, but these are switched off. Thus, in terms of spiritual responses and sensitivity to their cosmic surroundings, women are 'switched on'; men are 'switched off'. And the fate of each child is determined by the parent of the opposite sex.

Do we interpret this conundrum as a female conspiracy to exclude males from full communion with spirit worlds? Is this why male parents, themselves tuned-out, throw the torch of cosmic enlightenment to their daughters?

The genetic blueprint certainly explains why, intuitively, the rising monotheist religions were quick to exclude female spirituality. As early societies gravitated into fixed settlements, the religious laws of newly invented gods evolved as tools for social control. It may seem like a contradiction in terms, but those victorious gods of the early city-states served secular functions. Their priesthoods were police forces whose task was to enforce social conformity. The last thing required of priests was genuine spirituality. Females might serve spiritual roles as oracles and healers, but not as priests. Authority roles belonged to alpha males.

<blockquote>Priests as police</blockquote>

Earlier, we found that, prior to fifty-five hundred years ago, donors in what is now Denmark gave most votive offerings to *male* spirits. Three thousand years later the balance had shifted: twenty-five hundred years ago, more than ninety percent of offerings were clearly designed for *female* helper-healer spirits.

But then, quite suddenly, the climate of northern Europe changed for the worse. When that happened gifts were again given to male spirits. As a helper-healer, the compassionate Earth Mother was seen to fail: there followed centuries of crop failures, starvation, migrations, wars. British Celts dug massive ditch and bank defences at that time to keep the starving continentals out. The Danes turned to male war gods, Odin and Thor. Time to switch off female sensitivity. Male insensitivity and cruelty switched on.

Times and tides: Gods change sex | The Viking war gods raged triumphant until the climate improved again, about 1,000 years ago. Once more, Earth began cherishing her human children. Odin and Thor gave way, this time to Christ. But the Earth Mother returned as herself, and as the Virgin Mary.

In good times *yin* prevailed. But when population stress or crop failure demanded the slaughter of neighbors, *yang* came roaring to the fore.

How does this square with David Skuse's research about switched-on/off Nature? 'Well, [men] can *learn* social skills', he says, apologetically. 'Women will pick them up intuitively'. But why the elaborate genetic difference? 'It is an advantage to have boys socially unskilled so the dominant male in that group can impose a set of social mores', he suggests. War demands warriors.

We have seen how switched-off, brutish males preserved their proto-Danish tribe through thousand year cycles of adversity. Too often we forget that little bit of *yin* in *yang*, and *yang* in *yin*: Nature is herself a brute.

Denmark's prehistory offers an example of a society in which the feminine element was respected and honored in times of peace and plenty, then shoved aside in favor of maleness and brute force when catastrophe threatened.

There have been others. In *Woman as Healer*, Jeanne Achterberg, herself a healer at the University of Texas Health Science Center, cites—among other examples—the downfall of female healers in ancient Mesopotamia.

Around nine thousand years ago, humans in Mesopotamia learned to cultivate plants, and perhaps to breed animals. Given that women cultivate vegetable plots in traditional societies, the feminine touch may

City states and crops | have been largely responsible for the origins of agriculture. That is conjecture. But we do know that agriculture evolved in the fertile plain between the rivers Tigris and Euphrates. The birth of agriculture released humans from the day-to-day subsistence cycle. The result was that early city-states in ancient Sumeria accumulated the first wealth surpluses in human history. That wealth was reinvested across millennia to build impressive physical infrastructure and sophisticated social hierarchies. City-states of ancient Sumeria also left an extensive literature on baked clay tiles from

The twenty-first century must be female

which scholars have reconstructed a compelling history of a long-lost time.

Sumer's first, *agricultural*, revolution triggered another one several thousand years later. Here, five and a half thousand years ago, arithmetic and writing evolved to record stockpiles, distributions and rations of grain, promulgate laws, and describe motions of stars.

In its youth and full maturity, Sumerian society was rich in both gods and goddesses. A trinity of gods dominated the pantheon. Of four in the second rank, only Innana (Innin, Inanna) was female. Innana lived for so long in Sumerian religion that she enjoys the most elaborate resumé of any deity. Innana personified the vital forces involved in life's crises. Her titles included Queen of Heaven and Earth, and, in her manifestation as the planet Venus, she was Lady of the Evening *and* the Morning Star. Innana represented the very natural trinity of healing, love and birth. As an extension of these responsibilities, Innana was called upon to protect her sons in battle; so she became the goddess of battles, too. Through much of Sumerian history the majority of written prayers invoked Innana: she received the lioness's share of offerings, as well.

Unlike the solitary male God of Genesis, who first acted alone, and then created woman as a compensatory afterthought, ancient Mesopotamia's creation myths demanded the sexual coupling of male and female. The sex act was the wellspring of new life and being, a rite to be celebrated when fresh green shoots punched through the warm spring earth. A metre-high alabaster vase excavated from Uruk depicts naked priests presenting the year's first plant and animal offerings to the goddess Innana. She seems to preside over a procession including stalks of wheat, jugs of wine, baskets of food, date palms and flowing irrigation channels. The vase, in Baghdad's Iraq Museum, is one of the first known depictions of the Sumerian Spring Festival, *Akitu*. Here, the cult of Innana has given us the oldest female-inspired erotic hymns and verses. Skillful lovemaking was considered a form of high art.

We cannot claim that Innana was the Creation goddess of Sumeria, but she held creative powers as the loving mother who suckled kings. And, as the deity in charge of sexual procreation, she was but a step removed from cosmic control. It happened this way: having created the world, the supreme god, Enki, got drunk and assigned Innana his power over kingship, sexual relations, certain crafts, truth and lies, peace and victory. When the effect of drink wore off, Enki sent demons to reclaim those powers, but Innana escaped.

Goddesses

Then things began to go wrong. Not for the last time in human history, the apex of social success ripened the seeds that destroyed it. Success breeds envy. Semites attacked Sumerians; Sumerians warred against Semites. For centuries, city-states weakened themselves and each other in wars until Hammurabi, King of Babylon, conquered Mesopotamia. For a time he presided over a renaissant golden age: once more agriculture, trade and art flourished. These activities found their place in Hammurabi's Code of Laws.

Then, almost exactly 4,000 years ago, war and rebellion returned. A disintegrating social order went hand in hand with reports of widespread witchcraft: Hammurabi's Laws began to proscribe against sorcerers and witches. Threatened societies are quick to discover heretics and witches in their midst. Centuries later, the Catholic Church's fall from absolute authority would be marked by a similar, two hundred year pogrom against supposed witches.

Innana (Sumerian), Ishtar and Gula (Assyrian) had served as female deities of healing, birth and resurrection through several millennia. Then, almost exactly 4,000 years ago, with Mesopotamia adrift in troubled times, the goddesses' attributes began to change. Their healing natures were gradually suborned to sexual roles. The four thousand-year-old *Epic of Gilgamesh* sets male against female when King Gilgamesh—the hero—accuses Ishtar of promiscuity, and she retaliates by threatening to destroy the city. Thus a sublime, nurturing female deity became transformed into the Assyrian equivalent of a modern nuclear threat. The feminine nature, which supplicants had loved, was henceforth to be feared. In the best of times Ishtar's priestesses may have functioned like Japanese *geisha*, women who bestowed the goddess's blessings and their own sophisticated feminine company on men who brought offerings to Ishtar's shrines.

| Bad times bring male war gods |

As peace and prosperity slid into interminable wars, priestesses of Ishtar came to be described as harlots. Other women fared no better. During the good years—and there had been many—women had practised in two healers' guilds: one looked after spiritual aspects (perhaps we could call them shamans); others were herbalists, *vegetalistas*, pharmacists. As Sumeria entered its last troubled millennium, the healing professions disappear from lists of occupations appropriate for women. So do other respectable trades, including that of scribe. Henceforth, only men de/scribed society's decline. Even the goddesses lost their jobs, slipping down the pantheon to become wives, mothers and daughters to warrior-gods.

The twenty-first century must be female

The fate of feminine healers was similar in Greece, where their reputation lingered longer. 'I swear by Apollo the physician, by Asclepius, by Hygeia and Panacea and by all the Gods and Goddesses.' Those words of the Hippocratic oath echo through three millennia, recited by graduating classes of medical students to this day.

Graduating doctors are invoking powers vested in a family of healers working some 2,900 years ago. Asclepius' daughters, Hygeia and Panacea, represented prevention and cure. Pain sufferers addressed their prayers and offerings to Asclepius' wife, Epione.

Many of the temples dedicated to this healing family share a common feature, a large healing area, sunken, the better to concentrate incense near the floor. Here, perhaps aided by iambic chants or the burning of psychotropic drugs, patients lay down to drift into an altered state of consciousness. Healing deities or their earthly avatars came among them, working cures.

As in Sumeria, so in Greece. By Homer's time, depictions on pottery suggest that the many female healers were no longer deities but junior partners to their male kin.

We can conclude that societies under stress have, at certain times, replaced nurturing feminine values with aggression. Triumphant male usurpers justified this debasement, relegation or subservience of the feminine aspect in terms they deemed appropriate to their own worldview.

Joseph Campbell opined that the earliest humans regarded female procreative power as a wonder akin to the miracle of cosmic creation. We might take his analogy further: since the sheer survival of primal hunting societies depended on successful reproduction of humans *and* prey, procreation was creation. They were one and the same. (The Old Stone Age 'Venuses' of Europe and Siberia date from such a time.)

This is the epoch that archaeologist Marija Gimbutas describes when she tells us that scattered Stone Age communities across much of Eurasia held the world in all its forms to be divine. Their primary metaphor for that natural and sacred universe was the female human form. In the beginning, the female essence governed all that lived, all that was born, and all that needed to be healed. As the Earth Mother nurtured the Earth, so women nurtured the human condition. Gods were female, and were therefore the healers.

| The female essence |

This gave women in primal societies a 'prodigious power', in Campbell's view which, in recent millennia, the male half of the species has attempted to break or subordinate. Campbell found it 'most remarkable' that primal hunting societies all over the world shared a similar legend into recent times. The story described a 'still more primitive age' in which women were the 'sole possessors' of the magic arts. The son of a nineteenth century missionary, E. Lucas Bridges—he described himself as 'the third white native of Ushuaia'—recorded a myth from the Ona people of Tierra del Fuego, where Bridges was born:

> 'In the days when [the sun] and [moon] walked the earth as man and wife ... witchcraft was known only to the women of Ona-land. ... The girls, as they neared womanhood, were instructed in the magic arts, learning how to bring sickness and even death to all those who displeased them.
>
> 'The men lived in abject fear and subjection. Certainly they had bows and arrows with which to supply the camp with meat, yet, they asked, what use were such weapons against witchcraft and sickness? This tyranny of the women grew from bad to worse until it occurred to the men that a dead witch was less dangerous than a live one. They conspired together to kill off all the women; and there ensued a great massacre, from which not one woman escaped in human form'.[128]

The tale continues. Briefly, the men spared female children so that their sons would have wives. But children grow up, so the victorious men formed a secret society. From that day on, women were excluded from the inner council of tribal lore—such lore as remained. The Ona legend is poignant for having roots in a society that had changed little since the birth of this tale until the early years of the twentieth century, when Bridges wrote it down.

Since their inceptions, the modern sky-god religions of Europe and the Middle East have worked hard to restrict feminine roles. While not always invoking heresy or witchcraft to suppress women, theologians have nevertheless taken pains to ascribe male dominance to the most pious of motives—motives consistent with a male priesthood's internal logic.

Christianity has long resorted to the Cult of the Virgin (obedient, passive, meek, mild) as a tool for keeping women docile. For example, from the start of the twelfth century it was important to silence women's voices while the papacy wasted the blood of their men and treasure in several Crusades. So the Cult of the Virgin was encouraged to diminish women's opinions or ensure their compliance. Even so, some voices clung to older certainties. For Abbess Hildegard of Bingen (1098-1179) the feminine aspect of divinity was represented by an ancient concept—her name was Wisdom—whose tough/wise presence infuses the Hebrew Scriptures.

Wisdom has seldom triumphed, and certainly not in the twelfth century. Perhaps her time is now.

However, before we move forward, the motives from the past must stand revealed. It took an isolated tribe at the tip of South America to admit that the real reason for killing the women and destroying the keepers of the people's lore was perhaps resentment, and certainly fear.

TRUST IS THE OTHER SIDE OF FEAR ...

'And shamanic practices build that trust'. The speaker is Pa'Ris'Ha Taylor, industrial mediator, psychologist and shaman in the Eastern Cherokee tradition. Hers is not a lonely voice of the spirit crying in a materialist wilderness. Rather, Pa'Ris'Ha and the many women like her represent the new, dynamic cutting-edge of shamanism in North America—a force for healing in the largest sense.

Enlarging on that point, she said, 'The way indigenous and grassroots people work is to get back in touch with One Consciousness, and to know that we are all from One Creator, and that we are standing on common ground at all times'.

That common ground is important because, as Pa'Ris'Ha tells it, social forces tend to alienate people, keeping them divided from one another. Insecurity abounds. Its other name is fear.

> 'One of the greatest things I've been taught in our indigenous family is to realize that we must heal fear. We must replace fear with mutual understanding. ... To understand another person you have to first understand yourself. You consider the other person through the understanding of your ritual and your ceremony, so that you know you're talking to God every moment you're addressing anything. And this is beautiful'.

The modern North American shaman is an optimist, sensing a rising awareness of true value in difficult times for many people.

> 'Just the sharing of shamanic practices has awakened in people a greater sense of value in themselves, and therefore they can value other things. Trust is something our people have always had: they trust in Creator. And they know that reflections of that creator dwell in every living thing'.

THE TWENTY-FIRST CENTURY MUST BE FEMALE

Reflecting the creator's values from the spirit world into the here and now seems to fall most easily to women. Born into male-dominated Korea, Hi-ah Park shares in the view that people all over the world are waking to a desire for spiritual renewal. Women must lead the way. 'We have to wake up and put that life force to work, that inner energy that is our real empowerment', she says. 'Female shamans were the first truly liberated women—and a shaman's gifts of empowerment, of liberation, are for sharing'.

An empowered mind can do wonders for its body, we discovered earlier. An empowered mind can pull its body back to health. But surely people all over the world have rediscovered their real inner natures in times of crisis without having heard the words Animism or shamanism. Are people finding the shamanic way unknowingly?

Pa'Ris'Ha responds,

> 'Very much so. Shamanism is a Siberian word meaning "healer of the way". I don't think a person needs to work with a medicine bundle; the true medicines, the true power and source of balance, harmony and healing is inside the medicine bundle we call body and skin'.

Pa'Ris'Ha sees a groundswell of people seeking a return to the 'One Consciousness'. Brooke Medicine Eagle detects a rebirth, too:

> 'That kind of aliveness, that kind of approach to the world [shamanism] must live with enormous strength, because I believe it's emerging back up, not through tribal people only, but all people who are willing to pay attention to their spirit, to their wholeness, to the fullness of themselves, to healing at levels that we now call non-traditional'.

Medicine Eagle, the great-great-grandniece of Joseph, leader and holy man of the Nez Percé, was brought up in poverty on the Crow Reservation in Montana. In time, North Cheyenne medicine woman Stands Near the Fire became her spiritual teacher, eventually escorting her to the place of her vision quest on Bear Butte in the sacred Black Hills of South Dakota. There, lying beneath her buffalo robe, Medicine Eagle encountered her spirit guide, whom she calls Rainbow Woman. The spirit spoke, but Medicine Eagle did not so much listen as absorb the message through her navel. She did not at first understand the full message. But, as she puts it, more and more of it has become clear through the years. Speaking through Medicine Eagle, Rainbow Woman addresses her message to women: the thrusting, aggressive, materialist energy has thrown the earth's feminine, truly creative energies off balance; we have to return to receptive, nurturing ways.

Interviewed, Medicine Eagle likened the pace of modern life to 'electricity':

> 'A lot of our lack of healing is that we haven't been connected. We've forgotten that we *are* connected. Our lives have been so speeded-up and fast-moving that we really *have* forgotten to feel. Electricity! People naturally, when they're out of that 60-cycles-a-second and back in the earth at seven and a half cycles a second, begin to drop into a different selfness, a different feeling, a different energy. In surroundings without electricity we keep that heartbeat-drum going, and that really helps people slow down; it slows their brainwaves and their heartbeat and they breathe more deeply'.

Medicine Eagle speaks in a rush of words from which notions emerge, arranging themselves in broad brushstrokes of meaning. One senses that it is no great leap from the stillpoint of her self to cosmic consciousness.

> 'One thing I'm thinking about the future of shamanism is that if we simply turn our attention to that intuitive left side [of the brain] which is the side of dream and vision and other realities and different ways of seeing, the [shamanic experience] begins to emerge. ... I feel like in a part of everyday life and culture people are beginning to be more aware of these gifts, their usefulness, their power, their healing potential'.

Medicine Eagle likens environmental collapse to an 'underworld of darkness' which shamans are well equipped to tackle. 'Shamans understand our oneness and connectedness with all of life'. The shaman's approach is to confront the hard, disquieting facts and facets of our time, 'going through it and not denying it and working with our allies and the power that lives within us' to face all manner of challenges. Recognizing that a significant body of public opinion has prodded governments and international organizations into belated environmental action, Medicine Eagle adds, 'To me it's a fascinating thing, because we're in this sort of global shamanic healing process without many shamans to guide it'.

IN SEARCH OF SOUL

A 'global shamanic healing process' may be underway, but countless people are hurting on a personal level who cannot repair spiritual damage inflicted by life's shocks and strains.

Rape, physical or mental abuse, loss of a loved one, illness or accident are some of the shocks that result in lasting trauma. To cite an extreme example: in the decade after the First World War, British and European law courts and hospitals overflowed with defendants and patients who survived the terrors of the trenches only to fall into some sort of antisocial behavior as the result of 'shell shock'. World War II knew this as 'combat fatigue'; the era of the Vietnam War recognized the condition as 'post-traumatic stress disorder'. One need not go to war to be damaged. A significant percentage of prison inmates were abused as children.

Life-crippling trauma comes with many names. But even diagnosis may be elusive once a victim reaches adult life. Victims are left robbed of emotional balance, peace of mind and tranquility, as if they are not quite whole, aware that a part of them is missing. And it is

Life's normal stresses also take their toll. Shamans of old understood this state of affairs. They called it 'soul loss' and, through tens of thousands of years, shamans in widely separated cultures developed similar techniques to cope with partial loss of soul. Even Tibetan Buddhism (Lamaism) considered the old, shamanic, concept of soul loss worth recording in sacred texts. In Tibet as in much of Asia, a bad fright can have the effect of expelling a soul (*bla*) from its body. Sickness follows, requiring a specialist to perform the rite of 'calling the soul' back from its wanderings. Shamans from Nepal's largest ethnic group, the Tamang, have always held soul loss to be a form of disease in itself, one from which other diseases spring.

Soul loss

Sandra Ingerman is among North America's leading exponents of soul retrieval. Her book of that name, subtitled *Mending the fragmented self*, notes that shamanic techniques have been all but lost to the modern world; which is not surprising, because the very idea of partial soul loss is incomprehensible in the cultural context of the major religions. Those religions have enshrined the word as their own, implying an indivisible and eternal entity enduring past the grave. In a Christian context, for example, a soul may be damned after death or hauled into heaven, but never split. Contrast that view with Ingerman's …

'From a shamanic perspective, one of the major causes of illness is soul loss', she says, using the term to imply 'vital essence'. From a shamanic point of view, a trauma may result in a part of the soul leaving its body, the better to escape from the full weight of pain. Victims of long-term sexual abuse in childhood often grow to adulthood with no memories from that time. Counselors and psychiatrists describe such non-memories as 'blocked'; attempts to retrieve them through conventional therapy have raised serious questions about 'false memory syndrome'—but that is another issue.[129] Shamans know that such damaging memories are gone, flown, lost; never to be restored in ordinary consciousness.

Ingerman has a degree in counseling psychology and has worked on the faculty of the Foundation of Shamanic Studies, giving her a valuable trans-cultural view of things. She points out that modern psychotherapy can be highly effective, but it only works on those parts of the soul that are still 'at home'. Thus a patient may spend years in psychotherapy trying to recapture memories of an incident that led to long term trauma, but if the corresponding piece of the victim's soul fled, that information will be lost to ordinary reality for ever.

Soul that has been lost as the result of trauma must be retrieved. And, since that requires travel in an altered state of consciousness, that is a shaman's task.

'AS ABOVE, SO BELOW; AS WITHIN, SO WITHOUT'

'All metaphysical principles know this concept', Sandra Ingerman said in a telephone interview. Expressed simply, if one is in a vile mood, one's exchanges with other people are not likely to improve the day for anyone. One's external world reflects one's mood, be it anger or joy. Virgil put it: 'The mind can make a heaven of hell, of hell a heaven'.

Shamans describe this effect as 'mirroring', a principle Ingerman applies to the planet's health as well as ours. 'If we human beings have lost our souls, can that be why we are seeing that mirrored back to us by [a depleted] environment?' The health of the whole depends on the health of the parts.

And what of the health of the human condition, those parts? Pa'Ris'Ha Taylor believes it to be improving, especially among children.

'Children know they have to invest in their future. They are moving to the sound that the winds bring, the consciousness that's in the trees. Children are starting to view the earth as a living thing. And they are hearing her being called Mother. That's a very touching, very human thing for them to relate to, and they begin to understand the process of

Nature. Shamanic practices have been responsible for that. Intelligent people understand that shamanism is a way to give credence to change, to the ongoingness and the undeniable process of unconditional love that surrounds us. Children catch that'.

Then Pa'Ris'Ha talks about tree-friends:

'In the Eastern Cherokee tradition, parents symbolically return their child to Creator on its twenty-eighth day of life and plant a tree-friend to honor its birth. The child often visits its tree-friend to watch the sapling grow, gaining from the experience an understanding of that life which we all share. In the wider world, Nature is pointedly reminding us all of the tree-friend which she planted for each one of us at birth'.

I ask, 'Is this Mother Earth's counterattack?'

'All living things on Earth are starting to pound out her communication. Native peoples are really hearing the voices of the earth, the injury. They're hearing the fire of the Mother saying "Enough!" I see people every day who want nothing to do with New Age, or metaphysics or shamanism. But when you get through talking to them the seeds are there. ... We've complicated spirituality to the point where people think it's unobtainable.

> We are starting to hear the message

But now they are starting to hear. And that message is coming directly from the heart of the Mother. It's coming from the sky, from the sun. It's telling people: you are connected to everything, and inter-connectedness is what you have to cling to these days. The great cleansing that the earth is to go through, the great changes that people fear, we have been going through them. We will continue to go through them. There is nothing to fear'.

A TIME OF TRANSITIONS

12

Everything is energy; energy is everything

> *If our present cosmological model is accurate, 68% of energy in the universe is dark energy. Although our cosmos bathes and surrounds us, much of it is invisible, intangible and unfelt. That may explain why the great majority of humans cannot detect spirits.*

The remarkable thing about advanced shamanic thought is that it shares much in common with modern physics. This convergence will produce a reformation in the way modern humans perceive the fabric of their surroundings and the nature of their being. The approaching reformation will be one of perception. The iconoclastic New Age taking shape in the wings will in time become the icon—for better or for worse.

In one respect this new reformation will continue an intellectual revolution that overturned the study of physics in the years after 1900. Physicists lump together everything before that date as 'classical' physics. 'Modern' physics begins in 1900 with the old mechanical and physical models of the cosmos, the old certainties, being inched aside. There are no physical models any more. Mathematical equations have taken their place. And those equations have more to say about energy and its transformations than about matter. Most of us have yet to catch up.

| There's physics, and then there's physics.

It was Max Planck who revealed to the infant twentieth century that energy is equivalent to matter, in as much as neither can be subdivided indefinitely.

In 1905, Albert Einstein built on the result of a famous 1887 experiment to show that the speed of light is the only unvarying velocity; that an object's position and clock time have no absolute meaning.

In 1915 the force of gravity that we knew—and continue to experience—collapsed when Einstein showed that a mass alters the nature of space/time around it. Far from being a force, gravity is the consequence of space/time's altered nature in the presence of a mass. However, the human mind does not change swiftly: Einstein's theories met stiff resistance until 1935.

In 1927, Werner Heisenberg showed that it is not possible to predict both a body's position and its momentum for the same instant. This discovery shook a principle unchallenged since Thales gave us deductive mathematics twenty-four centuries earlier. In terms of predicting micro-events in physics, cause and effect is dead. Sequential, mechanical certainty in this cosmos has yielded to the Principle of Uncertainty.

In short, energy is equivalent to mass, the speed of light is the sole constant velocity, a mass determines the space/time around it, and nothing is certain. By 1927 the modern physics appeared as remarkable—and as incomprehensible—to many classical physicists as the transformative nature of energy-surfing shamanism appears to most of us today. 'Everything is energy' says the tantric shaman. 'Everything is energy' says the physicist.

After German-speakers (for the most part) had knocked the physical stuffing out of physics, three academics at Cambridge University studied the remaining entrails from a philosophical point of view. A Nobel Prize winner in physics, Sir Arthur Eddington, was struck by the fact that most people found 'solidness', which is to say physical mass, more *real* than the governing principles of natural law, expressed in equations. (He did concede that our healthy respect for solid things is well founded. No one has ever been killed by standing in front of a speeding equation.) And yet, were we to magnify the internal structure of a solid thing indefinitely we would find that matter is at root a void criss-crossed by atomic and electromagnetic forces, (which reminds us of the Anglo-Saxon shaman's web of wyrd.) David Foster suggests that Eddington was writing about physics on a writing desk that he knew to be mainly a void; that he 'could only be reconciled by considering them both as aspects of an Actuality which was based in the mind'.[130]

Eddington himself described his desk as 'a shadow table', adding: 'the frank admission that physical science is dealing with a world of shadows is one of the most significant advances of recent times'. The equivalent challenge in Buddhism or tantric shamanism is to reconcile the world of phenomena—things—with the realms of the Absolute (Emptiness). Theoretical physics and some spiritual disciplines are converging towards a unitary whole. Dare we invoke the term 'One Consciousness'?

> 'The stuff of the world is mind-stuff'

Everything is energy; energy is everything

Eddington seemed in little doubt. He summed up his dilemma: 'The stuff of the world is mind-stuff'.[131]

What sort of mind does this mind-stuff represent? Sir James Jeans, another of the Cambridge Three, concluded in 1930 that 'the Great Architect of the Universe now begins to appear as a pure mathematician'.[132]

It remained for A.N. Whitehead to add that the concept of matter—what was left of it—consisted of a long ladder of forces. Starting from simple organizations the ladder built up to complex organizations, which then achieved the complexity of an organism. In Whitehead's terms the simplest 'organism' was not a living thing: it was an electron. And not just any electron. Whitehead's organism is produced by force fields knitting themselves into ever more complex organizations, but 'the plan of the whole influences the very characters of the various subordinate organisms which enter into it'. He is saying that forces interact to knit organizations into organisms *from the bottom up*, but that these same forces are modified to fit the intended structure *from the governing principle down*:

> 'In the case of an animal, the mental states enter into the plan of the total organism and thus modify the plan of the successive subordinate organisms until the ultimate smallest organisms, such as electrons, are reached. Thus an electron within a living body is different from an electron outside it, by reason of the plan of the body'.[133]

Whitehead eventually sired process philosophy. Here we have the One Consciousness at work, sculpting form out of forces, trimming forces to fit form. We recall Saint Francis: 'What we are looking at is what is looking'.

Set beside the findings of the modern physics, the most esoteric of shamanic practices begins to seem mundane.

PROMETHEUS IS STRIVING TO BE FREE

In modern Europe, the Forward Studies Unit (FSU) is a European Community-funded think-tank, tasked with gazing into the future and offering guidance to Europe's political leaders. The FSU's very existence marks a sea change in the outlook of industrial powers: forward thinking now merits discussion in the cabinet offices and boardrooms of the largest trading bloc on earth. (Three thousand years after the shaman of myth was destroyed, the ancient man of forethought, Prometheus, may be returning.)

A member of FSU, Marc Luyckx is among the few scholars whom governments pay to gaze into a foggy crystal ball and find the future in it. Luyckx's 1996 essay *The Re-enchantment of Politics* was well received in the European press. Its first sentences read:

> 'The change we're seeing is a drastic, profound, and very important change. The political leaders are not the organizers of change; we are caught up by the depth and the rapidity of the change. We had not foreseen that. Nobody has mastery over the change. No one. ... '

This caught the public mood. Luyckx wrote of public dissatisfaction. Where society was heading and how fast, no one could say, let alone what course should be charted or who should chart it. People had lost faith in institutions. A sense of wonder at the triumphs of science had given way to frustration as people sensed that the way forward had become one of achievement without purpose.

Nineteenth century materialism never had such doubts. It knew how to celebrate its prowess: boldly! The coming of steam locomotion in the second Iron Age was an extraordinary phenomenon. To a significant degree, a sense of wonder abandoned religion in the nineteenth century, attracting itself to science instead.[134]

But now, as we establish ourselves in a new millennium, the miraculous has become mundane. Uncertainty has replaced the bold, assertive marchahead.

Hence *The Re-enchantment of Politics*. Our march ahead requires meaning. Addressing cultural change and scientists' ethical responsibilities, Luyckx argues elsewhere that the importance of capital in our society (the quantitative element) will yield to a world in which information (the qualitative element) will prevail. A holistic approach to solving problems will replace the reductionism that has marked so much of science.

Re-enchantment!

Vast computing power harnessed at ever-falling cost will lead the way in overturning the reductionist approach. Problems that scientists call 'grand challenges'—global climatic modeling, deep ocean temperature transfer simulation, ocean and atmosphere interface reactions—will yield their secrets. Linkages between all manner of natural phenomena will become apparent to Materialist Man as never before. Let us predict that, as science reveals the connections among the complementary energies of Nature's wonders, ecology will become the common basis for a new, and global, code of ethics.

Everything is energy; energy is everything

Aboriginal shamans have understood this since time out of mind, of course, because *tjukurpa* underlies all inter-reactions among existing things.

'Meaning and signification will slowly prevail over efficiency', writes Luyckx. The holistic/wholistic approach to natural phenomena will become respectable again. 'We are entering a society of signification (*société du sens*)'.

The first *sens* we must re-discover is one of purpose, of wonder, of enchantment. Luyckx writes: 'Re-enchantment begins when the people feel they can reconcile nature, time, meaning, soul, spirit and body'.

Suddenly we live in a world where a senior adviser to major governments can speak of 're-enchantment'—never mind that he is reciting a prescription for Animism—and he keeps his job!

Luyckx's comment sounds a lot like the root sense of *tjukurpa*, the Dreaming. Whether European Community leaders realize it or not, they seem to have sponsored a major report encouraging Burnam Burnam's call for *koompartoo*, a spiritual fresh start.[135]

Long ago, the spirits informing Animist cultures all over the planet were shoved aside to make way for the gods of rising city-states and their priestly enforcers for whom religion, not medicine, was the law. Those gods brooked no resistance. But now Prometheus, the 'titan power of the shaman', the 'man of forethought' in his many forms, is once more struggling to be free.

~ *'Re-enchantment begins when the people feel they can reconcile nature, time, meaning, soul, spirit and body'.* ~

13

To Heal the World

THE WORLD TREE SPROUTS AGAIN.
CONCLUSION

Humanity's history on Earth has taken an odd turn lately. In ancient times, when Nature was a threat, shamanism evolved in far-flung parts of the globe as a complex of spiritual methods for coping with natural forces, and harnessing them to humanity's advantage. Ambush and pitfalls lurked; the jungle was around us.

Recent human generations have witnessed the opposite state of affairs: the problems besetting our planet are now man-made. Deforestation, overgrazing, spreading deserts, unchecked population, famine and newly violent weather systems owe nothing to any force but us. The state of the planet reflects the imperatives of human society, the state of our collective will. The jungle is no longer an external threat. The jungle lurks within.

This is where history's 'odd turn' comes in. Quite suddenly, in a time when the inexorable iron rails of technological advance should guarantee a triumphal escape from all things primitive and natural, those rails are being torn up and turned in a new direction. The spiritual principles underlying shamanism, an ancient culture evolved to protect us from hostile Nature, is being rediscovered under a thousand different names to protect Nature, and us, from our collective self.

In 1871, at the top of Thunder Being Mountain in the Black Hills, a nine year old boy of the Oglala Sioux people experienced a vision which is among the most moving of all time: it rivals great religious writings in its raw predictive force.

The nine-year-old Black Elk received significant revelations from the Six Grandfathers (Mother Earth and Father Sky with the powers of the four directions). All six Grandfathers gave Black Elk valuable counsel; some gave him other gifts. Significantly, the Fourth Grandfather presented the boy with a bright red stick sprouting leaves, telling him that a sacred tree would grow in the centre of the nation. Then a yellow hoop appeared,

To heal the world

its color symbolizing new growth and healing, its circular form denoting the unity of all things. Black Elk planted the bright red stick—red being the color of plenty—which became a Sun Dance tree.

The Sixth Grandfather, symbolizing Mother Earth, briefly cast of an old man's years to reveal himself as a boy in whom Black Elk recognized himself. Becoming an old man again, the Sixth Grandfather told Black Elk that he would inherit the power of the Spirit of the Earth, and he would need it, for days were coming when 'your nation' (the Sioux, or humanity as a whole?) would be in desperate need of help from Mother Earth.

> Black Elk's vision

At the end of his vision, two spirit men gave Black Elk the daybreak star herb of understanding, which he scattered upon the world below, where it flowered, spreading its power far and wide.

Years passed. The buffalo were wiped out. The Sioux were finally defeated in battle and corralled on reservations. Starvation, disease, white settlement and missionary zeal took their toll on the physical and cultural health of the nation.

In 1931, sixty years after his vision, Black Elk persuaded his son, Ben, with writer John Neihardt, to take him back to the top of Thunder Being Mountain, the place of his vision. There, with tears running down his face, Black Elk prayed to Wakan Tanka (the Great Spirit), explaining that the sacred tree—'the bright red stick sprouting leaves'—was withered utterly:

> 'Again, and maybe the last time on this earth, I recall the great vision you sent me. It may be that some little root of the sacred tree still lives. Nourish it, then, that it may leaf and bloom and fill with singing birds. Hear me, not for myself, but for my people; I am old. Hear me that they may once more go back into the sacred hoop and find the good red road, the shielding tree'. [136]

Black Elk died in 1950, too soon to witness the cultural renaissance of his people, the resurgence of the Sun Dance or the onset of a worldwide environmental movement.

'There is no center any longer, and the sacred tree is dead'.

Black Elk

He could not have imagined that the health of trees, grasslands and forests, the waters, the very air, would within a few decades move international debate at high levels of government. This augurs well. Animists know that words impart the power to transform.

Black Elk had known a time when the plains were untamed and the Sioux hunted plentiful buffalo. Apart from his vision, his perception of better times lay in his past. Moses was at least permitted a glimpse of his promised land; Black Elk never lived to see the vision of his world restored. It is for the present generation and those who follow to ensure that an old man's plea to heaven did not rise in vain.

Black Elk scattered the day-break star herb of understanding on the world below, where it flowered, spreading its power far and wide.

Writer, lawyer and former fighter pilot Ed McGaa (Eagle Man, of the Oglala Sioux) compares the spreading herb of understanding in Black Elk's vision to the growth of the electronic information age in which we live. This will let us 'project knowledge to a higher state of harmony, unity, and growth', writes McGaa in his book *Mother Earth Spirituality*.[137] For the first time, instant global communication puts Earth's problems on display for all to see. There are no corners in which the rape of the planet can hide. Nature's plight will dominate the agendas of decision-makers' thoughts and acts through time to come. Solutions will be forced upon the majority culture painfully and reluctantly, but solutions will be found.

What solutions will we find? To which problems? In the dominant culture we must 'center ourselves before we can perceive the needs of the world through the eyes of Animist peoples and Black Elk. To do so we have to ask: who are we *vis-à-vis* them? Who are they *vis-à-vis* us?

For Western scholars and explorers, the concept of the 'noble savage' outlived the nineteenth century. Subsequently, following the lead of social Darwinists, the early twentieth century came to view 'primitive' peoples as being trapped in a backward state of social evolution. Franz Boas eventually dislodged this view by telling his learned colleagues that their harsh verdicts on other societies were in direct proportion to the degree of difference between 'our' intellectual life and 'theirs'. The Great War helped Boas to change the intellectual paradigm by slaughtering the best and the brightest along with the peasantry, blunting the argument of social Darwinists. With their own culture humbled by war and economic depression, the inter-war generation of scholars discovered enduring values in Animist societies—'stability envy', perhaps—finally conceding them a measure of respect. In the span of a hundred years, the majority culture has promoted the noble savage to noble philosopher capable of envisioning each mystery and every disease in a cosmic context. Which is as well, because we sorely need that quality. These days it is in short supply.

To heal the world

Primal cultures have maintained consistent worldviews for centuries. It is Western scholars' interpretations of Animist societies that have wandered all over the map: Animists and their shamans have always been perfectly centred. Stability and centredness are more easily achieved in 'Animist time' which, with its powerful component of 'past in the present', is circular rather than linear. Animists know who they are because they understand how they fit in the greater world around them. In a material age running on accelerating, linear time it is much more difficult to take lessons from the past, or to know our place in the cosmic scheme of things. Increasingly we do not. In the new millennium, a chorus of minds suggests that an understanding of the ancient order will help us reach a 'centre' for ourselves, and for our world.

What do Animist peoples regard as their all-important perceptual centre? Since Siberian shamanism is considered the prototype, let us return to the vastness of Siberia's forests, to a warmer epoch just after the last Ice Age when birches and willows grew almost to the shores of the Arctic Sea.

Here a shaman climbs a ritual tree, a tree of initiation, a symbol of his or her power and of foresight, because from its top the shaman will see far. The tree is a symbol of centredness for the shaman and his or her tribe. The shaman who climbs a ritual tree is climbing a powerful symbol: the World Tree, the Axis Pillar, the Central Tent, Lodge, Yurt Pole that Supports the Sky. The World Tree rises as the umbilicus, the 'golden navel of the earth' (Yakut), to connect the threefold worlds. Rooted in, and nourished by, the Lowerworld, the tree grows through the Middleworld, the here and now, and on, into the Upperworld to graze the clouds and part the winds. In some Siberian traditions such as the Goldi and Dolgan, human souls wait like birds on lofty branches, where shamans find them and bring them down to earth to enter infants at birth, inspiring them. In other traditions, each falling leaf (or conifer's needle) represents the passing of a soul.[138]

The Siberian tradition migrated far in space and time. In Norse mythology, the roots, trunk and branches of the sacred ash tree Yggdrasil unite the universe. Rooted in Hel, the trunk anchors middle earth, growing through it until Yggdrasil's top becomes wandering clouds and its flowers and fruit form stars. Which brings us to the brink of a modern Europe whose languages remember Norse gods in the names of four weekdays. Ancient Animists and their shamans were ever tough, resilient shape-changers. Nothing is ever fully cast away, and certainly nothing as fundamental to the human condition as the World Tree. Siberian shamans still honor the birch; native peoples of the Great Plains, cottonwood and lodge-pole pine; Nordic shamans, the ash; the Six Nations of the Iroquoian Confederacy celebrate the pine as the Tree of Peace and the symbol of a person's spiritual growth through life. For British Celts the World Tree was the oak, whose tough, enduring wood formed gateways into other worlds. (A Celtic word for oak may have given English its word for door.[139]) English villagers mark spring's passing by celebrating the fecundity of ancient male gods on May 29th, Oak Apple Day. And another tough old dæmon is emerging from Welsh and English woods to reclaim his place in the new millennium. The Green Man, fertility god and symbol of a fecund earth, has been carved respectfully in French and British Christian churches for fourteen hundred years. Now, in his own right, he is staging a return.

The idea of a 'sacred tree' at man's spiritual centre drives deep into the roots of consciousness. Psychologist Carl Jung detected a recurring image in the human psyche, which he described as a 'Philosophical Tree'. This tree is so basic to human needs and desires that it seems to embody any number of different ideologies. 'Tree' is an archetypal centering point in human consciousness for much of mankind.

> 'The complex body of ideas attached to that of a sacred tree at the center of the world was clearly essential to what is probably the oldest and most basic form of ideology and religious experience, shamanism'.
>
> Joan M. Vastokas, art historian

The tree is become a symbol, an image, a potent vehicle for imagination. In shamanic terms, such metaphors aid spiritual vision: indeed, visions speak through metaphors. Thus, shamans summon images of power animals to tap their qualities of cunning, speed and strength. Likewise, certain Tibetan Buddhists practise 'deity yoga', in which a practitioner envisions himself creating, then merging with, a deity-being embodying all virtue (i.e. Ngakpa Chogyam's merger with an 'Awareness Being', (*Chapter 8*). Navajo shamans and Aboriginal doctors use the power of metaphor to greet each dawn, drumming or singing their personal world into being anew every day. Imagination is a potent force indeed.

Extraordinary, parallel paths are leading to profound discoveries in the material worlds of engineering and science.

While researching this book, the author created and edited a series of magazines for a major computer company. The series dealt with a key requisite in modern engineering and scientific research. Computer-based experiments generate vast amounts of digital data that computer systems must turn into on-screen images so that a researcher's human mind can first visualize, then grasp, then interpret results. A picture is worth a billion bytes. Modern numeric-intensive science depends on computer-generated *visions*.

With one cerebral hemisphere in each camp, it seems that the spiritual vision quest of shamans is fast converging in intellectual space with the computer-generated cyberspace visions of data-driven scientists and engineers. In our new millennium, the two will surely meet.

We have entered an era when pharmaceutical companies design medicines in digital computer space. No test tubes. Few guinea pigs. Just visions in cyberspace. Computers simulate the actions and interactions of molecules, pathogens and experimental drugs as electronic images, revealing their molecular shapes and reactions as visualizations on a screen. Interviewed, Dr Malvin Kalos, Director of the Cornell Theory Center, told me, 'Visualizations are metaphors. In science, metaphors have real value. We can wrap our intuition around them. Even the reality of simple things is complex. When we bring all our data together, visualizations have a way of creating these powerful metaphors that our mind can grapple with'.

To earn her Ph.D., Carolina Cruz-Neira created a device called the Computer Assisted Virtual Environment (CAVE). An experimenter stands in a darkened room, the CAVE-space, while computer-generated images project on the ceiling, walls and floor. The researcher wears stereoscopic eyeglasses that are in fact miniature television screens connected to the central processor, ensuring that, as he or she moves, computer-generated images change their perspectives accordingly. Argonne National Laboratory's Rick Stevens told me: 'To interact with the simulation you use a wand. The central processor tracks its movement. You can grab a piece of [computer-simulated] molecule and turn it, or fit it into another molecule'. Cruz-Neira, now at Iowa State, and Paul Bash of Argonne's Center for Mechanistic Biology and Biotechnology, have used CAVE to try and create computer-simulated prescription drug molecules. In attempts to prevent HIV virus from producing an enzyme that breaks down human protein, they have tried to dock small, computer-visualized test molecules into the visualized-HIV's receptor sites.

Along these lines, British cancer specialists stated in 1995 that, by 2020, patients and their doctors would be studying virtual reality images of tumors, discussing tailor-made therapies. That study advances.

From here, the mind flies off to a sequence of free associations: from the CAVE to caves where wall-painted animals looked down on shamans invoking that best of medicines, a good hunt; to shamans everywhere, extracting foreign objects without surgery to let their patients heal; to the work of physicians whose patients visualize cancer cells as gremlins, then expel them.

While powerful computers imagine potential medicines and therapies, the Cornell Theory Center is running computer-simulated models of forest growth. A computer program sows theoretical seeds of theoretical trees on theoretical bare ground, mixes the several species in many proportions, then runs growth and decay cycles through several centuries.

No, Black Elk, the sacred World Tree is not dead. Its return to health has only been postponed. And the daybreak star herb of understanding is indeed spreading its power far and wide, though not as fast or in the form of power that you envisioned. The *deus ex machina* coursing through silicon entrails is studying optimal methods of reforestation and the greening of the planet. And it uses time-compression algorithms worthy of a shaman.

PROMETHEUS UNBOUND

We must not regard state-of-the-art computer-based science as a panacea for the world's ills. Scientists do not determine policy; nor do shamans. But we can now create computer models that predict future climatic and land use trends with some degree of confidence. If we program the variables and start the machine, we can skip ahead for a decade or a century, or two. Like Prometheus of old, society is once more becoming far thinking. To a substantial degree environmental sciences can now visit the future in order to rescue it by revising policy decisions made today. We are developing the capacity to envision and map the outcomes of bad policy in time to head them off. This effectively represents time travel as shamans know it.

The need to envision is but one referential tool that shamans and scientists share. Another is their mutual need to adjust the scale of their mind-work to fit the size and complexity of tasks. Computer scientists call this 'scalability'. If a problem conceived on a laptop can also run successfully on the several hundred processors of a massive research computer, then the experiment's protocol is said to be 'fully scalable'. Shamans describe the equivalent metaphysical relationship between small events and the cosmic as 'mirroring'. Mirroring relates the shaman to the clan, the local to the global, the microcosm to the macrocosm, the earth to heaven. A far-seeing shaman is fully scalable!

'As above, so below. As within, so without'. That is how Sandra Ingerman defines mirroring. Ingerman, whom we met practising soul-retrieval, reflects that the loss of balance—the loss of soul—in millions of individual lives cannot help but be mirrored in the wounds of a bruised planet. Interviewed, Ingerman said, 'On a lot of levels the planet itself is mirroring back to us our own state of health. So my belief is that, if we can start working on a personal level to get a significant number of people back into a state of balance again, the planet will have no choice but to mirror that positive state of health'.

That sounds a lot like the high-level call by the European Community's Forward Studies Unit, demanding the reconciliation of 'nature, time, meaning, soul, spirit and body' in order to attain 're-enchantment'.

But re-enchantment is hard to achieve when every medium of mass communication stresses negative news to the exclusion of positive views. More than forty years ago, Adlai Stevenson defined newspaper editors as 'men who separate the wheat from the chaff, and then print the chaff'. Fast-forward to a modern television mindset: If it bleeds, it leads. Shamans know better than anyone that constant emphasis on negative things breeds negative energy, creating a loop of self-reinforcing negative feedback. As long as tales of social upheaval and environmental collapse dominate our visions of the greater world, the collective psyche will continue to wither in passive despair.

The modern human tribe has discarded Nature as an unworthy model, setting in its place a 'reality' best exemplified by the distilled and distorted mirror of violent current events. This negative spirit is a moloch of our own devising. But it is one that the tribe must transcend before we can once again envision the world in beauty and wholeness.

That is why shamans like Ingerman work hard to restore balance, so 'the planet will have no choice but to mirror that positive state of health'.

With thousands of years of experience behind them, shamans are well equipped to help restore our tribal equilibrium. And, as spirit-guides, they are well qualified to assist us into a future built on a positive frame of mind.

Perhaps our post-industrial society is slowly pointing itself in the right direction. But it is doing so shame-facedly, with groveling apology to the purely human artifice of demand and supply economics. Thus, forests are said to be worth preserving because they represent a hitherto undiscovered source of potential drugs, because they serve as carbon dioxide sinks, or because science has not had time to catalogue the utility value of their doomed biota. The same tautology is applied to any disputed habitat. Preservation in an economic culture demands an economic excuse. Nature must be part of the economic model, to be squeezed into the human economic scheme of things.

We have become so successful at taming Nature that we no longer recognize ourselves in Her, or Her in ourselves. To city dwellers—most of us—even the night sky is lost. We are de-Natured and denatured, excluded and disconnected. As long as Nature remains an inventory of economic resources to which no intrinsic values attach, we will continue to know exactly what we have, what we own, and what we are worth in monetary terms—but little of what we are. Recall the Taoist axiom: A man is wealthy who knows that he has enough.

We have important, positive roles to play, as do our coeval species on this planet. In 1979, James Lovelock took the world by storm with *Gaia: A New Look at Life on Earth*, a hypothesis named for a goddess of ancient Greece. In addition to its pantheon of deities, the world of Animist, classical Greece was a hive of conflicting omens and spirits. Spirits imbued each mountain, rock and tree, propelled each watercourse and drove the ever-restless air. Some were benign, others malign. And of course this multitude of earthy, airy and watery spirits comprised a snakes'-nest of seething contradictions. But, in her quiet wholeness, one goddess embodied them all. She was the ultimate feminine spirit, the Earth-goddess, Gaia.

In developing his modern, scientific Gaia hypothesis, Lovelock drew on geology, geochemistry, atmospheric chemistry, climatology, physiology and biology—Gaia's enabling spirits, in Animist terms. From a shamanic point of view, Lovelock has used scientific disciplines as if they were power animals, tapping their intellectual strengths to show how every reaction forms an integral link in a single chain. From Earth's core to her lithosphere, from her oceans to her atmosphere and biosphere, Lovelock proposed that Earth as a whole behaves like a huge, self-regulating organism. Vladimir I. Vernadsky reported some of these manifestations earlier, in *The Biosphere*.[140]

Ideas may take years to ferment: Lovelock credits earlier work by ecologist Eugene Odum, philosopher Stephen Zivadin and other 'geophysiologists', to use his expression. But it was not until he collaborated with biologist Lynn Margulis that 'the skeleton Gaia hypothesis grew flesh and came alive' in 1973. At that point it took flight as a theory of Earth as a living organism.

To heal the world

'Gaia theory forces a planetary perspective', writes Lovelock. 'It is the health of the planet that matters'. To that end, he 'came to realize that there might be the need for a new profession, that of planetary medicine'.

Predictably, the Gaia hypothesis was lauded by environmentalists and scorned by many scientists. The hypothesis went into eclipse for a while. It seemed too unworldly, too whole/istic, too New Age. Skeptics abounded ...

But Gaia rebounded. Why? We previously heard of the dramatic recovery of Ojibway shaman/artist Norval Morrisseau after a shaman changed his name. James Lovelock did the same for Gaia. He changed her name to Geophysiology. The British *Independent on Sunday*[141] quotes him: 'By calling [Gaia] geophysiology, I thought [scientists] would be kept happy'. They were. Dick Holland of Harvard University, a prominent former critic of Gaia, became a founding member of the Geophysiological Society. The name change won for Lovelock's patient the long-overdue attention of the appropriate doctors—the research community.

Other factors helped bring about a positive change of attitude. Physics had long assumed that we live in a universe grounded in chaos and scattered by entropy—the gloomy promise of the Second Law of Thermodynamics. But recent research seems to support A.N. Whitehead's conclusion that atomic and molecular interactions demonstrate an inherent orderliness at the most basic levels. Something—Nature, if you will—imposes order. Molecular construction, destruction and change seem to be explicitly *designed*.

That raised the thought: if order imposes itself on the microcosmic world of atoms, is it also at work in the macrocosm?

Driven by that question, science is again exploring Gaia—Geophysiology—this time in a more holistic frame of mind. Gaia's ordering is fully scalable: from the microcosm to the macrocosm, from the scale of atoms to the planet's envelope. By way of example, let us pull just one straw from a haystack of facts: *Emiliana huxleyii* is a marine organism, a single-celled green plant, blooms of which cover vast areas of the deep oceans. 'Emily' removes carbon dioxide from the air and replaces this heat-trapping gas with oxygen. Moreover, Emily and her kind generate vast amounts of dimethyl sulfide gas, which rise into the atmosphere to form an aerosol of sulfuric acid droplets. These droplets become nucleii around which water vapor condenses, forming clouds. Since oceans cover two thirds of the planet, the resulting cloud cover contributes powerfully to reflecting solar radiation, thereby cooling the atmosphere. Lovelock and others suggested that marine microorganisms generate sufficient dimethyl sulfide to cool our gaseous envelope to the same degree that carbon dioxide warms it.[142] From life, to gas, to heat-reflecting liquid, to continued conditions for life. Animate, inanimate; *yin* and *yang*. All critical parts of the wheel. Tiny components directing the whole. Gaia as self-regulator. Gaia as medicine and healer.

Earlier, Sandra Ingerman introduced us to mirroring, the metaphysical principle governing the relationship between small events and cosmic; between local events and global; between the health of humans and the health of the world. Scientists now realize that the chemical elements of which we are made were once forged in the nuclear fusion-fires of long-dead stars. Musing along those lines, Jesuit astronomer William Stoeger of the Vatican Observatory Research Group comments that modern cosmology shows how humans are woven into the skein of the cosmic network. It stands to reason, then, that a creation should experience its creator. I suggest that the pragmatism of physical, secular science is joining hands with a new spirituality to lead us back to the spirits defined at the start of this book: 'A natural world in which every phenomenon is endowed with cosmic force makes itself manifest to human perception by means of spirits. ... Spirits are simply the manifestations by which shamans and sensitive people experience the cosmic world. Spirits represent the healing power of the cosmos'.

As, for example, when the healing powers of microorganisms help regulate the temperature of the planet's atmosphere and facilitate life-giving rainfall. Here we have Gaia as shaman.

Discovering the intricate perfections of Earth's abiding systems, I am reminded of Pa'Ris'Ha, shaman of the Eastern Cherokee, who told me: 'Our prophecies state that man will never annihilate himself, that the great intelligence that created him will always arouse again the nature of God in him. ... That message is coming directly from the heart of the Mother, from the sky, from the sun'.

The first play in a trilogy by Æschylus was *Prometheus Bound* (c. 488 BC). In this book, *Spirit in Health*, Prometheus falls near the end of *Chapter 1*. Now, however, we are at the point where *this* section takes the name 'Prometheus unbound' (which was likely the name of the third, lost play in Æschylus' trilogy).

The future history of our species on this planet stretches ahead. It is we who will help to write the missing part.

To heal the world

Soon, the human ape may re-discover something that its shamans have not forgotten: There are many manifestations, but only one Ark. We and our partners on this hurtling ball of rock are locked in an intercourse of spirit and spirits—a common sacred heritage, if you prefer. Discovering that, we will be able to re-integrate ourselves into the greater scheme of things, in the process discovering what we are.

Bibliography

Achterberg, Jeanne. *Imagery in Healing: Shamanism and Modern Medicine.* Shambhala, Boston, 1985.

Achterberg, Jeanne. *Woman as Healer.* Shambhala, Boston, 1991.

American Theosophist, The. Fall Special Issue, 1985.

Barnouw, Victor. *Acculturation and Personality Among the Wisconsin Chippewa.* American Anthropological Association memoir, no.72. Menasha, Wisconsin, 1950.

Bates, Brian. *The Way of Wyrd.* Harper, San Francisco, 1992.

Bates, Brian. Interviewed by Janet Allen-Coombe in *Shaman's Drum* 27, p. 20.

Blodgett, Jean. Curator of Eskimo Art, The Winnipeg Art Gallery. *The Coming And Going of the Shaman: Eskimo Shamanism and Art.* Catalogue of the exhibition, March 11 to June 11, 1978.

Bogoras, W. *The Chukchee.* Memoirs of the American Museum of Natural History, Vol. 11 (F. Boas, editor).

Bridges, E. Lucas. *The Uttermost Part of the Earth.* Hodder and Stoughton, London, 1948.

Campbell, Joseph. *The Inner Reaches of Outer Space: Metaphor as Myth and as Religion.* Alfred van der Marck Editions, New York, 1986.

Campbell, Joseph. *Primitive Mythology: the Masks of God.* 1959. Re-issued by Penguin Books, 1976.

Carpenter, Edmund. *Eskimo Realities.* Holt, Rinehart and Winston, New York, 1973.

Castaneda, Carlos. *The Teachings of Don Juan: A Yaqui Way of Knowledge.* Ballantine, New York, 1969.

Cawte, John. *Medicine Is the Law.* The University Press of Hawaii, Honolulu, 1974.

Chetwynd, Tom. *A Dictionary of Sacred Myth.* Unwin Paperbacks, London, 1986.

Cloutier, David. *Spirit, Spirit:Shaman Songs, Incantations.* Versions of previously recorded texts. Copper Beech Press, Providence, R.I., 1973.

Cousins, Norman. *Anatomy of an Illness as Perceived by the Patient.* W.W. Norton & Company, New York, 1979.

Cowan, James. *Mysteries of the Dream-Time: The Spiritual Life of Australian Aborigines.* Prism Press, Bridport, Dorset & Unity Press, Lindfield, NSW, 1989.

Crow Dog, Leonard and Richard Erdoes, *The Eye of the Heart.* Harper & Row, New York.

De Angulo, Jaime. 'Indian in Overalls' in *A Jaime de Angulo Reader*. Berkeley, Turtle Island, 1979.

Dickinson, Emily. 'The brain is wider than the sky'. *The Complete Poems of Emily Dickinson*. Thomas H. Johnson, editor. Little, Brown and Co., Boston, 1960.

Dioszegi, Vilmos. *Tracing Shamans in Siberia*. Humanities Press, New York, 1968.

Dioszegi, Vilmos. 'Tuva Shamanism...' *Acta Etnographica* 11:143-190 (Quoted in Harner, p. 51)

Doidge, Norman. *The Brain That Changes Itself: Stories of Personal Triumph from the Frontiers of Brain Science*. James H. Silberman Books, 2007.

Doore, Gary, ed. *Shaman's Path: Healing, Personal Growth and Empowerment*. Shambhala Publications, Boston, Mass., 1988.

Dorsey, George A. Sun Dance. *Handbook of American Indians North of Mexico, Part 2* (Frederick Hodge, ed.) pp.649-652. Smithsonian Institution Bureau of American Ethnology Bulletin 30. Washington D.C. U.S. Government Printing Office. 1910.

Dossey, Larry. '*The Inner Life of the Healer: The Importance of Shamanism for Modern Medicine*', (In Doore, q.v. p. 89)

Drury, Nevill. *The Elements of Shamanism*. Nevill and Susan Drury Pty Ltd., 1989. Element Books Limited, Shaftesbury, Dorset.

Eagle Man, see McGaa

Eddington, Sir Arthur. *The Nature of the Physical World*. Cambridge University Press, 1935.

Eliade, Mircea. *Shamanism. Archaic Techniques of Ecstasy*. Translator, Willard R. Trask. © 1964 by the Bollingen Foundation, No. 76 in the series, Princeton University Press.

Elkin, A.P. *Aboriginal Men of High Degree*. 1945. Second edition, University of Queensland Press, 1977.

ETHOS, Journal of the Society for Psychological Anthropology, Volume 10, Number 4, p. 344. Winter 1982.

Engblom, Johan. 'Bridge to Heaven...' *Shaman's Drum*, Number 26, Winter 1991-92, p. 53.

Fenton, W.N. *The False Faces of the Iroquois*. Oklahoma.

Fire, John (Lame Deer) and Richard Erdoes. *Lame Deer, Seeker of Visions*. Simon & Schuster, New York, 1972.

Foster, David. *The Philosophical Scientists*. Dorset Press, New York, 1985.

Fowles, John. *Islands*. Little, Brown and Company, Boston and Toronto, 1978.

Gaddis, Vincent H. *American Indian Myths & Mysteries*. © 1977. Indian Head Books, 1992.

Gelfand, Michael. *Witch Doctor: Traditional Medicine Man of Rhodesia*. Harvill Press, London, 1964.

Bibliography

Goodman, F. *Speaking in Tongues: A Cross-Cultural Study of Glossolalia.* Chicago, 1972.

Grim, John A. *The Shaman. Patterns of Religious Healing Among the Ojibway Indians.* (The Civilization of the American Indian Series; v.165) University of Oklahoma Press, Norman, Oklahoma, 1983. Second printing, 1987.

Grinnell, George Bird. *Blackfoot Lodge Tales.*

Guedon, Marie-Françoise. Interviewed on CBC Radio's *Open House*, February, 1992.

Guest, Lady Charlotte, translator. *The Mabinogion from the Red Book of Hergest.* (The original is in the Jesus College, Oxford, library.) 1838. Second edition, Bernard Quaritch, London, 1877.

Haft, Nina Otis. 'Initiation into Ecstasy: An Interview with Hi-ah Park, Korean Mudang'. *Shaman's Drum,* Number 26, Winter 1991-92, p. 39.

Halifax, Joan. *Shamanic Voices: A Survey of Visionary Narratives.* E.P. Dutton, New York, 1979.

Halifax, Joan. *Shaman: The Wounded Healer.* Thames and Hudson Ltd., London, 1982.

Hammerschlag, Carl A. *The Dancing Healers: A Doctor's Journey of Healing with Native Americans.* Harper & Row, San Francisco, 1988.

Harner, Michael. *The Way of the Shaman.* 1980, 1990, Harper & Row.

Hurley, J. Finlay. *Sorcery.* Routledge & Kegan Paul plc., 1985

Huxley, A. *The Devils of Loudon.* Chatto and Windus, London, 1961.

Ingerman, Sandra. *Soul Retrieval: Mending the Fragmented Self.* Harper Collins, San Francisco, 1991.

Ingerman, Sandra. 'Welcoming Our Selves Back Home. The Application of Shamanic Soul-Retrieval Techniques in the Treatment of Trauma Cases' *Shaman's Drum.* Number 17, Mid-summer 1989, p. 25.

Jaynes, J. *The Origin of Consciousness in the Breakdown of the Bicameral Mind.* Boston, 1976.

Jeans, Sir James. *The Mysterious Universe.* Cambridge University Press, 1930.

Jenkins, C.D. 'Psychological and Social Precursors of Coronary Disease', *The New England Journal of Medicine* 284: 244-255, 1971. (Cited by Dossey, q.v.)

Jilek, W.G. 'Altered States of Consciousness in North American Indian Ceremonials' (See *ETHOS* entry, p. 326).

Jilek, W.G. *Salish Indian Mental Health and Culture Change: Psychohygienic and Therapeutic Aspects of the Guardian Spirit Ceremonial.* Holt, Rinehart and Winston, Toronto and Montreal, 1974.

Johnston, Basil. *Ojibway Heritage.* McClelland & Stewart, Toronto, 1976, 1990.

Katz, Richard. 'Accepting "Boiling Energy": The Experience of !Kia-Healing among the !Kung'. (See *ETHOS* entry, p. 344)

Kalweit, Holger. *Dreamtime & Inner Space: The World of the Shaman.* Shambhala, Boston, 1988.

Kilpatrick, J. & A. *Run toward the Nightland*. Dallas, Texas, 1967.
Krippner, Stanley. *Shamans: The First Healers*. (In Doore, p. 105)
Kühn, Herbert. *Auf den Spuren des Eiszeitmenschen* (On the Trail of Ice Age Man), Brockhaus, Wiesbaden, Germany, 1953.
Lao Tzu. *Tao Te Ching*. D.C. Lau, translator. Penguin Classics, 1963.
Lao Tzu. *Tao Te Ching*. Feng, Gia-fu & Jane English. Knopf, New York, 1972.
Lame Deer and Richard Erdoes. *Lame Deer: Seeker of Visions*. Simon and Schuster, New York, 1972.
Larousse *World Mythology*, Pierre Grimal, editor. Hamlyn Publishing Group Ltd. 1965.
Landes, Ruth. *The Ojibwa Woman*. Columbia Contributions to Anthropology, No. 31. New York. 1938. (Quoted in Grim, p. 121)
Lao Tsu. *Tao Te Ching*, translator Gia Fu-feng, Alfred A. Knopf, New York. 1972.
Lejeune, Father Paul. *Relations*, 1634 or 1637. (Quoted in Gaddis, p. 154)
Lévi-Strauss, Claude. *Structural Anthropology*. Basic Books, New York, 1963.
Lot-Falk, Evelyne. Also given as Lot-Falck, Evelyne. *Les Rites de chasse chez les peuples sibériens*. Paris, 1953.
Lowie, Robert H. *Primitive Religion*. 1924, re-issued by Grosset and Dunlap, 1952.
Matthews-Simonton, see Simonton.
McGaa, Ed. Eagle Man. *Mother Earth Spirituality: Native American Paths to Healing Ourselves and Our World*, Harper, San Francisco, 1990.
Men, Hunbatz. *Secrets of Mayan Science/Religion*. Bear & Company, Santa Fe, New Mexico, 1990.
Mikhailovski, V.M. 'Shamanism in Siberia and European Russia, Being the Second Part of *Shamanstvo*'. Trans. Oliver Wardrop. *Journal of the Royal Anthropological Institute* 24 (1894). (Quoted in Grim, p. 45)
Miller, Jay. *Shamanic Odyssey: The Lushootseed Salish Journey to the Land of the Dead*. Anthropological Papers No. 32, Ballena Press, Menlo Park, California.
Morford, Mark P. O. and Robert J. Lenardon. *Classical Mythology*. New York and London. Third edition, 1971.
Myerhoff, Barbara G. *Peyote Hunt: The Sacred Journey of the Huichol Indians*. Cornell University Press. Ithaca, N.Y. 1974.
Neihardt, John G. *Black Elk Speaks*. University of Nebraska Press, Lincoln, 1961.
Nequatewa, Edmund. *Truth of a Hopi*. Northland, Flagstaff, Arizona. First published 1936.
Neher, Andrew. *Electroencephalography and Clinical Neurophysiology* 13 (13): 449-451, 1961. Also *Human Biology* 34 (2): 151-160, 1962.
Newsweek Magazine, June 24 1991 46-53. Lead writer, Jerry Adler.
Nicholl, Charles. *Borderlines: A Journey in Thailand and Burma*. Viking Penguin, New York, 1989.

Bibliography

O'Keefe, Daniel Lawrence. *Stolen Lightning: The Social Theory of Magic.* Vintage Books, 1983.

Okladnikov, A.P. *Yakutia: Before its Incorporation into the Russian State.* Henry N Michael, Editor, for the Arctic Institute of North America, McGill-Queen's University Press, Montreal and London, 1970.

Ostermann, H. *The Alaskan Eskimos, as Described in the Posthumous Notes of Dr Knud Rasmussen. Report of the Fifth Thule Expedition 1921-24,* Vol. X, No. 3, Nordisk Forlag, Copenhagen, 1952.

Oswalt, Robert L. *Kashaya Texts.* University of California Publications in Linguistics, Vol. 36. Berkeley and Los Angeles. (Quoted in Harner)

Parry, J.J, translator. *The Life of Merlin: Vita Merlini.* Urbana, University of Illinois, 1925.

Physicians for the Twenty-first Century: Report of the Project Panel on the General Professional Education of the Physician and College Preparation for Medicine. Association of American Medical Colleges, 1985. (Cited by Dossey, q.v.).

Prince, Raymond. 'Introduction' (See *ETHOS* entry, p. 299)

Prince, Raymond. 'Shamans and Endorphins: Hypotheses for a Synthesis'. (See *ETHOS* entry, p. 409)

Prince, Raymond. 'The Endorphins: A Review for Psychological Anthropologists' (See *ETHOS* entry, p. 303)

Ramakrishna. Swami Nikhililananda, translator, *The Gospel of Sri Ramakrisha,* New York, 1942.

Rasmussen, K. *Across Arctic America (AAA).* Narrative of the Fifth Thule Expedition, 1921-24, G.P.Putnam's Sons, 1927; Greenwood Press, 1969.

Rasmussen, K. *Intellectual Culture of the Hudson Bay Eskimos (ICHBE),* translated by W.E. Calvert, pp. 52-55. Report of the Fifth Thule Expedition, 1921-24, Vol. 7. No.1. Gyldendalske Boghandel, Nordisk Forlag, Copenhagen, 1929.

Rasmussen, K. *Intellectual Culture of the Iglulik Eskimos (ICIE),* translated by William Worster, Report of the Fifth Thule Expedition, 1921-24, Vol 7, the first part. Gyldendalske Boghandel, Nordisk Forlag, Copenhagen, 1930.

Rasmussen, K. *Netsilik Eskimos: Social Life and Spiritual Culture (NE),* translated by W.E. Calvert. Report of the Fifth Thule Expedition, 1921-24, Vol. 8, Numbers 1 & 2, 1931.

Raudot, Antoine Denis. 'Memoir Concerning the Different Indian Nations of North America', in *Relation par lettres de l'Amérique Septentrionale.* (Quoted in Grim, 102.)

Recovered Memories of Childhood Sexual Abuse: Implications for Clinical Practice. Report to the Royal College of Psychiatrists, 1996.

Reichel-Dolmatoff, Gerardo. *Beyond the Milky Way. Hallucinatory Imagery of the Tukano Indians.* UCLA Latin American Center, Los Angeles, 1978.

Rogers, Spencer L. *The Shaman: His Symbols and His Healing Power.* Charles C. Thomas, Publisher, Springfield, Illinois, 1982.

Rosenwasser, Penny (editor). *Visionary Voices: Women on Power—Conversations with Shamans, Activists, Teachers, Artists and Healers.* Aunt Lute Books, San Francisco, 1992.

Roth, H. Ling. *The Natives of Sarawak and British North Borneo.* 1887. (Cited in Eliade, p. 57)

Ruspoli, Mario. *The Cave of Lascaux: the final photographs.* Harry Abrams, N.Y. 1987.

Sandner, Donald. 'Navajo Symbolic Healing'. *Shaman's Drum.* Number 1, Summer 1985, p. 25.

Shapiro, Arthur K. 'Factors contributing to the placebo effect'. *American Journal of Psychotherapy* 18, 1961, pp. 73-88.

Shapiro, Arthur K. 'The placebo effect in the history of medical treatment: implications for psychiatry'. *American Journal of Psychiatry* 116, 1959, p. 298.

Shepard, Paul & Sanders, Barry. *The Sacred Paw: The Bear in Nature, Myth, and Literature.* Viking. Viking Penguin Inc. New York, 1985.

Shternberg or Sternberg, Lev or Leo I. Divine Election in Primitive Religion (including material on different tribes of N. E. Asia and America), in *Congrès international des Americanistes,* pp. 176-178. Compte-Rendu de la XXIe session, 2eme partie tenue à Goteborg en 1924. Kraus Reprint (Kraus-Thomson Organization Ltd.), 1968.

Shirokogoroff, S. *Psychomental Complex of the Tungus.* Kegan Paul, Trench, Trubnor, London, 1935.

Simonton, O.C, Matthews-Simonton, S, and Creighton, J.L. *Getting Well Again: A Step-by-Step, Self-Help Guide to Overcoming Cancer for Patients and Their Families.* First edition, J.P. Tarcher, 1978. Bantam edition, from 1980.

Sinclair, Lister and Pollock, Jack. *The Art of Norval Morrisseau.* Methuen, Toronto, 1979.

Smith, Curtis G. *Ancestral Voices. Language and the Evolution of Human Consciousness.* Prentice-Hall, New Jersey, 1985.

Snyder, E. *Hypnotic Poetry.* Philadelphia, 1930.

Speck, Frank G. *Naskapi: The Savage Hunters of the Labrador Peninsula.* Volume 10 in 'The Civilization of the American Indian' series. University of Oklahoma Press, 1935. New edition 1977.

Spencer, B. and Gillen, F.J. *The Northern Tribes of Central Australia.* London, 1904. (Cited in Eliade, pp. 47-50)

Stewart, R.J. *The Mystic Life of Merlin.* Arkana, London and New York, 1986. See also Parry, J.J.

Stein, R.A. Tibetan Civilization. Stanford University Press, Stanford California, 1972.

Bibliography

Stones, bones and skin: ritual and shamanic art. An artscanada book. The Society for Art Publications, Toronto, 1977
Sucking Doctor, a film showing the work of the Pomo shaman, Mrs Essie Parrish. University of California Extension Films, Berkeley, CA
Sun Bear and Wabun Bear. *The Medicine Wheel.* Prentice Hall, New York, 1980.
Sullivan, Lawrence E. *Icanchu's Drum: An Orientation to Meaning in South American Religions.* Macmillan, New York, 1988.
Tart, Charles. *States of Consciousness.* El Cerrito, California: Psychological Processes, 1983.
Taussig, Michael. *Shamanism, Colonialism and the Wild Man.* University of Chicago Press, 1987.
Teish, Luisah. *Jambalaya: The Natural Woman's Book of Personal Charms and Practical Rituals,* Harper & Row, San Francisco, 1985.
Thalbitzer, William. 'Les Magiciens esquimaux, leurs conception du monde, de l'âme et de la vie'. *Journal de la Société des Américanistes,* N° 22, 1930. (Cited in Eliade).
Thubten Jigme Norbu & Colin M. Turnbull. *Tibet.* Simon and Schuster, N.Y., 1968.
Thompson, Lucy. *To the American Indian.* 1916. Reprinted with amend-ments as *To the American Indian: Reminiscences of a Yurok Woman* by Heyday Books with Peter E. Palmquist, Berkeley, CA, 1991.
Tolle, Eckhart. *The Power of Now.* New World Library, 2004.
Torrey, E. Fuller. *Witchdoxtors and Psychiatrists: The Common Roots of Psychotherapy and its Future.* Harper and Row, 1986. Originally published as *The Mind Game,* 1972.
Van der Post, Laurens. *The Heart of the Hunter.* Hogarth Press, 1961; Penguin Books, 1965.
Van der Post, Laurens. *The Lost World of the Kalahari.* Penguin Books, 1958.
Varagnac, A. 'The Problem of Prehistoric Religion', Larousse *World Mythology,* Hamlyn, 1965.
Vastokas, J.M. & R.K. *Sacred Art of the Algonkians: A Study of the Peterborough Petroglyphs.* Mansard Press, Peterborough, Ontario, 1973.
Vernadsky, Vladimir I., *The Biosphere,* 1926 Russian, 1998 English.
Walsh, Roger N. *The Spirit of Shamanism.* Jeremy P. Tarcher, Inc. New York, 1990.
Whitehead, A.N. *Science and the Modern World.* Cambridge University Press, 1926.
Wood, Rev. J. G., M.A., F.L.S. *The Natural History of Man, Being An Account of the Manners and Customs of the Uncivilized Races of Men.* Routledge and Sons, London. Vol I, 1868; Vol. II, 1870.
Work in America: Report of a Special Task Force to the Secretary of Health, Education and Welfare, Cambridge: MIT Press, 1973. (Cited by Dossey, q.v.)

Endnotes

1. LeJeune, Paul. *Relations*, c. 1634. Quoted in Gaddis, p. 154.
2. Lao Tsu, ch. 47 (Feng).
3. Rasmussen (ICIE).
4. Rasmussen (ICIE), p.112.
5. Harner, p.23.
6. van der Post, *The Heart of the Hunter*, p.57. After Bleek.
7. Guédon, Marie-Françoise, CBC Radio broadcast, 1992.
8. Armstrong, Karen, *A Short History of Myth*, p.34, Knopf Canada
9. Carpenter, p.81.
10. van der Post, *The Heart of the Hunter*, p.35-36.
11. Carpenter, p.106.
12. *The Siberian Times*, 'First glimpse inside the Siberian cave that holds the key to man's origins', by Anna Liesowska, 28 July 2015
13. Lot-Falk, Evelyne. Also Lot-Falck, Eveline. See Bibliography.
14. Okladnikov, pp.268ff. Cites *Arkhiv Yakutskogo filiala, Lenskiye pesni*, pp. 28-29.
15. Campbell, *Primitive Mythology*, p.251.
16. Mikhailovskii, p.138.
17. Shternberg.
18. Eliade, p.36.
19. Ibid. p.36-37.
20. Dioszegi, p.62.
21. Campbell, *Primitive Mythology*, p.261.
22. Okladnikov, p.277.
23. Ibid. p.344.
24. Rasmussen.
25. Taboo: a socially sanctioned behaviour by which members of the living generation cope with cosmic forces by emulating the learned experience of those who came before.
26. Rasmussen (AAA).
27. Rasmussen (AAA), p.81.
28. The goddess Sedna has many names: Arnapkapfaaluk ('Big Bad Woman') to the Copper Inuit. To others, she is Arnakuagsak, Arnaqquassaaq, Sassuma Arnaa, Nerrivik, Arnapkapfaaluk, Nuliajuk, Takánakapsâluk
29. Ibid. p.131.
30. Ibid. p.81.
31. Ibid.
32. Rasmussen(ICIE), p.113.
33. Halifax, Joan. *Shamanic Voices*.

34 Rasmussen (AAA), p.125-6.
35 Ibid.
36 Ibid. p.126.
37 Ibid. p.119.
38 Johnston, p.119.
39 Bibliography: See Fire, John (Lame Deer)…
40 Fire, op. cit by Halifax, Joan, *Shamanic Voices*, p.74
41 McGaa, p.83.
42 Sinclair, p.70. This passage accompanies Morrisseau's picture *The Mishipashoo* on the facing page (National Museums of Canada number III-G-1103).
43 Grim, p.103.
44 Ibid, p.102. See Bibliog. under Raudot.
45 Johnston, p.119.
46 De Angulo. Quoted by Achterberg in Doore, p.115.
47 Eliade, Mircea.
48 Ibid. p.xvii.
49 Jilek, 'Altered States…' p.331.
50 McGaa, Ed. Eagle Man.
51 Oswalt, Robert L.
52 Barnouw. Quoted in Grim, p.107.
53 Fenton, W.N.
54 Men, Hunbatz.
55 Modern English is not far removed from an Animist's understanding in this regard. The *Shorter Oxford English Dictionary* gives an early definition of Intuition as: 'The immediate knowledge ascribed to angelic and spiritual beings, with whom vision and knowledge are identical'.
56 *Ayahuasca* derives from two Peruvian Quechua words: *aya* (spirit or ancestor) and *huasca* (vine or rope). The psychedelic brew is made by boiling down the stems of the vine *Banisteriopsis caapi* with at least one other psychotropic drug.
57 Taussig, p.467.
58 Ibid, p.467.
59 Bridges, Lucas.
60 Campbell, *Primitive Mythology*, p.308. Cites Kühn pp.91-94, q.v., to whom Bégouën gave an oral account in 1926.
61 Ruspoli, p.83, quotes André Leroi-Gourhan.
62 Rasmussen, (ICIE) p.126.
63 Morford, p.97.
64 Larousse, p.97.
65 Morford, p.42.

Endnotes

66 Ibid, p.53.
67 Ibid, p.104. *Odyssey* 4. 435-450.
68 Ibid, p.60. *Metamorphoses* 1. 211-121.
69 *The Mabinogion*, Welsh translation by Lady Charlotte Guest. See Bibliography: Guest.
70 Stewart, pp.25 and 55.
71 Ibid, p.69.
72 Carl Zimmer, *New York Times*, September 21, 2016. And, from the National Geographic Society's Genographic Project, published in the *American Journal of Human Genetics*, April 2008: The Khoi and San people in South Africa 'appear to have diverged from other people between 90,000 and 150,000 years ago'.
73 Scientific debate re the *tablier*: Stephen Jay Gould, 'The Hottentot Venus' in *The Flamingo's Smile*, p.291, 1981.
74 Van der Post, *The Lost World of the Kalahari*, Chapter 8.
75 Katz, p.348.
76 Ibid. p.352.
77 Ibid. p.357.
78 More recent work, published in the *Transcultural Psychiatric Research Review* (XXV, 4, 1988, p.249) leaves the involvement of endorphins 'rather inconclusive', according to Raymond Prince, who chaired the 1980 conference in Montreal. Personal communication to the author, 1992.
79 *The Guardian*, 22 September 2016, reports research published in *Nature*. Nature, *A genomic history of Aboriginal Australia*, reference 18299.
80 *Shaman's Drum* magazine, No. 14, Fall 1988, p.29.
81 Cowan, pp.47-8.
82 Wood, Vol.II, p.85.
83 Cawte, p.28.
84 Ibid, p.33.
85 For full declaration, search: *Burnam Burnam declaration England*
86 Milirrpum v Nabalco, Supreme Court of Northern Territory, Alice Springs, April 27, 1971. Federal Law Reports 17 F.L.R. Quoted from pp. 270-1.
87 Northern Territory subsequently enacted legislation (1976) requiring negotiation with Aboriginal land users. Since 1788, British settlement in Australia had refused to recognize undocumented property rights; from a legal viewpoint the land was uninhabited (*terra nullius*). In 1992 a landmark decision by the High Court of Australia overturned *terra nullius* (Eddie Mabo and Ors, Plaintiffs. F.C. 92/014).
88 Special to *The Toronto Star*, December 22, 2016. By Jessica Wynne Lockhart, Port Douglas QLD, Australia.
89 See Bibliography: Haft.

90 *American Theosophist*, p.387.
91 Thubten Jigme Norbu, late, the eldest brother of Tenzin Gyatso, the fourteenth Dalai Lama. See Bibliography: Thubten.
92 India knows Lopon Rinpoche as Padmasambhava, the Tantric or Lotus-born Buddha.
93 Ibid.
94 Reported by Leslie Scrivener in the *Toronto Star*, January 18 1998, p. C1.
95 See Bibliography: Stein.
96 Shamanic Practices in Tantric Buddhism. *Shaman's Drum* Number 20, Summer 1990.
97 Cited by Donald C. Robinson in intro to Norval Morrisseau Exhibition, 'Honouring First Nations', Kinsman Robinson Galleries, Toronto, 1994. Source: Nat'l Gallery of Canada.
98 Torrey.
99 Lévi-Strauss, p.193. Quoted in Torrey, p.19.
100 Teish, p.62.
101 Torrey, p.27.
102 Katz, p.352.
103 Ibid. pp.350, 365.
104 Bibliography: *Physicians for the Twenty-first Century...*
105 Dossey, *The Inner Life of the Healer*, in Doore, ed. p.93.
106 Halifax, *Shamanic Voices*, p.85.
107 Hampton Sides, *The New York Times*, September 12, 1997.
108 New England Journal of Medicine, December 1976.
109 Achterberg, *The Wounded Healer*, in Doore, p.121.
110 Sandner, p.25.
111 Simonton, Bantom edition, p.6.
112 Shapiro. 'The placebo effect...' p.298.
113 Doidge, Norman. *The Brain That Changes Itself: Stories of Personal Triumph from the Frontiers of Brain Science*, James H. Silberman Books.
114 Prince, Introduction, p.299.
115 Cited in Jilek, 'Altered States...' p.328.
116 McGaa, p.85.
117 Prince, Shamans and Endorphins, p.421.
118 Rasmussen (ICIE) p.147.
119 Kalweit, *Dreamtime* p.1.
120 Campbell, *Primitive Mythology*, p.275.
121 Katz, p.348.
122 Campbell, *Primitive Mythology*, p.275.
123 Ibid. p.363.
124 Bibliography: see Guédon.

125 Elkin, p.66.
126 Jeans.
127 David Skuse, of the Institute of Child Health, London, collaborated with colleagues from the Wessex Regional Genetics Laboratory, Salisbury. Source: e-file from the *Guardian Weekly* (19/6/1997) reported by Tim Radford.
128 Bridges, Lucas, p.262.
129 A scathing report on techniques that 're-discover' false memories was prepared for, and submitted to, the Royal College of Psychiatrists, in 1996. After internal dissent, a watered down report was published in the *British Journal of Psychiatry*, in April 1998. See Bibliography: *Recovered Memories…*
130 Foster, p.12.
131 Eddington.
132 Jeans.
133 Whitehead.
134 A reaction to the relentless march of technology set in near the turn of the twentieth century. Relief from railways, steam, machines and the moloch of progress triggered a counter-fascination with fairies, things spiritual, seances and astral projection.
135 Burnam Burnam, who did much to reawaken his own people and to inspire many white Australians with a long-suppressed sense of natural justice, died in 1997.
136 Remembered mainly for *Black Elk Speaks*, John G. Neihardt became Nebraska's poet laureate. Television personality Dick Cavett chaired a 1992 campaign to fund a museum in Neihardt's name. This passage comes from page 273.
137 McGaa, pp.16-17.
138 Eliade, pp.269ff.
139 Every Celtic language in northern Europe uses a variant of the Sanskrit *drus* to express oak. Modern Welsh has *derw*. The first professor of Gaelic studies at Oxford University, John Rhys, found the word in place names meaning entry, passage or door. The main entry point for waves of ancient migrants to Celtic Britain preserves the name Dorset.
140 Vernadsky, Vladimir I., *The Biosphere*, 1926 in Russian; 1998, English.
141 *Independent on Sunday* magazine, August 4, 1996, p.40. *Healing the Rift*, by Oliver Tickell.
142 The contribution of phytoplankton does not end there. Terrestrial plants need traces of sulphur that most soils lack. Earth's rich flora may owe much to ocean-derived sulphur falling in rain.

Index

!*kia* altered state, 89-90, 121-122
!Kung, 89, 91, 121-122, 124, 137
!Wi, (Bushman), 90

A

Aadja (Yakut), 24
Aborigines, 3, 7, 11, 90, 93, 95-96, 99-100, 129
Absolute, the, 55, 113-14, 156
Achterberg, Jeanne, 126, 130, 142
Æschylus, 76
Akachu (Jívaro), 59
Amaringo, Pablo, *vegetalista*, 60
Anatomy of an Illness, title, 126, 132
Angakoq (Inuit), 29-30, 72, 77
Animism 4-5,
  defined, 15, 76, 148, 158
Animist time, 163
Anishnabegs, (Ojibway), 39
ApErshat, (Inuit), 7
Armstrong, Karen, 10
Arnapak (Netsilik Inuit), 32, 122
Aroe, 62. See also *bope* (Bororo)
Asclepius, 144-145
atherosclerosis, 123
Aua (Inuit), 26-28, 30, 33
Australian Medical Assoc., 96
Australian Transpersonal Conference, 92
Awareness being, 115
Ayahuasca, (*yagé*), 7, 59-61

B

Baay-Bayanay (Yakut), 25-26
Barren Grounds, the, 29, 129

Bates, Brian, 78-79
Bear, 34, 38, as power animal 42
Beast Gods, 43
Benson, Dr Herbert, 125
Berndt, R.M. and C., 138
beta-endorphins, 24
  See endorphins
Black Elk, vision, 160-162, 166
Black Hills, 148, 160
Blackburn, Justice Richard, 101
Blackfoot, 43, 47, 134
buffalo drive, 41
Bladud (Wales), 80
Blessing Way ceremony, 128
Boas, Franz, 163
Bope, 62-65. See also *aroe* (Bororo)
Bororo (Brazil), 62-65
Bridges, E. Lucas, 65-67, 146
Bronze Age Europe, 19, 74
Buddha, 9, 100, 106, 110, 113
Buddhism, 4-5, 110-113, 150, 156
Buffalo Calf Woman, 47, 134
Bungai, *manang* (Iban), 135
Burnam Burnam, 92-93, 98-101, 158
Buryat, shamans by descent, 22
Bushmen (San, or !Kung) 5, 11, 85, 87-89

C

Cain and Abel, 12
Campbell, Joseph, 9, 12, 21, 24, 136-137, 145
Candid Camera, 126
Caribou (Willow-folk) Inuit, 29
Carpenter, Edmund, 11, 28

Castaneda, Carlos, 5, 121
Cawte, John, 95-99
Chest (Lakota Sioux healer), 36
Clanton-Collins, Jan, 92
clever-men, 3, 95-6, 98, 128, 138
clown quality, 107, 136
Coast Salish people, 24, 42, 134
Cófan (Colombia), 59-60
Cole, Dr Steve, 131
Computer Assisted ...
 environment, (CAVE), 165
 computer-generated visions, 165
Conibo (Peru), 44, 59, 61
Copper Thunderbird,
 See Morrisseau
cosmic forces, 4, 54, 58
Cousins, Norman, 126, 132
Cowan, James, Dream Journeys, 93
Creighton, James, 130
Creole Religions of the Caribbean,
 title, 124
crisis of mind, 7
Crocker, Jon C., 62-65
Crow Dog, Leonard, 35, 123
Cruz-Neira, Dr Carolina, 165
Cult of the Virgin, 146

D

Dances, 24, 40, 99, 107
 healing 34, in rites 43
 Sun dance, 46-49
dancing, 40-43, 46-47, 108,
 ritual and trance, 10
Dark Sovereign, title, 112
de Angulo, Dr Jaime, 41
Dené people, 10, 138-139
Denisova cave, Siberia, 19
Denmark, pre-history, 74
deprivation, 7

Desana people, 58
Destroyer, the, 108
Dioszegi, Vilmos, 23, 45
disease, born in the mind, 128
dismemberment visions, 25, 31
Dossey, Dr Larry, 123
Dream Journeys (the Dreaming), 93
Dream Time, 11
Dreaming, the, 92-95, 98, 100, 158
dreams, 6-7, 11, 13, 15, 23, 38-39,
 51-52, 65, 77, 79, 101
drum, 19, 21; as tool 24-25, 32,
 34, 43-46, 51, 56, 68, 109,
 134, 149
'drum is our horse' (Siberia), 24
drumming, 24, 44-49, 56, 79,
 113, 133, 165

E

Earth Mother, 74-75, 141-142, 145
ecstasy, 5, 43, 48, 61, 95, 100,
 107, 133, 134
ecstatic dance, 107, 109
Eddington, Sir Arthur, 139, 156
ego, 113
Einstein, Albert, 155
Eliade, Mircea, 5, 9, 43, 56
Elkin, A.P., 95-96, 138
Emiliana huxleyii, 170
endorphins, 24, 91, 129, 133
energy, 4, 9-10, 42-43, 50, 55-59, 89-
 91, 101-104, 108, 114-115, 121,
 125, 130, 135-139, 148-149, 155-
 6, 168
enlightenment, 8-9, 22, 29-30, 33,
 59, 73, 113, 141
Epic of Gilgamesh, title, 144
Epione, 145
Erdoes, Richard, 36

Index

F

False Face tradition (Iroquois), 52
Fenton, William, 52
Fontana, B.L., 121
Foundation for Shamanic Studies, 50
Fowles, John, 73
Freeman, Derek, 135
frequencies, 9, 24, 31, 45, 99, 108, 115
Freud, Sigmund, 119
Freyja, 74-75, 79
Furst, Peter, 57

G

Gaia, 82, 168-171
  A New Look at Life on Earth, title
  Gaia, as geophysiology, 169
Galen, 125
Gangele, Toby, 94
Ganieda, Earth Mother, 81
Garfein, Jack, 84
Gelfand, Dr Michael, 129
Getting Well Again, title, 130
Gilgamesh, See *Epic*
Gimbutas, Marija, 145
Great Spirit, 31, 37, 47-49, 161
Greece, ancient, 75-78, 144-145, 169
Grinnell G.B., 41
guardian spirit, 25, 42-43, 121 124, 138
Guédon, Marie-Françoise, 10, 138

H

Hadu'i (Six Nations), 52
Haft, Nina Otis, 106, 109

Halifax, Dr Joan, 56-57
Hammurabi's Code of Laws, 144
Harner, Michael J., 7 9, 15, 44, 51, 59-61
Harper, Stephen, 102
healing dance, 89-91, 106, 121-122
Heisenberg, Uncertainty Principle, 155
Herodotus, 86
Hesiod, *Theogony*, 77
Hiawatha, 122
Hildegard of Bingen, 146
Hippocrates, 125
Hole of the Spirits, 71
Holland, Dr Richard, 169
Homer, *The Odyssey*, 77
Hong Kong, 103-105
Hopi, 51-52, 54; dancers, 43
Houshken (Ona), 66
Huichol (Mexico), 56-58
Hunab K'u (Mayan), 55
Hungry Ghost Festival, 140
hunt, 11, 20, 25-28, 46, 48, 64-68, 99, 166; in pre-history, 10
Huxley, Aldous, 133
Hygeia, 144-145

I

Iban, 135, 137
Igjugarjuk (Inuit), 29, 58, 129
Iglulik, 26, 31
Imagery in Healing: Shamanism and Modern Medicine, title, 130
incense, 104
In Tune with the Infinite, title, 132
Ingerman, Sandra, 45, 150-1, 167-170
initial crisis, 9, 22

Innana (Sumerian goddess), 143-144
Inner Eye, 95
intellect vs. intuition, 107
Inuit, 7-11, 26-34, 55, 58, 61,
    71-72, 77, 109, 122, 129, 135
Ishtar (Assyrian), 144
Ivanov, Pyotr (Yakut), 23

J

James, William, 22
Jeans, Sir James, 139, 156
Jilek, Dr Wolfgang, 46, 49
Jívaro, 7, 9, 59-60, 62, 109, 112
John the Baptist, 9
Johnston, Basil, 39
Jung, Carl, Philosophical tree, 164

K

Kachina masks, 43, 51, 54
Kalahari, 5, 11-12, 32, 85-88
Kalos, Dr Malvin, 165
Katz, Richard, 89-91, 122, 124, 137
Káuyumari (Huichol), 57
Kinachau (Bushman), 90, 122
Kinalik (Inuit), 29
koompartoo, a fresh start, 98-99, 158
Kootenay healers, 42
Krippner, Stanley, 58
Ksenofontov, G.V., 23
Kwakiutl, 42-43
Kyzlasov, 23

L

Labyrinth, 45, 73
    See also Maze
Lacnunga, Anglo-Saxon spellbook, 79
Lame Deer (Lakota Sioux), 36, 40

Landes, Ruth, 39
Lascaux cave, 21, 68-69, 70-71
LeJeune, Fr. Paul, 3, 119
Leroi-Gourhan, André, 71, 188-189
Les Trois Frères cave, 68, 70-71, 73, 82
Lévi-Strauss, Claude, 120-1
Life magazine, re Inuit, 29
Lightning Man, 92, 94
Logos, 76; See also *Mythos*
Lopon Rinpoche. See Rinpoche
Lot-Falk, Evelyne, 20, 27, 93
Lovelock, James, 168-170,
    Gaia theory, 82, 168
Lowerworld, 5-6, 20, 31-32, 71
Luna, Luis Eduardo, 60-61
Luyckx, Marc, 157-158

M

Mabinogion (Wales), 80
Mahayana, 110
maikua, 59
manang, Iban shaman, 135
mandalas, 71, 72
manitou, 7, 38, 40
mantra, 114-115
Marbe, Karl, 138
Marx Brothers movies, 126
Masks, 34, 41-43, 52-54, 71,
    112,125,136; See Kachina
mathematics, in ancient Greece, 76
Matsúwa (Huichol), 56-58
Matthews, Dr Dale, 125
Matthews-Simonton, Stephanie, 130
mazes, 71-3; maze-lore, 82
McGaa, Ed (Eagle Man), 37, 48,
    162
Medicine Eagle, Brooke, 35,
    148-149
Medicine Is the Law, title, 96

medicine men, 3, 36-7, 47-8, 66-7, 129-30
Men of High Degree, 95
Men, Hunbatz (Mayan), 55
Merlin, 9, 81, 107
Middleworld, 5, 20
Mikhailovskii, V.M., 22
millelba, spirit-brother, 97
Miller, Jay, 44
Mimi folk, 93, 94
Minoan Crete, 73
Minotaur, 73
Mishipashoo (Ojibway), 37
mist of knowledge, 78
miwi, 138
Mohammed, 9
Morrisseau, Norval, 38, 119, 169
Moses, 7-8, 13, 81, 114, 162
Mother Earth, 48, 81-82, 152, 160-161
Mother Earth Spirituality, title, 162
Mother Goddess, 75
Mother of Sea Beasts, 28, 31, 77
mudang (Korea), 3, 106-107
Museum of Civilization, 44
Mycenaean culture, 76
Mythos, 76. See *Logos*

N

N/um healing energy, 89-91, 121-124, 136-137
Najagneq (Inuit), 28
nanandawi, 39, 51
　See Sucking-doctor
Navajo, 53, 54, 61, 128, 165; sand painting 53
Neher, Andrew, 45
Neihardt, John, 161
Nerthus, 74-75

New York Times, quoted, 125
Newsweek, re drumming, 45, 56
ngak, awareness spells, mantras, 114
ngakpa and *ngakma*, 114
Ngakpa Chogyam, Rinpoche, 114-115, 165
ngangas (Shona healers), 129
ngathungi, pointing stick, 138
Norbu, Thubten Jigme, 111-115

O

Odin and Thor (Norse), 75, 141-142
Ojibway, 7, 35-39, 51, 119, 169
Okladnikov, A.P., 21, 26
Olatunji, Babatunde, 56
Olmos, Margarite Fernández, 124
Olympus, 14, 77
Ona (Tierra del Fuego), 65-66, 146
Orpheus, 76
Ovid, *Metamorphoses*, 77

P

Paabo, Svante, 19
Paksu (Korea), 106
Pa'Ris'Ha, See Taylor
Panacea, 144, 145
Paravisini-Gebert, Lizabeth, 124
Park, Hi-ah (Korea), 106, 109, 115, 147
Parrish, Essie (Pomo), 49-51, 60
peyote, 57
physics, old and new, 155
Pit River language, 41
placebo, 129, 131, 132, 137
power animals, 15, 42, 65, 75, 107, 121, 130, 165, 169
Power of Now, The, title, 133

Prince, Dr Raymond, 46, 133-134
Prometheus, 12, 14, 76-77, 81, 100, 102, 136, 157, 159, 167
Prometheus Bound, 76, 171
Prose Edda, 75
Proverbs, Book of, 125, 131
psychic surgery, 109
psychosomatic, 96, 108-109, 121
Pwyll (Wales), 80

Q

QuamanEq, 8, 30.
    (See enlightenment)

R

*R*ai, 7
Rainbow Serpent, 92, 94, 99
Rainbow Warrior, 108
Rainbow Woman, 148
    See also Medicine Eagle
Rasmussen, Knud, 8, 10, 26-32, 72, 135
Re-enchantment of Politics, 157
Reichel-Dolmatoff, Gerardo, 58, 60
Reid, Bill (Haida), 44
Relations, title, 3
Revelations, Book of, 61
Rinpoche, Lopon, 111-114
Rinpoche, S.M. See Sakyong
Risse, Dr Guenther, 128
Roudot, Denis, 38
Rudd, Kevin, 101

S

Sakyong Mipham Rinpoche, 114
saman, name origin, 19
Sami (Lapp), 82

Samutchoso (Bushman), 88-89
Sandner, Donald, 128
Sanimuinak (Inuit), 31
Schweitzer, Dr Albert, 132
Sedna, 28, 32, 77
seer, 6, 8, 14-15, 81, 88, 103, 107
Semyonov, Semyon, 22
Shaman's Drum magazine, 114
shamanic personality type, 22
shamanic state of consciousness, 7, 11, 23, 31, 33, 42, 44, 72, 122
Shamanic Studies, Foundation, 150
Shamanism, 5, 14;
    defined 15, 65, 128, 148
Shamanism, Celtic, 78
shamans, 3-9, 12-16, 21-25, 28-33, 43-45, 49-51, 58-65, 70-71, 74-80, 82-83, 100, 104, 106, 109, 111, 119-122, 124, 126, 130, 132, 136, 140, 144, 148-151, 158, 163-168, 171
Shamans and Endorphins conference, 49, 91, 133
Shapiro, Dr Arthur, 131
Shiva, dancing, 108
Shona, 129
Shternberg, Lev, 22
Siddhartha, Buddha, 110
Sila, 28-29
Simonton, Dr Carl, 130
sinbyong, initiatory illness, 107
Skuse, Dr David, 140-142
Sky Heroes, 92, 94, 98-99
Sky Woman (Ojibway), 39
Smith, Loren (Pomo), 58
Solitary Journey, film, 109
Sorcerer, of *Les Trois Frères* cave, 21, 68-69, 70-71
soul loss, 6, 25, 126, 150

soul retrieval, 150
Soul retrieval, mending the fragmented self, title, 150
soul-flight, 24, 58, 71-2, 74, 97, 123-124
spirit guardians, 43, 58
spirit helpers, 6-7, 9, 29-30, 32, 59-62, 65, 107, 109, 121, 124, 130
spirit-canoe, soul recovery, 43-4
spirit-journeys, 6, 24-5, 32, 70
spirit-medium, Hong Kong, 103-5
spirits, 3-4, 6-7, 10-15, 20-23, 25, 27-35, 37, 40, 42, 44, 48, 51-53, 55, 57-58, 60, 62, 64-65, 68, 71-72, 74-5, 77-79, 88-90, 94-95, 97, 103-107, 109, 111-112, 115, 122,124-126, 134-135, 137, 140-141, 158, 169, 171; defined, 15, 19, 190-191
spiritual dismemberment, 7, 25, 31
St Francis, 10, 12
St George, shaman-hero, 135
St Paul, 7, 13
Stands Near the Fire (North Cheyenne), 148
Stein, R.A., 114
Stevenson, Adlai, 167
Stewart, R.J., 81
Stoeger, Fr. William, 170
Stone Age England, 74
Studies on Hysteria, title, S. Freud & J. Breuer, 97
Sturluson, Snorri, 75
sucking-doctor, 39, 49, 51, 119
sucking cures, 41, 50-51, 64, 98
Sucking Doctor, film, 50
Sumeria, 143-145, goddesses, 143

Sun dance, 46-49
Spring Festival, 143

T

T- and B-cells, 125-126
taboos, 28, 121, 123
Ta-da-da-ho (Onondaga), 122
Takánakapsâluk, 28-29, 32
 See also Sedna
Talth. See Thompson, Lucy
Tantric shamans, 114
Tantricism, 115
Tao Te Ching, title, 8, 120
Taoism, 5, 110, 120
Tart, Dr Charles, 23, 72
Taussig, Michael, 59, 60
Taylor, Pa'Ris'Ha, 147-8, 151, 171
Teish, Luisah, 121
Tenzing, Dawa, 109-110
Thales, 155
Thero, Nandisvara Nayake, 109
Thompson, Lucy, 40-41, See Talth
Thunderbird, 39
Tibet, title, 111
Time magazine re Morrisseau, 38
Tiuspiut (Yakut), 22
Tjangala, Barney (Walbiri), 98
tjukurpa, 92-96, 98-101, 158
To The American Indian, title, 40
Tolle, Eckhart, 133
Torngarsoak, See Great Spirit, 31
Torrey, E. Fuller, 119, 124
Tree-friends, 151
Tree of Life, the, 20
tree spirits, 38
Trickster, the, 107, 135-137
Trine, Ralph Waldo, 132
Trois Frères cave,
 See *Les Trois Frères*

tsentsak, 7, 59, 60, 62, 109
Tso, Natani (Navajo), 128
Tsodilo (Slippery) Hills, 87-89
Tsosi, Denet (Navajo), 128
Tungus, 19, 21-22

U

Upperworld, 5-6, 20
Uvavnuk (Inuit), 30

V

Van der Post, Laurens, 11-12, 85-89
Vanir, the, 75
Vastokas, Joan M., 164
Vegetalistas, 60-61, 144
Virgil, 151
Virgin Mary, as Earth Mother, 142
visions, 6, 9, 11, 15, 25, 29, 31, 35, 38-39, 48-49, 57, 59-61, 65, 71, 76, 131, 134;
of dismemberment, 25, 31
visualization, 129-130
visualization videogame, Re-Mission, 131

W

Wakan Tanka, Great Spirit, 47-49, 161
Walbiri (Australia), 92, 97-98, 102
warrior spirit, 108
Watson, Lyall, 137
Waubosse (Ojibway), 39
Way of the Shaman, The, title, 59
Whitehead, A.N., 156-7, 170
Williams, Mrs P.
(Six Nations), 52

Wiradjeri (Australia), 9
Witchdoctors and Psychiatrists, title, 120
Woman as Healer, title, 142
Wood, Rev'd J.G., 95
World tree, the, 26, 160, 163-6
Wyrd, web of, 78-9, 83, 109, 156

X

Xhabbo (Bushman), 10

Y

Yagé, (ayahuasca) 7, 59, 60
Yakut, 19-25, 109, 163;
epic poems (olonkho), 25
Yakutia, title, 21, 26
yang, 106-107, 141-142
yin, 4, 54, 79, 104, 106, 140-142
yin and *yang*, 4, 54, 79, 140, 170

Yirrkala NT, Australia, 100
Yurok people, 40

Z

Zeus, 76-77

www.ingramcontent.com/pod-product-compliance
Lightning Source LLC
Chambersburg PA
CBHW032113090426
42743CB00007B/334